Get Thee Behind Me

Get Thee Behind Me

MY LIFE AS A PREACHER'S SON

by Hartzell Spence
Author of "One Foot in Heaven"

ILLUSTRATED BY DONALD MCKAY

New York WHITTLESEY HOUSE *London*
MC GRAW-HILL BOOK COMPANY, INC.

253.2092
Sp 3 8

GET THEE BEHIND ME

Copyright, 1942, *by* HARTZELL SPENCE

First Printing, August, 1942
Second Printing, August, 1942

19129
October, 194

PUBLISHED BY WHITTLESEY HOUSE
A division of the McGraw-Hill Book Company, Inc.

Printed in the United States of America

TO

EILIE AND FRA

Get Thee Behind Me

CHAPTER ONE

*T*HE PARSONAGE was quiet. Not even the scrape of a carpet sweeper or the sizzle of roasting meat desecrated the silence.

In two big Douglas fir trees that framed the front door's vista of snow-capped mountains, birds perched songless. A grocer's boy on a bicycle stopped whistling at the corner and did not resume until he had passed the parsonage and was well down the block. The postman tiptoed up the porch steps, eased his letters into the box, and cat footed away.

The upstairs windows were open, their curtains swaying in an almost guilty flirtation with the morning breeze. A screen swung outward on its hinges. A dust mop emerged, shook vigorously but without throat. Holding the mop handle in both hands, a boy watched the petals of dust drop like parachutes to the hedge below. Then he pulled in his head and noiselessly latched the screen hook.

Inside his bedroom he announced softly, "Mother! I'm done!"

"Sh-hh!" murmured the parson's wife, entering the room swiftly. Then she asked, in an even more muffled tone, "Did you dust under your bed?"

A nod.

"And take those snakeskins out of your closet?"

Another nod.

Mother looked around, searching for neglected Saturday-morning chores. She remembered the bathroom.

"Did you clean the washbowl?"

"Shining."

"And the floor?"

"Scrubbed."

"The corners?"

"Clean."

"Well, I guess that's all. Do you want to go to the store now, or later?"

"Later."

"Just before lunch then."

From an apron pocket she took a 25-cent piece and handed it to me. "Here's your allowance. Now be careful, dear," she warned. "No noise. Father is going over his sermon in the living room."

"Yes, mother."

For three hours I had scrubbed and polished and now was free. My Ingersoll watch said ten o'clock. Mother softly descended the stairs, and I crossed the hall to join my fifteen-year-old sister, Eileen. She was sewing in her room, and for a while I watched her, saying nothing; Saturday-morning conversation was prohibited. Through the window I could see my brother, Fraser, inspecting basement rubbish for salvage before throwing it in the brick-lined incinerator at the alley end of the property. Even at the age of five Fraser had Saturday work to do.

An automobile I was constructing from laths and an old wagon stood, like an enticing sin, before the cellar door; but on Saturday I must not hammer and pound.

I wanted to build a wireless set but lacked $2.25 for materials—nine weeks' allowances. Bright cherries on a tree across the alley offered an escape from boredom, but only for a moment. Everyone else in the neighborhood might rifle that tree, but not the preacher's son.

I left Eileen and returned to my room. Lazily I inventoried the possessions that I had removed that morning from the closet floor and had deposited neatly in a new wooden chest: a football, deflated; a basketball, bladder broken; a rusty erector set; a camper's mess kit; a knife; a whistle; and two cartons of old electric trains and track.

The electric train attracted me. Listlessly I set up the track and began running the engine. This lasted only a moment, for a call came from downstairs.

"Hartzell! What's all that racket?"

I switched off the train and was already dismantling the track when mother appeared.

"It's a lovely morning, son. Can't you play outside?"

"Nobody to play with."

"Where are the other children?"

"They're all at Elitch's."

Elitch's was Denver's little Coney Island, with a roller coaster and an outdoor pool. The whole neighborhood had gone there for the first swim of the season. Because Elitch's also had a dance hall, we were forbidden to go near it.

Mother was wise enough not to comment. She understood my disappointment, for she found nothing evil in a swimming pool patronized by almost every member of the church. But the law had been laid down, and she, the good policeman, must enforce it.

[5]

"Do try to find something outside."

"Can I play tennis?"

"*May* I play tennis?" she corrected me.

"All right. *May* I play tennis?"

She deliberated. On one side of the house was a stretch of brick wall, a perfect backstop for tennis practice. A chalk line marked the net, high on the wall, and I had spent hours there, slamming the ball from the center of the adjacent lawn until father decided the living-room window was in danger and forbade the game. But this morning mother was desperate.

"All right," she consented. "But don't hit the balls too hard. Father will hear them, if you do."

Before long, unheeding mother's admonition, I was in a furious game of singles against "Big Bill" Tilden. He returned my crashing serves, my smashing volleys. Rules of the game were quite well defined, and I was honest with them. Sometimes the ball would strike a rough brick and lob high in the air, where I could deliver a smash not even Tilden could handle. Occasionally I'd outmaneuver him, catch him off balance, and score a point. When the ball bounced crazily off the brick and did not come back to me, that was Tilden flubbing a hot one.

I missed many smashes, too, when the ball ricocheted off the wall in such a way that I could not return it, although it was within the confines of my imaginary tennis court. I'd look across the net, into that white-brick wall and say with a look but without a vowel, "Nice shot, Bill."

The score was 5-4 in my favor when I came up to serve the tenth game. If I could ace out, I would win a

set from the great Tilden. My service had a twist that,
if it caught the brick just right, jumped the ball off the
court—an ace. Absorbed in the game, I tossed the ball
to serve, smashed down a crasher with all the side spin
I could pull from my shoulder and body.

Something went wrong. The ball flew off my racket
and shivered through the living-room window.

Father's head appeared where a moment before there
had been glass. His eyebrows were up; his black eyes
were flashing. Bill Tilden, the center court at Forest
Hills, the cheering spectators, the annoying referee, all
were gone. Father alone was there, a match for all of
them. His great nose, his clear broad forehead, his
clamplike jaws, caught the sun through the glassless
window. I froze, one leg crossed, left arm holding the
guilty racket at the finale of my tennis serve.

Wrath billowed, electric, tremendous. Father was a
mighty man: mighty with God in the pulpit, mighty
with compassion for children who could not learn the
catechism, mighty with mirth in conversation, mighty
with twinkling eye among the ladies, and mightiest of
all when dangling a razorstrop of chastisement in his
massive, hairy hand. No breach of discipline approached in cataclysm the interruption of his Saturday
sermonic meditations.

"How many times have I told you not to bang that
ball against the house?"

"Mother said I could," I answered defensively.

That cooled him off a little.

"Have you finished your chores?"

"Yes, sir."

[7]

"Oh, you have? Then *I'll* give you something to do."

A moment later he was on the lawn. "How much money have you?"

"A dollar and a quarter that I'm saving for a wireless set."

He appeared highly satisfied.

"All right, I'm going to teach you a lesson—in setting glass. Evidently it's something you ought to know."

He ordered me to take my money to the hardware store to buy glass, putty, and a putty knife. He was waiting for me on the lawn when I returned, led me to the window, and supervised replacement of the broken pane. But he did not help me with the job. Nor did Fraser, who watched from behind a lilac bush.

When I was done, father inspected the work.

"Very well," he said and retired to his sermon.

My score with Tilden, however, was still 5-4.

Cautiously I picked up my racket.

"You aren't going to play *again?*" Fraser whispered from behind the lilac bush.

That settled it.

"Sure, why not?" I asked and batted a few balls to get father's reaction. There was none.

Fraser departed discreetly as the hard-hit volleys began again. With the handicap of father just inside the window, I was no opponent for Tilden. He drew even, passed me at 6-7.

This was serious. Eileen, I noticed, now was watching from an upstairs window. Threatened with defeat, possessing a real gallery, I forgot father and went to work.

The first point was mine, a wicked ace; the second a hot rally that finally came to me on a smashing pass off the champion's backhand. Eileen smiled down her applause. Inspired and exultant, I delivered another service ace and brought myself within a point of winning a love game.

A great moment had arrived, one that would be

talked about for years. The unknown, who came out of the unseeded list into the finals, battled the seven-time champ to a standstill and broke him with a love game. Everything I had went into the next serve.

Like a well-aimed rock the ball spun from my racket, shattered the window, and smacked father on the cheek in final sacrilegious defiance.

This time father did not inspect the damage. He slammed through the front door and seized me by the arm.

"What's the matter with you?" he barked.

"Nothing, sir."

"There's more to this than disobedience. Why didn't you quit that game of yours?"

"I was playing Bill Tilden. We were in the middle of a match."

The eyebrows relaxed; the flame ebbed, as when a fire is banked for the night. He barely controlled a smile.

"You were winning, no doubt?"

"Yes, sir."

"You should be playing real tennis down at the park, not imagining these games by yourself."

"Will you play with me?"

That stopped him. He looked across the alley to a vacant lot where usually the neighborhood children congregated. Today it was untenanted. He asked no further question.

"No, son," he said. "I can't play with you. But suppose we fix that bloomin' window. There's a draft through the whole house."

This time he helped me.

CHAPTER TWO

MY BIRTH was so old-fashioned that it occurred at home.

There was no proper hospital in the little county seat of Clarion, Iowa, on Valentine's Day, 1908. Had there been, my mother would not have stood for any such nonsense. I was born in the parsonage, where father was serving his second year and was just starting to be called "that bright young man, William Spence."

Old Dr. Murray, whose horse stood out front in a late-winter blizzard, held me up by the heels, I'm told, slapped life into me, and turned to my father.

"Well, Parson, you got a boy, all right. What a wonderful world for a son to be born into!"

That was a few minutes after midnight on February 15. My mother had wanted the baby to be a Valentine. As it was, my birthday parties always were on Valentine's Day, with presents from mother, my grandmother in Canada, Eileen, and Fraser; but father would not participate in this misrepresentation. To his last year he waited until the honest proper day to offer his gift alone and with great dignity. He would not cheat honesty for the sake of a party.

It was a secure world to be born into. Clarion, population 2,743 and the largest town in the county, was prosperous. For miles around spread the rich, fat soil of Iowa farms. And the rich, fat farmers drove into town on Saturday morning, where they loitered around the courthouse while their women went shopping, and in the afternoon fraternized at Schwartzendrover's hardware store until time for the evening chores.

A few farmers employed hired men, but not many; the majority had growing sons. The town banker, who lived in a big house with white pillars, owned two farms, on which there were tenants. To Banker Price, jovial, white-haired collection-plate passer at the Methodist church, the tenants were "my boys," and at threshing time he took off his shirt and worked with them in the fields.

Every living came from the land; my father's too, for such a collection of cabbages and onions and carrots as the parsonage accumulated in lieu of cash church subscriptions! Nobody had much actual money except Banker Price, and his was all in the bank, not in his pocket.

On Saturday night at nine Clarion shut up as tight as a jewelry shop, and everyone went home to study his Sunday school lesson. On Sunday money changed hands only at the churches, although Druggist Allbee would run down to mix a prescription if the matter was urgent—postponing payment until the morrow, of course. If a man ran out of pipe tobacco on the Sabbath, he borrowed from a neighbor or went without; but that never happened to the Methodists, who didn't smoke even on weekdays.

Old Mrs. Bobeau, who was president of the Ladies Aid, sat up with mother when I was born, clucking to and fro from kitchen to bedroom with the hot water.

She went home at dawn but not to sleep, for she had to be out mighty early to spread the news about the baby over at the preacher's.

According to father's story, Mrs. Bobeau was a little sorry it wasn't Monday, for then she could have shouted her tidings across the fences. All the ladies would have been out in their yards early, racing to get the wash on the line ahead of the neighbors even in February, when the wet clothes froze into sheets of ice.

But it was Thursday. She lingered at home only long enough to make herself a cup of scalding coffee before she wrapped a gray shawl around her head and ploughed through a foot of snow to the home of the Shacklefords, where my year-and-a-half-old sister was spending the night. Mr. Shackleford was an engineer on the M. & St. L. Railroad and a very prosperous and distinguished man because of it.

"Yes," she said, as Mrs. Schackleford let her in and helped warm her at the kitchen range, "it's a boy at the Spences'."

"My, isn't that nice!" Mrs. Shackleford responded. "He'll have to grow some, though, to be as big as his six-foot daddy."

"He's poorly, it's my opinion," Mrs. Bobeau said confidentially, "but I'm not the one as told you."

Out again into the crisp cold she went, to the Duffields and the Sperrys and the Shanks and the Turnipseeds. They all knew why she was coming. They could see her high black button shoes treading down the snow long before she reached the gate; and they knew from the set of her plump body that she brought good news.

[13]

She was not bent over enough nor breathless enough to be a harbinger of disaster.

By midmorning the whole town knew about the Spences' boy, and into every oven was popped an extra tidbit for the minister, poor man, such a handsome fellow and nobody to feed him properly for several weeks to come.

An hour later the ladies began to drop in, bringing meat loaves and muffins and their very best preserves and arranging a schedule among them as to which half day they would tend the children and feed the pastor. The little parsonage was a hubbub of chatter and excitement with an overcast smell of boiling coffee. My sisten Eileen was not forgotten, either; castoff neighborhood toys were brought to her, and a shiny new doll with real eyelashes was sent by Banker Price.

Through it all father pranced, I'm told, genially yielding first attention to the new baby; but the day was really his. He loved people, and he knew exactly how to act amid a gang of buzzing women.

"Come in, come in," he would whisper from the door to each new visitor, his *sotto voce* not so much for consideration of my mother in her room as for the dramatic effect. "So nice of you to come. I knew you would. I said to Hope only an hour ago, 'It's eleven o'clock. In twenty minutes the cinnamon rolls will be out of the oven, and in thirty Mrs. Storer will be over here in her new blue hat.' And here you are."

Mrs. Storer handed him the cinnamon rolls, on her best hand-painted Haviland china plate that left the dining-room shelf only on great occasions. Father lifted the embroidered linen napkin and sniffed admiringly of the sweet bread, while Mrs. Storer threw off her coat and shawl and hurried to the bedroom to make a fuss over mother and to exclaim over me.

"I do declare if he isn't the image of his mother!"

"Yes," father agreed, coming in after putting the rolls in the kitchen, "it's Eileen who's my baby. Hartzell's going to look like his mother."

"So it's Hartzell, is it?" the ladies asked. They had been waiting for this. Father explained how, as a medical student, he had felt the call while listening to Bishop Hartzell at a revival meeting in Toronto.

"So it's only proper we call the baby Hartzell. One day he'll be a bishop, too."

I remember nothing of Clarion. A snapshot in an old album purports to be me, seated prim and neat on the parsonage porch watching Eileen attempt, with an innocence belying her temper, to take an orange away from Ruth Shackleford.

It was usually like that with oranges and all luxuries. We saw them occasionally in the hands of others but rarely tasted any ourselves. Mother's ingenuity was stretched to keep plain food in our stomachs. If there was chicken on our table, it probably was an old hen that had stopped laying; if there was beef, it was round steak, very thin. Mother herself existed on tea when there wasn't enough food to go round.

From Clarion, we moved to Fort Dodge, Iowa, where we lived eight years. Then there were nine months at Omaha and three years at Sioux City, Iowa. Eileen emerged from childhood at Sioux City. My adolescence began a year later, about the time we reached Denver,

an exciting modern city with a junior high school, de-
partmentalized classes, home rooms, and a football
team. The girls wore gym bloomers to school in the
morning and kept them on all day, a ghastly impro-
priety, and every Saturday afternoon the children in
our neighborhood went to the Bluebird Theater to see
a film.

Across this new horizon my sister and I would have
bolted like colts turned out to pasture in the spring.
But father was there, restraining us with a ministerial
bit between our teeth.

Father was a towering man, strong and big handed,
and he knew how to be firm with such finality that not
even a bishop would argue with him. He could thunder
like Isaiah, but rarely did so, preferring the New Testament Gospel, "Be kind, one to another."

Stern to the peak of puritanism in his personal life,
he expected like character in his children. He realized
that Christianity could be lived many ways, and the
immortal soul was his concern, not the body in which
it dwelt. He had only one axiom concerning the human
race: it was weak. Otherwise there was no such thing as
a race—it was a collection of human individualities. He
approached each person as cautiously as he'd shoe a
mule. He had no patience with psychologists who
pooled human reactions and drew behavioristic pat-
terns, like spools of varicolored thread, out of a drawer.

Yet father did not understand his own children. Perhaps because we were part of his being he assumed that
we were out of the same moral mold. "Like father, like
son" was a truism of his, and we were supposed to be
untroubled by doubt, immune to temptation, selfless,

and content with spreading the Gospel to the exclusion of all else. When brought up short by some incomprehensible demonstration of our worldliness, father would retire to his study to meditate upon it. Sometimes he would admit we were right. He was not stubborn for the sake of willfulness or insistent on a decision merely because he had made it. Indeed, he was delighted if anyone could prove him wrong. "My value ends where my leadership errs," I heard him say many times, but it was usually in connection with parishioners. Where we, his children, were concerned, he was more often unyielding than pliant.

At Denver father was for the first time pastor of a smart suburban charge, with members who belonged to golf clubs. The neighborhood definitely was upper middle class, with building restrictions and boulevards. But the church was dingy and the parsonage shabby.

Down our street lived prosperous family people: a dealer in railroad equipment, a commission broker, a successful young surgeon. They all had automobiles, phonographs, neat lawns, and children the age of Eileen, Fraser, and me.

Because there were so many pastimes we might not share, we were often alone. We would devise games until, in time, we became the game inventors for the neighborhood. We had to, or be left alone.

No matter in what direction we turned, we were sure to end up in trouble. On the east was father's stern code, on the west mother's attempts to make our lives Christian, on the south the rigid parish customs for a ministerial household, and on the grim, cold north public opinion.

[17]

Normal adolescence in other children was deviltry in us. Had we been the rankest of sissies, against the parsonage background we should still have appeared as imps of Satan. Often we resorted to the command in Matthew, "Get thee behind me, Satan," and even then we weren't safe. Someone in the church was sure to spot him over our shoulders.

CHAPTER THREE

ESTRICTED as we were, parsonage life would have been a miserable existence had it not been for certain advantages, the most enjoyable being that we knew the gossip of the whole town.

Father was the confidant of everyone, and he did not believe in concealing professional secrets from the family. He discussed them over the dinner table on the theory that if we ate surrounded by man's mistakes we would profit by them. We did, too. Our English themes were intimate character sketches, slices from life itself.

The hopes, tragedies, and difficulties of our neighbors flowed across our dining table like a motion picture thrown on the wall with every meal. Father would come home to lunch, acquaint us with the morning's fateful developments, and hurry away again. Sometimes the complete account of a spicy private life would be narrated at a single sitting. Occasionally father would point up his narrative until it reached a crisis, then rush off as though he were a dramatist ringing down the second-act curtain, leaving us tantalized by curiosity until the next meal. He had a fine appreciation of suspense, and he did not dull his effect by any admonition such as "Now, not a word of this to anyone!" He assumed that we would not gossip, and we never did.

Nothing we did was little or insignificant. The ac-

[19]

quisition of a new piece of furniture or a ride into the mountains were great moments. When on Saturday afternoon my sister successfully begged two cups of sugar from mother and made fudge, we had as much fun over it as we would have had at a circus.

The grating of the sugar in the pan as the cocoa was mixed with it, the first titillating aroma of the bubbling mixture, the pot about to overflow, the victorious instant when the beaten mass turned creamy under the spoon, the elaborate ceremony of licking the pan: all these were epic, to be lived intensely. Our neighbors, to whom a pan of fudge was commonplace, did not share the wonders we experienced. If they spoiled two cups of sugar, there was more in the cupboard. In our house sugar was rationed in peace as well as in war.

The position of prestige we occupied in the church as children of the minister was flattering. Parishioners were considerate and respectful—until they caught us in wrongdoing. Parents made a fuss over us in the vestry, which compensated somewhat for the indifference of their children.

We lived in an adult world, and, looking back, I know our playmates were envious. Conversations never were scaled down for us, a very gratifying state of affairs. We were assigned parts in Sunday school pageants; we were presidents of the Epworth League. My sister played the piano for her Sunday school department; I led the singing at father and son banquets and League meetings. If there was a prize given anywhere for memory work or quotations from the classics, Eileen and I won it.

In school it was easy to excel. Homework was simplified for us by our parents' ability to unravel our scholastic dilemmas. Father was trained to give assistance wherever it was needed. When we required help, we got it; father was not at an office downtown but in the next room when our algebra was baffling or when a sonnet needed a rhyming line.

Father's collection of books was so extensive—the equal of many public libraries—that hundreds of times Eileen and I found at home the source materials we needed at school. Once Eileen's English assignment was to locate a poem which made significant use of the word "And." Father stepped into his library and returned a few minutes later with a book of verse in which sixteen consecutive lines began with "And." Eileen drew an A for her English lesson that day.

In the matter of required school reading we were years ahead of our class. When, as a junior in high school, I complained that I had forgotten the little details of Charlotte Brontë and Charles Dickens that my English teacher expected to find in my book reports, father bought a twenty-volume set of condensations from the classics to refresh my memory. The rule was, though, that I might not consult a condensation of a novel unless I had read the complete work.

Father directed my reading without letting me realize it. When, at the age of twelve, I was in the hospital with a mastoid, he introduced me to James Fenimore Cooper, Walter Scott, and Alexander Dumas and kept my hospital table flooded with enticing literature. He did so after discovering that Gordon Fogg, who lived next door, had brought me *Tom Swift among the Diamond Makers* and an Edgar Rice Burroughs novel

[21]

about life on the planet Mars. "I've some yarns you'll like better," he said simply.

There was always great excitement when father, ever unpredictable, stepped out of his role of preacher and became a father. The occasions were rare, and were accompanied by a sensational élan.

While concluding a building campaign in Fort Dodge, Iowa, father neglected us for months. Then one bright May morning, after the structure was completed, all the money pledged, and the dedication plans approved, father realized that for a few weeks he had nothing to do except keep an eye on a quarrel among the members of the furnishings committee, all of whom had different ideas about interior decoration.

He said as much to mother, and she, piqued at his complete absorption in ministerial duties, replied, "In that case, how would you like to get acquainted with your children? You do recall that you *have* children?"

Father laughed, whereupon mother turned on him, "Tell me what color your daughter's hair is—tell me!"

He couldn't.

Half an hour later he appeared at Eileen's school with the story that he had urgent need of his daughter. Wonderingly, the teacher excused Eileen from class, and, no less bewildered, Eileen accompanied father home. There she found her suitcase packed for a journey. Without a word of explanation, father boarded the noon train with her, and they disappeared.

Until that trip father had been pretty much her pastor. Now she became acquainted with her father. She discovered that he hated to shave; that a battered hat became him; that, while he did not go so far as to desecrate their holiday Sabbath by fishing, he conveniently forgot to take her to Sunday school; that he knew a perch from a pickerel and how to catch both; and that he could gain the admiration of his fishing guide by other than pastoral accomplishments. Not many children can number among youth's great experiences the discovery that their father is human.

In Fort Dodge our connection with the parsonage unexpectedly provided a great treat. One church member, E. T. Lizenby, jovial dealer in farm implements, had no offspring of his own. On July Fourth about ten in the morning he dropped in to chat with father. My sister and I, who were on the front porch, had shot off all our firecrackers. Only two Roman candles and a box of sparklers, which we were saving for evening, remained.

Mr. Lizenby noticed the frayed red papers of exploded fun and saw across the street the sons of Johnson, the wallpaper dealer, still noisily at play. He scanned the whole block; on every porch children were setting off loud explosions and yelping with excitement. He sat down on the step beside us.

"Yours all gone?" he asked sympathetically.

We shook our heads glumly.

"That's no way to celebrate the Fourth! Why, you just escaped being English by the skin of your teeth." (Both father and mother were Canadian born.) "If anybody ought to celebrate Independence Day, it's you kids. Will," he called into the house, "I'm taking the children for a walk. Be back in a minute."

Downtown we went to Main Street, where a drugstore displayed fireworks. As the morning was half over, a sale was in progress.

Mr. Lizenby began to buy, by the dozen packages, firecrackers of all sizes, flares, colored lights, and rockets. A huge sack was filled until the tempting merchandise bulged out the top.

"How much?"

"Four-seventy-five."

"Throw in that dollar balloon, and I'll make it $5 even," said Mr. Lizenby, and we held our breaths. Only the very rich celebrated the Fourth of July with balloons.

The deal was closed. Like puppies, we heeled Mr. Lizenby back to the house. Then such a disturbance began as never before profaned a minister's porch. We were glutted with fireworks. Long after every other cracker on our street had been spent, the parsonage clatter continued. All the children among whom we had been unwelcome at ten o'clock because we could not contribute to the fun had assembled at our house by midafternoon. Mr. Lizenby then went home with the promise to return at dusk.

That night our house was illumined as for a rich girl's wedding. Skyrockets swished upward; chasers ran back and forth along the clothesline. Finally, in an elaborate ceremony presided over by Mr. Lizenby and father, the balloon was sent aloft.

Each Independence Day as long as we remained in Fort Dodge Mr. Lizenby appeared about ten in the morning with his bursting sack. No other children in the neighborhood possessed half so many fireworks as we.

[24]

Christmas always was an exciting holiday. The family was a unit as at no other time, and father, who throughout the year had been big brother and uncle to the entire community, was remembered by scores of parishioners as though he belonged to their own households.

One of our greatest Christmases occurred at Fort Dodge. It was the last of the old-fashioned yuletide festivals, for war had come before the winter of 1914, and after the war Christmas was not quite the same.

In 1913 the merchant had not yet become the beneficiary; Christ in the manger was still worshiped. Most of the people of Fort Dodge made their own gifts, supplementing them only by such items as sleds and skates, which they could not handily produce at home. The parsonage celebration began two weeks earlier than that of our neighbors because of the ceremony of packing a box for our Canadian relatives. A week's lull followed, until a box arrived from Canada, after which we turned our attention to preparations for the church Christmas; we were not permitted to forget that first place was reserved for the Christ child, whose birthday the holy day was. We children learned verses and attended rehearsals for the Christmas pageant. A few days before Christmas a committee appeared at the house with tubs of candy and nuts and packed sacks for Santa Claus to give every member of the Sunday school on Christmas Eve. We loved this, because any candy left over was ours.

Then downtown on the day before Christmas went the whole family to select the Christmas tree. Father examined it for durability, mother for size, we children for symmetry. We went to Woolworth's to augment the ornaments saved from year to year. Eileen, Fraser, and I would have run riot here had not father and mother patiently curbed our extravagance both in money and taste. If mother shook her head, we rejected a gaudy ornament in favor of one more conventional; if father frowned, we were overreaching the budget.

Home again with our booty, we shared the intoxicating excitement of dressing the tree, which father enjoyed to the extent of writing his sermon on a clip board in the living room instead of in his study. When the ornaments were in place, we opened the big bundle from the Canadian relatives and hefted, rattled, and sniffed the individual packets for possible identification, father as curious as the rest of us. At the same time we helped father and mother to sort packages from other towns where father had served as pastor, and we arranged the offerings from his parishioners in Fort Dodge.

In the evening we went to the church and after the Christmas Eve service hurried home to appear in the window when the choir came by to sing carols. We smiled and beamed our appreciation, and then Eileen and I went outside to join the carolers on their round of the hospitals, the jail, and the homes of shut-in church members. This lasted until ten o'clock, or later if falling snow enhanced the festivities.

Christmas morning we were up early. Church members began to call at seven o'clock and continued to drop in throughout the day, bringing gifts and messages. There were a few presents we could count on: the Mohnike girls' homemade candy, Tony Roffel's cut glass or Haviland, Mr. McCutcheon's barrel of apples. Father waited anxiously for the appearance of the Men's Brotherhood, hoping that their remembrance would be in cash, but it wasn't; they contributed a leather chair.

By noon the tables overflowed with presents: hand-made lace, wearing apparel, preserved fruits, cakes, candies, oranges, nine scarves, four pairs of mittens, and for father seven pairs of knitted socks with ties to match. The gifts were tokens of love from men and women who had no other way of expressing their grati-tude and devotion to the pastor who counseled them, freed their children from escapades, solved their do-mestic problems, found employment for them, and lent them money when he had it.

The lace, for example, that Sister Hawkins had been tatting since August had a story in it. Joe Hawkins, a farmer, had been stricken with a ruptured appendix just as the oats ripened. Father had managed the farm, helped to harvest the crop, and put up hay that would have been ruined by imminent rain. Joe Hawkins' hired man said the parson should have been a farmer, and that was reward enough for father. Mrs. Hawkins had spent every spare moment since on the lace.

The story of the six jars of plum butter from Mrs. Aiken was ten months old. The previous March Mrs. Aiken had contracted diphtheria and had been taken to the County Hospital for Contagious Diseases. Father had sent the Ladies Aid to the rescue, and their vol-unteers had kept the Aiken house running and the three children and husband fed until the mother could return. Daily father had called on her at the hospital, delivered letters to her from her family, and bolstered her spirits. One day when she said, "Oh, Mr. Spence, I'll never be able to thank you," he had laughed it off. "You just make me some plum butter next summer, and we'll be even." She had put up the butter, all right; it was her Christmas gift.

People who were that generous with their preacher did not forget his children. We received candy enough to last, with careful hoarding, for six weeks or more and many games, which father inspected carefully to be sure that they could not be utilized for gambling. When he carried one to the furnace, we didn't mind; what was one among a dozen?

From time to time the great of the outside world visited the parsonage. Because the church auditorium was the largest hall in town, public lectures, concerts, and recitals that had no connection with Methodism were held there. The building would be rented to a local promoter for the occasion, and not infrequently the speaker or recitalist went to the church to test the acoustics before the performance. There, by coincidence, they also met the pastor. If a celebrity expressed a desire to escape club women and autograph hunters for a few hours, father brought him home. Many a concert artist practiced on the parsonage piano, and many a lecturer shared potluck with us. If the guest was an excellent conversationalist, father particularly enjoyed him; if not, all the better, for the company could listen to father.

We children benefited by these contacts. But lest we succumb to the hypnotic glitter of worldly influences, father would also deliberately invite to our table some floater from the Salvation Army wayfarers' home or a tramp who had knocked at the back door. We were shown in this way that the world is not all art and tinsel.

If a bishop was within fifty miles of us, he stayed at our house. Such an occasion was supposed to be a highlight in our lives. But the churchman was very apt to talk shop all evening—and very unimaginative shop at that.

Father did not realize, of course, that my sister and brother and I found the bishop dull, or that we fervently admired the bearded transient who cut an apple into segments and with toothpicks assembled it into a duck that waddled across the table. It was he, not the bishop, who awakened our ambitions, arousing in both Fraser and me the determination to become hobos and causing Eileen to feel put out because we were positive that girls had no place in such a glamorous profession.

CHAPTER FOUR

WHEN we moved to Denver, Eileen was fourteen, I was twelve, and Fraser was six. Eileen and I were in junior high school, and Fraser was in the first grade.

"Why, you children are growing up!" father exclaimed suddenly one morning at breakfast, and his eyes settled on me. "Aren't you twelve?"

"Yes, sir."

"Then you're old enough to join the Boy Scouts. You can't learn everything at home."

The Boy Scouts met in the church basement on Thursday night. I was not keen about them; there were enough Bible verses and catechism to be memorized without additional oaths and routines. But I enrolled. There was no question about it. The troop was sponsored by the church.

Father bought me the scout manual, and I presented myself to the scoutmaster, Mr. Seeley, who was distinguished by bulging arm muscles, light-footedness, and an inclination to lisp. Sometimes he would start to speak and then, conscious of his sibilants, try to escape the sound of his voice by busying himself with the arrangement of a group of chairs or knotting a rope. Mr. Seeley was also a school gymnasium instructor and an amateur boxer. Athletic boys worshiped him.

I, however, was not muscular. When I first walked

into the church basement, where thirty boys were shouting over Indian wrestles, I was overcome by the brawn about me. I did not like the look of it or the noise of it or the pungent smell of it. Until then I had never been in contact with boys outside the Sunday school, and the prospect of mingling with these boisterous athletes, who shouted and laughed as they played tricks on each other, was as terrifying as if I had entered a cage of gibbons.

Into a corner I edged, hoping to remain there in seclusion. But Mr. Seeley found me.

"Come, now," he beckoned, "the meeting is about to begin."

I joined the others, who by now stood at attention, serious, ready to recite their scout oath. I felt better. It was a little like Sunday school. So was the half hour of instruction that followed. Interesting too were the calisthenics and military drill. I was shoulder to shoulder with big fellows, following identical movements, executing identical commands. I began to be proud of myself.

Then came the recreation hour and boxing gloves. Adversaries paired off, but no one challenged me. I was the new preacher's kid, not a neighbor, not a pal to anyone, stamped immediately as a half boy, who had never in his life owned a tool chest or a bicycle, gone on a hike, or smoked a corn silk. I was the kind of guy who recited Bible verses and hung up his trousers at night.

Into the lonesome corner I withdrew again to watch the fisticuffs unobtrusively.

Mr. Seeley was persistent.

"Come, put on the gloves with me!" he called.

This was something special. I could sense it by his tone and also by jealous eyes that focused quickly on me.

I shook my head.

"Come on, fellow," he invited, "be a sport."

Still I declined.

"What's the matter? Don't you feel well?"

My face burned. I longed to put on those gloves and acquit myself. I thought of the hundred times in Omaha when, enroute home from school, the sons of packing-house workers had waylaid me and taunted me for being small and a preacher's kid. Often I had flown at the gang of them, fists flying, until I learned to fight so well that Mr. Pond, who lived on the corner, would leave his office early in the evening to watch the battles. He gave me a silver dollar every time he saw me emerge from a fray, bloodily defeated but unhumbled.

This, however, was different. I could not admit that never in my life had I donned a pair of boxing gloves. Why, I wouldn't even know how to lace them. The snickers of the scouts when they found this out would suffocate me.

One of the older boys joined Mr. Seeley.

"He's scared of you, Al," he said. "Maybe we can get somebody his own size."

Everyone roared.

"I can lick you!" I said.

Mr. Seeley appraised me critically. He glanced at my adversary, Bud Eaton, one of his patrol leaders, a strong, quick boy.

The Eaton boy laughed good-naturedly and turned away, but Mr. Seeley took his arm.

"Wait a minute, Bud," he said. "Hartz says he can lick you. You know the motto of this troop: Be prepared to prove everything you say, or don't say it. He's said it; give him the chance to prove it."

Bud hesitated, gloves dangling on sunburnt arms that were nearly as long as my whole body. The other boys left their play.

"I *can* prove it," I insisted sullenly.

"Then do so," commanded Mr. Seeley, tossing me the gloves.

I put the left one on backwards, heard laughter, quickly corrected my mistake. As I laced the gloves, the troop drew into a square, in the center of which I eyed Bud Eaton.

"Three-minute rounds," Mr. Seeley directed. "Go!"

I'll show them, I thought, and next time they'll *want* to put on the gloves with me. I ploughed into my opponent with such fury that he backed into a corner. The scouts screamed with surprise. Bud circled, amused by the bantam before him, misconstruing my humiliation for personal dislike. I charged in again, and his right guard biffed me on the head. The blow was light, but I was lighter, and went down on the padded floor. Aware of a din of shouting, up I bounced, blinded by uncontrollable anger at the shouting, at the dark corner out of which I had come, at the strangeness and the newness. I flew at Bud, again went down, cut over one eye.

"Are you all right?" Mr. Seeley asked anxiously.

For answer I spun Bud around in a clutch, whacked

him on the head, ploughed my fists and head into his ribs. He backed away, blowing. The din grew louder.

"Time," called Mr. Seeley. "One minute's rest. One more round will be enough."

I panted in my corner, sprang on signal to the center of the ring, met Bud coming out. He had not once tried to hit me; the blows from which I had gone down were the result of my own rush against his protecting guard. He did not know what to do.

But I did. I hit him on the cheek with everything I had. That dispelled his indecision. He went after the bantam then to give him what he deserved. Mr. Seeley looked on meditatively but did not interfere. The blows fell. I swung back but would not give way; I could not retreat an inch nearer that howling, yelling gang at my back and on either side. I did not feel Bud's blows. As in Omaha when I had been battered and blackened without feeling, so now I was insensate to pain.

Bud grew tired after a minute and dropped his guard.

That was my opportunity. I was in again, head down, fists in his face, fists in his stomach—fists like a swarm of angry hornets that had no sting.

"Time!" shouted Mr. Seeley and entered the ring laughing. He held up my hand. "The winner," he called, "for aggressiveness!"

Everyone laughed.

At home father spotted the cut over my eye, the chafed cheeks.

"What happened to you?"

"Nothing."

"Son, have you been fighting?"

"No, sir. I was at scout meeting."

He looked at me. For a moment I thought he was going to ask questions. Instead he said simply, "I didn't know that scouts had an initiation," and I went up to bed.

But not to rest. For half an hour I was in the ring with Bud, bruising and pounding him, and the scouts were cheering me. In tears, I went to sleep.

Next Thursday I did not want to go to scout meeting. Father was unsympathetic.

"Nonsense," he said, "it's good for you. Besides, what would people say if my own son ignored the church troop?"

I went, but everything done by the boys was alien to me. I did not even know "squads right" or a proper "about face." I could not clean a .22 rifle; there had never been one in our house. I could not tie a knot properly; we had never possessed a boat or a horse. I could not make a mortise and tenon joint. The scouts' pride was in manual achievement, and I had never used my hands except to scrub the kitchen and bathroom and to carry groceries.

At each meeting I grew more despondent. Mr. Seeley tried to bolster me. Without seeming to do so, lest I be ridiculed, he coached me through the scouting manual, through the tenderfoot stage, up almost to the badge of second class.

Then school adjourned for the summer, and to end scouting for the season Mr. Seeley proposed a fourteen-mile overnight hike. The announcement was greeted with whooping and jostling.

"What is it?" I asked Allen Thamer. The idea seemed silly to me.

"Oh, you know," he answered.

I went in search of father, but he was not home. Mother was as ignorant as I on scouting matters. So she telephoned Bud Eaton's mother and learned that the boys would leave at noon Monday, walk to a grove in the country, cook their supper, sleep in the open, and hike back to town next day. I would need blankets, a scout cooking kit, a can of beans, a steak, and some bacon—the necessities for a short outing.

Monday morning father presented me with a water canteen. I already had a mess kit, a Christmas present from an enthusiastic camper at Sioux City, and had bought the steak, bacon, and beans. But when I assembled all the equipment in a pile, I had no idea what to do with it.

"Put it in a suitcase," mother suggested, and, knowing no better, I did so. To my embarrassment mother insisted on walking with me to the corner where the troop had gathered. Mr. Seeley looked at us and pointed to the valise.

"You're not taking that, are you?" he asked.

"Why, yes," mother bridled. "It's just the thing for an overnight trip."

Mr. Seeley did not reply. Before we had walked half a mile, the suitcase had the weight of a double trunk. I fell behind. By the time we reached the city's outskirts, I was trailing the troop by a hundred yards.

Mr. Seeley and Bud Eaton then showed me how to roll my provisions in the blankets and how to carry this bedroll on my back. They also relieved me of the suit-

case, rigging it between them like a water bucket on a scout stave. Light and buoyant, I hurried to the head of the procession to be among the leaders. Several times I looked back to see what had happened to the suitcase. Mr. Seeley and Bud seemed to be a very long way behind. Finally, by means of signal flags Eaton flashed a message to a first classer, who looked at me and said, "They want you."

I waited until they caught up. Mr. Seeley was angry.

"Since you have so much energy now, you can carry this yourself," he said and left me alone. I arrived at camp with a swollen wrist, ten minutes behind the others.

That night I hid the suitcase in the woods. Next day I returned home without it, and father inquired. He did not appreciate my explanation.

"That's the silliest nonsense I ever heard," he fussed, "leaving a perfectly good suitcase in the woods. We'll go get it right now."

He handcranked the Ford, which stood in the yard because there was no garage, and we rattled out of town, gulping the miles that had been interminable afoot.

We stamped into the woods. Father fretted continuously. Was I too lazy to return something I had borrowed when I finished with it? Had I no respect for other people's property?

But when I uncovered my humiliation from under a pile of twigs and a dead branch, he grunted a little at the care with which I had buried it.

"What the mischief did you hide it for?"

"You don't take a suitcase on a hike."

"Why not?"

"You can't carry it. It gets heavy."

"What did the other boys do?"

"They wrapped everything up in blankets and strapped the roll over their shoulders."

"Hm-m—"

"I hid it as soon as I got here."

"Hm-m—" He took the suitcase from me. "I'll carry it," he said, his voice husky. When we returned to the car, he shoved me into the driver's seat. "How would you like to learn to drive?"

Had he not pushed me behind the wheel, I would not have believed him. The car was inviolably his, ready at all times to dash to any bedside in the community. Not even mother was allowed to drive. No one dared touch the car except father. He oiled and greased it incessantly, grooming it as though it was a thorough-bred. He affectionately called it "Good Old Maud."

To be behind the wheel when the car was parked and the engine cold was a privilege, indeed. Now to be invited to drive!

I looked at father. His face was relaxed, his eyes kindly, his smile tenderly paternal. He was not often in this mood.

"I think I know how to drive," I said. "I've watched you."

"Get set then; I'll crank her."

Systematically he went through the rattling ceremony of cranking: gas throttle down on the notched bar to the spot that had worn smoothest; a quick jerk or two on the priming wire, which projected from the radiator; a squaring of the shoulders and spreading of the feet in preparation for a jump either way in a crisis; a violent spin accompanied by a pull of the choke wire; then the racing noise of the motor accompanied by a shout, which was my signal to yank down the spark lever and throw up the throttle.

Father stood on the roadway, beatified by the radiant smile he bestowed on Sunday upon a teeming collection plate.

But my foot slipped from the clutch pedal too suddenly, and the engine died. So did my heart, for this would end my driving. Instead of relieving me, however, father recranked "Maud" and hopped into the car.

We drove noisily homeward. Father sat beside me, indulgently pretending not to notice when I detoured two blocks to go past Dorothy's. The whole neighborhood was on the corner, playing kick the can. Their game stopped in awe as we rattled by.

On our own street a dog ran out before us, and I veered to avoid hitting him. One wheel jumped the curb. Father offered no assistance. He let me master the difficulty. He even let me drive through the alley into the back yard, where I honked the horn jubilantly to bring Eileen and mother to the window.

Father reached into the rear seat for the suitcase, but it was not there.

"What the mischief!" he exclaimed, realizing that he had left it by the side of the road where he cranked the car. He looked at me and I at him, but I kept a straight face.

Back we went, I driving. When we were again in the yard and the engine was dead, he spoke.

"When a dog barks at you," he said, "pay no attention to it. You watch the road, and the dog will look after himself. If you see a cow or a horse, you want to stop; and if you see a mule, get clear out of the car."

That's all he ever told me about driving.

CHAPTER FIVE

AFTER the hike there was a farewell meeting of the scouts to distribute merit badges won for excellence in camping, cooking, and woodcraft. As I had done nothing of merit, Mr. Seeley, with one eye on father and the other on my morale, appointed me a patrol leader. Perhaps Mr. Seeley suspected that without this incentive I might avoid scouting in the fall. If so, it was a bull's-eye hunch.

The meeting was short, and there was an hour of warm June night to spare before we were all expected home. On the street a group of older boys began to whisper. As I, the new patrol leader, approached, they widened their ranks to include me.

"Let's get some of Mrs. Hibbard's plums," someone proposed.

Mrs. Hibbard was the community's richest widow; her plum trees stood behind a four-foot red-brick wall in the Hibbard garden; they were very precious trees because with their fruit she refreshed the Episcopal minister and her Auction Club. The plums were not yet ripe, but that made them no less desirable to us.

I had misgivings, of course. My parsonage training seized me by the lapels and murmured, "Get thee behind me," but my desire to be a real fellow in the eyes of these older and bigger boys was overwhelming.

Trembling with excitement, I followed them over the cloistral wall and up a tree until my pockets were filled with stolen fruit. We had almost stripped one tree when Mrs. Hibbard discovered us.

"Boys," she screamed. "Get out of my orchard! Police!"

We ran, fleet, bulging shadows, over the wall in a leap, down the alley, across a vacant lot to the sanctity of a cave, which I had never before been invited to enter.

The green plums were delicious, the danger stimulating, the conversation invigorating. This was the life!

We sought bolder amusement. Why not pull trolleys? They said this was a great sport that required nice timing, agility, and fearlessness. To Twenty-third Street we went. Two boys stood at a corner. When the next streetcar came along, they signaled it to stop. As the noisy hulk responded, I slipped from the sanctuary of a convenient tree trunk and ripped the trolley cord behind the car. Amid a shower of sparks the lights burst off, the tram stopped, and an angry motorman descended from his controls. By this time we had vanished into the night to meet our comrades at a pre-arranged rendezvous.

After three successes our excitement abated.

"Let's pull the fire alarm," someone exulted.

That was our undoing. The police, called by Mrs. Hibbard and attracted to Twenty-third Street by reports of rowdyism, encountered us as we fled from the red box on the corner of Twenty-third and Elm and nabbed the three whose legs were shortest. They caught me first.

We were in our scout uniforms, and the police knew us all by sight. Hauled to a precinct station, we were interrogated concerning the identity of our escaped companions. We would not answer. In ten minutes father, a stern ecclesiastical figure of parental wrath, arrived at the station.

A newspaper reporter dropped in, too, on his night rounds. He asked many questions of my father and the other two fathers when they appeared. Three names went down on the dreadful blotter. The charge was malicious mischief, which possibly involved an appearance in Judge Lindsey's juvenile court. The reporter reached for the telephone as father led me away.

Enroute home father was grim, too stunned to talk. Such conduct transcended his experience. When he could find no words, he acted. I knew what that meant. I had been taken to the basement before, and it wasn't fun.

At the parsonage we headed in the direction of the cellar entry.

But around the house came Charles Archer, a lawyer with four sons, a short, red-swarthy fellow with a once-broken nose. Even in the dark I could see his amusement.

"By Joe, Brother Spence," he exclaimed, "I didn't know he had it in him."

"Eh?" said father.

"News travels fast when the preacher's in trouble," Mr. Archer went on. "I'm not soliciting this case, but I'm your lawyer and I'd consider it a pleasure to handle it. After all, boys will be boys."

"Eh?" father repeated. "Oh. I guess so. Come in the house. I want to talk to you."

I waited outside for my trip to the basement, but father and Mr. Archer talked a long time in the front room. Through the window drifted fragments of their conversation.

"There was a watermelon patch that belonged to an Irish family named Higgins," Mr. Archer was saying. "Well, Brother—" Here his voice huddled into a confidence. Occasional lifts propelled strange phrases. "But that was just the beginning— When we got the hayrack up on the church roof— The presiding elder whooping down the road after us in his nightshirt, trying to get that horse back—"

Father's memory, thus primed, began to flow.

"That reminds me of a prank we played on an Irishman in Newbridge— Well, Shaughnessy had the finest outhouse in the county. It took eight of us to move it, and half the night— But there it was next morning, in front of the schoolhouse (laughter)—and to get into the building you had to go through it. We had cut another door and on the outside had painted in red the name of Timothy J. Shaughnessy—"

Mr. Archer departed very late. Father locked the door and went up to bed. From the lawn I watched the light in his room and saw his shadow cross the window shade. The light went off. The shade opened. Father stood for a moment in the window, looking off toward snow-capped Mount Evans, at which a third-quarter moon was nibbling. His shadow was at ease. There was nothing in his big frame except peace.

When he saw me, he leaned out the window.

"You're locked out."

"I can go up the rainspout."

"Then you'd better do it," he said; "you've been out long enough tonight."

When I came down to breakfast in the morning the paper was in his hand. He called me to him and pointed to a long story on the front page. I read it through, and he cleared his throat.

"I'm not going to punish you for what you did last night," he said. "The court will do that. But I want you to take a good look at this paper. Every member of the church is reading it."

His eyebrows were close together, black and heavy. "You will notice that your name is in the first paragraph, and mine, and that of the church. The other boys are not mentioned until the third paragraph."

He read the headline aloud, " 'Preacher's Son Leads Scout Troop in Park Hill Pranks.' "

I said nothing.

"How does that sound?" he went on. "The first two words tell the whole story. Preacher's son. That's all that matters to the newspapers. It was a preacher's son. That you were accompanied by a doctor's son and an undertaker's son is nothing."

Father cleared his throat and continued to read: " 'Not only was the diminutive thirteen-year-old culprit the son of the minister of Park Hill Church, but he was last night appointed a patrol leader of Troop Fifteen, which is sponsored by the church and holds its meetings in the church basement. It is believed his companions were members of his own patrol, but only two were apprehended. They were—' "

Father stopped reading and said a few words on his own behalf. "People are always waiting for the preacher's son to get in trouble. When a preacher, who tries hard to correct evil, cannot keep order in his own house the reflection is on him, not on the culprit; it is on me, not on you. And not on you so much as on scouting, for the scouts made a leader of you, and you abused your leadership."

He gave me opportunity to defend myself, but I knew better than to start an argument.

"Even if you did not initiate last night's pranks, you are responsible, for as leader you should have put your foot down and you did not. I hope you are thoroughly ashamed of yourself and sorry for the disgrace you have brought to your family and to scouting. You may eat your breakfast."

I ate quickly.

Chastened, I went timidly that morning to the store for the day's groceries. The Palmer boys were on their porch down the block. I saw them from afar and hoped to pass them unobserved. They used to make fun of me in scout troop, jeer at my leading the singing in church, and ridicule every game I suggested when the boys were playing in the street.

Pretending not to notice them, I approached their house. But they saw me, and Bob jumped from the porch swing. Hot-faced, I quickened my pace. I could take father's reprimands, but I dreaded the sharp tongue of the Palmer boys.

"Hey, Hartz, come here a minute!"

"I've got to go to the store."

"I wanna ask you something."

"I'm in a hurry."

"What are you doing this afternoon?"

I paused, fearful of a trap.

"We're going out to snare rabbits—wanna go?"

Did I want to go! Incredulously happy I went to the porch.

Snaring rabbits was sport of the big kids: the Palmers, the Keelers, and fellows like Dudley Joy, who knew how to play poker. Often they had pedaled their bicycles to the tumbleweed prairies a few blocks away for gophers or rabbits, but I had never been included. And I knew all about gophers, having trapped them in Sioux City for the 25-cent bounty the county paid.

"Sure," I said, at once an authority. "What do you get them with, rope or twine?"

"Twine."

"That's right. What do you smoke 'em out with?"

"Smoke 'em out?"

"Sure, smoke 'em out. How do you expect to get a rabbit out of his hole unless you smoke him out?"

"Did you ever catch any that way?"

"Sure, dozens. Gophers, too. Ever snare gophers?"

They hadn't.

"I'll show you," I said, and we agreed to meet after lunch.

Nearer the corner Howard Gange, my own age, stepped off his porch. "Hey, Hartz, how d'you feel?"

"Okay."

"You do?"

"Sure, why not?"

"Didn't you get licked or anything?"

"No—"

Howard pressed me for details, which I provided, at first reluctantly then more confidently as the Bramley boys abandoned their perch on the drugstore railing to gather round. What had the police said to me and I to them? What questions had the reporter asked? When was I to appear in juvenile court? I supplied exhaustive answers to all queries, including some on which I had no information. I even began to hope I *would* be taken to court.

Wondrously, I realized, I had become a hero. Here was something I had not counted on. Father had said the whole community would be ashamed of me, but he didn't know what he was talking about.

Finally Howard Gange asked a question that added authority to dignity.

"Hey, Hartz, what's the best way to make a hoop-stick?"

"Depends on the hoop," I said, inventing a large number of qualifications and specifications for various types of rolling wheels. Howard was impressed. So were the others.

All week long I was consulted—and included. The gopher snaring was a great success, because of the smoke. The cave was remodeled under my direction.

During the week father and I made a trip to the police station downtown, where I was given a solemn lecture and released from the threat of a court trial, much to father's relief and my disappointment. This second contact with the law I told and retold in the cave over cigarettes made from tea and newspaper. Everybody listened to me.

The greatest triumph of all came on Sunday. I had been afraid to anticipate what might happen when I faced father's parishioners and the girls at Sunday school and church, especially Dorothy Snell, whose attention I was trying to divert from Junior Ramsay.

On the lawn the elders who had arrived early smiled in amusement, and I went into the junior department to lead the singing with considerable pride. As usual, after the bell had quieted all noisy voices and mother had taken her seat behind the table where she presided, I arose with the hymn book and called a number that mother had selected. It was A. J. Gordon's devout and adoring:

> *Lord Jesus, I love Thee,*
> *I know Thou art mine.*

The children waited for my forthright pitch before taking their own. Eileen plunked the piano. The hymn was one I knew by heart. Earnestly I belayed it, beating time with my left hand, holding the hymnal in my right. The second verse started:

> *I love Thee because*
> *Thou hast first loved me—*

Dorothy was looking at me! She was singing to me! There was no doubt about it. With a little shock I recoiled momentarily from the profane purpose the hymn was serving and mustered a little piety on the next two lines:

> *And purchased my pardon*
> *On Calvary's tree.*

When she continued to smile through the next two lines and cast an impish, disdainful glance at my rival,

Jordan Ramsay, Jr., I responded. Her implication was mighty, her blue eyes round and significant:

> *I love Thee for wearing*
> *The thorns on Thy brow.*

I smiled. She smiled. We finished the hymn beaming on each other:

> *If ever I loved Thee*
> *Lord Jesus, 'tis now.*

The convocation yielded to instruction classes. Dorothy was in another room. Junior Ramsay, however, was in my class, and I had a feeling he knew. He seemed mighty uncomfortable and mighty jealous.

After Sunday school I saw Dorothy in the church lobby waiting for her father and mother.

"Hi," she called softly.

"Hi, Dorothy. What you doing this afternoon?"

"Nothing."

"I might come over."

She smiled wonderfully. "I'll make some candy if you do," she invited. "But don't tell Junior."

"Oh, that Junior!" I said deprecatingly and went to join mother in our pew.

CHAPTER SIX

In JUNIOR high I had met some fellows who lived on the hem of City Park, a considerable distance from home. They played baseball and football and went to the movies on Saturday. They also had an organization, the Two Gun Club, which shortly after my escapade with the police I was invited to join.

The glamour of the Two Gun Club was its quarters, a tree house in a large oak behind Walter Lenahan's house. Since Walter's parents were away all day operating an insurance business, there were no adults around to pry into secret meetings. Mrs. Lenahan atoned for her absence by leaving large quantities of Hires root beer in the icebox and elegant "store cookies" in a cakebox.

The Lenahans encouraged Walter to use his home for his social headquarters and generously financed his hobbies. He had a tool chest with an electric lathe and freight as well as passenger cars for his electric railway. As club members we shared his toys, ate his store cookies, drank his root beer, and in return contributed to the tree house decks of forbidden playing cards, parentally disapproved books, certain pictures of movie stars, tea leaves for cigarettes, and an occasional pilfered cigar.

We all had wooden revolvers, some with notches on the barrels, and when a member in the clubhouse heard someone scrambling up the tree trunk, he cocked his wooden gun with a rubber band fitted to the bolt. Not until the proper signs were exchanged did he relax his "drop" on the interloper and permit him to enter. Our password was "Cheese it, the cops," the door signal two staccato raps, two legato raps, and then, after two answering thuds from inside the door, three very quick raps. Our identification signals were an index finger hooked over the nose, which meant "Hello, brother gunman"; thumb and index finger stroking right ear, which signified "Danger"; and a pat on the cowlick at the back of the head, which pleaded "Come to the rescue!"

The Two Gun Club specialized in cowboy stories, which we read in magazines and then reenacted. We were all riders for the Bar-X Ranch. Our ring, bought for fifty cents from a Chicago novelty house, was the shape of a horseshoe with an inset bar and the letter X. This brand we put on all our possessions.

Father had no reason to worry over my daily absence in another part of town. I told him about the tree house. He could not see me gallop over fences and through alleys so far from home.

The club had five members besides Walter Lenahan. Because Walter owned the tree house and sports equipment and was proprietor of the saloon (basement playroom in which he dispensed root beer), he was our president. His title, however, was Foreman of the Bar-X Ranch.

Walter was growing out of his last pair of short pants

and tried to snag them on nails all summer to hasten his debut into long trousers. His legs were spindly, knocky at the knees, and not quite coordinated, and his expression was always a little startled, as though he had just heard something shocking. He was neither a leader nor a follower but entered happily into any sport suggested, though occasionally protesting the abuse of his toys with a halfhearted "Aw, gee."

Our real leader was Shorty Sloane, a chiropractor's son with a quick eye for deviltry. He knew all the rules of card games, was a pretty good cusser, and commanded us in any enterprises requiring fisticuffs. Shorty was a runt and usually sniffed from a head cold. But these physical drawbacks did not prevent him from fighting, by voice if possible or by action if necessary, when someone opposed his will. Shorty did not find it difficult to manage Walter and to intimidate Joe Henry Longwell, Steve Fuller, Chris Torcher, and me.

Joe Henry was gangly and nimble. Whenever we needed a bundle of laths from a building project or a magazine from a drugstore, Joe Henry was the boy to swipe it, even though his father was a superior court judge.

Steve was a whiz at algebra, a builder of model airplanes and kites. Naval aviation was all Steve really cared about, and although he rode earnestly for the Bar-X Ranch, sometimes you'd hear him purring to himself as he galloped down the alley, and you knew Steve was zooming high above the arroyos and mesas, playing a game of his own. His teeth were in straighteners, and his mother made him practice on the violin.

Chris Torcher, who was larger and heavier than the

rest of us, played left end on the junior high football team. When the club was receiving orders for some project, Chris would lower his heavy head, grit his teeth, and listen intently. Then suddenly he'd smile. "I got it," he'd say. "Let's go." We knew then that the instructions would not be misunderstood by any of us.

I was the sixth member of the club, commonly called either Pretzel (a bastardization of my given name) or Shrimp. I was admitted because of my prestige. No other member had been in trouble with the police. My other outstanding asset was that I could supply, from mother's tea chest, the makin's for our cigarettes.

Summer progressed excitingly. We dramatized one Wild West story after another with great success. Two blocks away another secret order had headquarters in a barn. On rainy days we challenged our rivals to boxing matches and poker games. On sunny days we raided each other's headquarters and carried away trophies and toys. By agreement these forays were not conducted after dark, on Tuesday morning when everyone was at music lessons, or on Saturday afternoon when movies were shown at the Bluebird.

In the Two Gun Club I learned to play card games for pennies and matches, to cuss a little, and to get along with other boys in competitive sports. I compensated for my smaller size by verbal fluency, furnishing the picturesque speech for our cattle rustling and other predatory activities. Without knowing it, mother was a great help to us by directing me to Jack London and Bret Harte, whose dialogue I adapted liberally to our uses.

One day Joe Henry Longwell "appropriated" a magazine because its cover illustrated a masked cowboy riding hell for leather through sagebrush. The leading story described a character worthy of our mettle. We read the lurid tale aloud, each of us mentally selecting the part he cared to play, when abruptly the narrative ended at a thrilling climax. It was a continued story.

No matter. We assigned roles and performed it anyway, and as each new issue of the magazine appeared we enacted new scenes.

All went well until, in Chapter XVI, a heroine appeared. That stumped us. Until then we had shunned all communication with girls. Not even Arline Trowbridge, who was Walter Lenahan's "girl," had been in the tree house. Any story that so much as hinted at "mushy stuff" we had scorned. But the white-masked bandit had too strong a hold on us by this time to be readily discarded. He was our hero, our example, our pal.

Shorty Sloane's voice stumbled as he read aloud the description of Adelia Dell and of our hero leaping from his horse and doffing his hat to make her acquaintance. At the bandit's praise of Adelia's beauty, Shorty stopped reading altogether.

It was as though a traitor had been discovered in our midst. A terrible silence wallowed through the tree house. No one looked at anyone else. If Dutch Patterson and his barn gang had raided us then, we'd have been trapped like the sheriff's posse the white bandit had exterminated in Suicide Gulch. Steve Fuller brushed aside ashes with his little finger from his tealeaf cigarette and expressed the general sentiment.

"Shucks!" he said.

But after a desultory, heartbroken argument we decided not to let down our pal, the white-masked bandit. If he was going soft, that was his business; the gang had to stick together. We decided to play the sorry story to its end.

This required a female. We suggested inviting Arline, but Walter wasn't sharing his girl even with the blood brothers of the Two Gun Club.

Our second choice was thirteen-year-old Betty Havenor, who lived across the alley. She was brown haired, pretty, and cooperative. By emphatic agreement she was not, under any circumstance, to share club secrets or the clubhouse, and she was to be dropped as soon as the bandit story was concluded.

Almost too willingly she consented to be our heroine and to abide by our restrictions. In fact, when the boundaries of her fellowship were explained, she said, "I wouldn't think of going into your rickety old tree house. I can smell it from here, and that's enough."

Somehow, complications crept upon us. Betty's mother refused to let her remain a captive of the sheriff's posse in the Havenor-garage "jail" for two days. Betty recruited a substitute. Before long plump Agnes Angell had a part in our play, then red-haired Mary Byron, and, suddenly, noisy, scatterbrained Sally Phipps.

"Who invited Sally?" Walter whispered when she appeared.

No one knew. There she was and there she stayed.

Shorty called an urgent meeting in the saloon.

"Who do these dames think they are anyway?" he asked belligerently. "They aren't running this show."

But they were. We were being squeezed out of our own drama.

Slowly we drank our root beer, depressed by the sordidness of a world in which white-masked bandits fell for skirts. Girls spoiled everything.

"Well," Shorty said finally, "that's what we get!" But in the same breath he voiced an inspiration. "What's all that stuff?" he asked, pointing to the boxes that contained electric-train equipment. As Walter inventoried his stock, Shorty looked out the window to the broad lawn with its S-shaped birdbath and generous flower beds.

"Let's build a railroad *outside*," he shouted, and the white-masked bandit was forgotten.

The girls could not understand why our wonderful game ended or why we became engineers, firemen, and dispatchers. But they knew better than to invade Walter's yard. They had tried that before.

Somehow or other I could not forget Betty. She had been a good sport, following us over fences and hiding in the tumbleweeds, heedless of scratched knees and broken fingernails.

Often I looked across the alley and caught her watching us. She would lower her head, looking down at her book, until all I could see was her long curls and the tip of her nose.

One Saturday morning while I was doing my weekly chores at home, Dr. and Mrs. Bramley drove up in a new Dodge and invited father and mother on a trial spin over Lookout Mountain and down Bear Creek Canyon.

Their departure left me alone in the house, since

Eileen and Fraser were visiting friends for the day. I sauntered to the back yard, where the Ford was parked, and immediately had an idea.

Why not invite Betty to the movies? Driving up in front of the Bluebird with a date would be the sensation of the summer.

Father need never know. I'd be home ahead of him. I could buy a gallon of gasoline.

The only obstacle was the matter of capital: two tickets 20 cents, one gallon of gas 26 cents, peanuts or popcorn to eat during the show 5 cents, ice cream cones later 10 cents—total 61 cents, a fortune.

Thoughtfully I rambled the house, taking inventory: allowance for the week 25 cents; in my bank, subject to withdrawal by manipulation, 13 cents. I tried Fraser's bank. Empty. Likewise Eileen's purse. In the kitchen there was a jug for coins to pay the iceman. It, too, was empty. But in the china cupboard on the lowest shelf was a quarter, Eileen's allowance, as yet unclaimed.

Betty's face appeared temptingly, and the triumph of driving with her to the Bluebird grew more and more desirable, well worth the risk of Eileen's anger.

I telephoned Betty.

Her high voice, always a little excited, exclaimed, "Oh my, just a minute. I'll ask mother."

Mrs. Havenor came to the telephone.

"Is anyone going with you?" she wanted to know.

"No," I said, "just the two of us. I have the car for the day, and I thought—"

"Oh, you have your car. Well, I don't know—"

"Please, mummy," I overheard Betty whisper behind the telephone, but Mrs. Havenor hedged.

Would we come straight home? Yes, indeed. Would I drive carefully? I should say so. Then, "I guess it's all right," she said.

I went again to look at that 25-cent piece which was not mine. All during my lunch of cold beans and ham I pondered the grave consequences of borrowing. Appropriating another's money was a crime subject to terrible punishment.

Eventually 12:45 came. It was time to be on my way. Eileen's allowance was still on the cupboard shelf. Quickly and guiltily I took it and hurried from the house. But after the car was cranked, I thought of father. What if he came home and found the car gone?

Back into the house I ran; wrote a note, "I have taken the car; I will pay for the gas"; and hung it on the hall tree where father always put his hat. Then off to Betty's I rattled, elated by my first solitary drive in an automobile and by my first date.

At the Bluebird Betty and I ate popcorn, cheered the hero, and gauged our friends' reaction to our being together. Of whispers I was tolerant and to giggles impervious; all these others had walked or come on bicycles. I had brought Betty in a car.

Betty played up to me, made me understand that I was now a being set apart as a man who drove a car. I became aware of her breathing, of the kicking of her heels as they swung back and forth in time with the piano music.

After the show we bought ice cream cones at a corner drugstore, then returned to sit conspicuously in the front seat of the car. Everyone we knew saw us. But suddenly I had a most uncomfortable feeling. Dorothy sauntered by, and the glance she gave me was not one of admiration. It was timid, frightened, hurt, as though I had called her a name. Betty noticed it, too.

"Who's that?" she asked.

"Oh, just a kid that lives up by my house."

Betty wisely changed the subject and began to signal members of the Two Gun Club and friends of her own. We were eight in the car when we left the Bluebird, ten when we reached Betty's house to eat cookies and drink lemonade.

About five o'clock I excused myself. Father would be home soon. Glowing over a good-by smile from Betty, I started toward Park Hill, but the car seemed to move slowly now. As I turned into our block, I saw father on the porch.

To duck him I took the car up the alley and parked it in the side yard, where it belonged.

But this was a bad maneuver, for just inside the kitchen door I met mother, whose eyes were stern.

"We found your note," she said sharply. "It amused your father but not me."

"What's wrong, mother?" Surely she could not be angry after I had offered to pay for the gas.

"Where did you get the money to finance your ride this afternoon?"

Obviously she had discovered the truth.

"Is Eileen home yet?" I parried.

"It makes no difference whether she is or not. You took her money, didn't you?"

"Yes, but—"

"You used her allowance to have a good time by yourself."

[60]

"I'll pay her back."

"And what will she do meanwhile?"

This problem had not occurred to me.

"Go ask your father," mother commanded, "to advance you next week's allowance. Tell him you took Eileen's money."

"Oh, gee, mother. I—"

"Tell him the truth."

"Oh, mother, I can't—"

"That's all," she said and went about the business of getting dinner. Slowly I went toward the sound of the creaking porch swing. I was in for it now. But at the door mother recalled me.

"By the way," she asked, "why did you need so much money today?"

There it was. Mother was much too wise.

"I took Betty Havenor to the Bluebird."

"Who is Betty Havenor?" she asked.

"She lives across the way from the Lenahans. She used to play with us."

"Do I know her parents? Are they church people?"

"They're Congregationalists, friends of the Lenahans."

Mother sighed and turned to stir a cream sauce on the stove.

"So you have taken a girl to the movies—a girl I don't even know."

I was unable to diagnose the implications of that one.

She went to the pantry, returned with a kettle of potatoes and a paring knife, and handed them to me. As I sat down on a high stool and set to work, she put her arm around my shoulders and pressed me tightly.

"Oh, son," she said.

"What's the matter?"

Whatever it was, she shook it off. "Nothing's the matter," she answered, her voice bright now, "but I wonder what Dorothy will think about you and Betty?"

The paring knife dropped into the pan. My flirtations over the hymnbook these past four Sundays had not gone unnoticed.

"Oh, that." I was uncomfortable.

"I think, son," mother laughed, "it's time your allowance was increased. I'll lend you enough to repay Eileen. We'll see father about giving you a little more money."

The potatoes flew through my hands into the pot. I wanted to get up and hug mother to let her know how I felt. But something warned me I'd better just let well enough alone.

CHAPTER SEVEN

*W*HEN my allowance was increased from 25 to 50 cents a week, Eileen quickly negotiated a like increment for herself. Nearly sixteen, she was becoming boy and clothes conscious, and 25 cents a week did not go very far.

Before our door every afternoon there was a bicycle and in the porch swing its owner, a tribute to my sister's personality, because parsonage daughters don't chase boys, and young men don't usually date around a preacher's house.

Eileen's curly hair was golden, her brown eyes large and full of mischief, her smile provoking. She also had a quick-flaring temper, but it was mostly histrionics to compete against father. Even when her dander was genuine, it was nothing to be afraid of for she melted quickly into a butter-soft remorse that was perhaps her most appealing mood.

Father had kept a proud eye on her during childhood. Hers was the photograph that was sent to the Canadian relatives every Christmas. But because of her beauty father kept her close to home. He wasn't taking any chances.

When we moved to Sioux City, Eileen was eleven years old, and mother decided to work on father to give her a little more freedom. The campaign was beginning to show a few results when an incident renewed father's determination to cloister her.

Father was not sure whether Eileen, who played the piano well, possessed all the talent he attributed to her or whether his judgment was warped by parental fondness. So he arranged an audition for her when Rudolf Ganz came to town.

Ganz listened while she brushed off Chopin, Beethoven, and Debussy, then turned to father.

"She undoubtedly has talent," he said, "but don't waste too much money on it. She's so pretty she'll marry the first man who takes her fancy."

Father continued to provide music lessons, but every time a lad showed up at the house to court Eileen, father interpreted literally Ganz's prediction. He was serious even about her twelve-year-old "crushes." Eventually her existence contracted to the entertainment of girls only. She was fast becoming a prissy, demure shell of a girl. She was so sheltered, in fact, that when a course on "the next generation" was introduced into the seventh grade of Sioux City's schools and her sixty-two-year-old maiden teacher, forced by curriculum to talk about the mating of birds and bees, began to explain natural function, Eileen was terrified. Other children had a good idea what life was all about but not Eileen; the pastor's child is last to learn about such things. She walked into group sex education cold and emerged from the first lesson so frightened that she would not walk home from school with me.

This was the period of the First World War, of the influenza epidemic, and of postwar adjustments. Father and mother, after listening to the troubles of parishioners all day and half the night, had no strength for juvenile difficulties at breakfast and dinner. Eileen did not bother them about her troubles, which to her were no less acute than those of the butcher, the war veteran, and the oil-stock salesman.

Even on week ends and holidays father was too busy to give Eileen close attention. On Sunday he was in the pulpit all morning, in meditation all afternoon, in the pulpit all evening. On every holiday he made a speech somewhere. He was in great demand as a public speaker. Because, an American citizen but not American born, he loved the country of his naturalization with a devoutness unappreciated by many who had always taken their citizenship for granted, he was particularly glad to speak on July Fourth, Memorial Day, and Labor Day.

The money he earned in this way was often the margin between eating and going to bed hungry, and I can remember one Labor Day when, mother having told him that with all bills paid there remained only $6 to last until midmonth, he responded: "Well, I get $25 for my speech today, thank God."

Eileen often told me that she would have preferred an empty stomach if she could have walked with father in the woods on a holiday and discussed her problems with him. The opportunity, however, never arose.

As a result Eileen turned to Grace Lake, one of mother's friends, who proved to be a benefactress. Grace understood the cruel confinement of a daughter in a preacher's house because her own father had been a shouting Methodist circuit rider. Married and affluent, with a summer cottage at a smart resort and no children of her own, she was in a position to be a real friend to a growing girl. Grace's home, her cottage, and her friends became Eileen's; and father, a respecter of Mrs. Lake's Methodist background, approved.

He didn't know about the post-office games Eileen played with boys whose parents also had summer homes or about her proficiency at cribbage under the tutelage of Grace's husband, a livestock-commission merchant. Certainly father was unaware that Frank Lake brought home the latest jazz records for Eileen to dance to and that Grace's icebox was always filled with the sort of provender to attract boys from miles around.

We had not been long in Denver before a fellow who had met Eileen at school made the mistake of parking before our door in the largest red Packard in town and emerging from it in a suit with wide purple stripes, a two-button vest, and trousers cut like a bullfighter's.

Father, who did not know that eighteen-year-olds were for the moment influenced by the fashion of a certain movie actor named Rudolph Valentino (he had not seen the heart-throbbing epic *Blood and Sand*), took one look at Joe and retired to his study to pray for the younger generation.

From that time on Joe was *persona non grata* around the parsonage, even when he appeared, as ultimately he did, clad in an exact duplicate of father's own favorite pin stripe, with the added conservative touches of a black four-in-hand tie and standard white collar. Joe even visited our church, though by inheritance an Episcopalian, and sat three Sundays in the third row, where we all saw him put 50 cents in the collection plate. It made no difference. As far as father was concerned, Joe had shown his true colors with his red car and purple pants.

Eileen's girl friends danced. They gave theater parties at Elitch's Gardens. They played a game called bridge. They enjoyed picnics with boys in the mountains. Eileen might join mixed parties only for ice skating and for boating on City Park Lake, which shows how wide of the mark parental decisions can be, for Eileen, boating on the lake, had to jump out and wade ashore one afternoon to escape being kissed in public.

All the other girls had bobbed their hair, but father would not permit this frivolity. "If a woman have long hair, it is a glory to her," he quoted I Corinthians with finality.

In Sunday school Eileen assisted in the cradle roll, which is the children-in-arms department. She sat in a conspicuous seat during the morning-worship service and afterward fraternized with the adults, inquired after the sick, and jollied old men who tried to hold her hand. Frequently she was an officer in the Epworth League, usually being stuck with the fourth vice presidency, which is the party chairmanship. She played the piano at League meetings, which necessitated her punctual and meticulous attendance, and she always led off the sentence prayers as an inspiration to others.

She also belonged to the Queen Esthers, who in addition to money-raising for missions gave an annual play. Eileen could not take too prominent a part nor too lean a one. If the former, there were jealousies; if the latter, she shirked her Christian duty.

Preparations for the plays started with the assignment of roles, the first reading of lines, and the selection of a costume for the pastor's daughter that would be adequate and at the same time not rob the food budget.

One year, I remember, the city junior tennis champion had the lead in a dramatic version of Tennyson's poem *The May Queen*. With great effect, after forty minutes of preamble, she was to say, while someone combed her long blond hair, "Call me early, mother, for I'm to be queen of the May," the catch being that she doesn't waken in the morning, having gone to join other Queen Esthers in Heaven.

Eileen was assigned the part of the mother, which nobody else wanted. In middle-age make-up, she had to run errands for the May queen and trudge on and off stage to single lines such as "No, my precious daughter," and "Yes, my sweet, delicious daughter." It was that last line that got her. At home she looked up the meaning of the adjective "delicious." "Affording exquisite pleasure, especially to the taste," she read aloud, threatening that if she had to act an old woman and say such a stupid line in public, she would give the hair a good tug, even if the May queen was going to die before morning.

On the night of the performance Roberta, the heroine, made a capital appearance, for she had caught a bad cold playing tennis and sounded as though she was in the ultimate phase of throat infection.

As the hair-combing scene approached, father, mother, Fraser, and I held our breaths in good 35-cent seats. Eileen shot us a glance.

"Yes," she said, altering the line a bit, "you great big delicious thing, you," and yanked the hair hard.

"Ouch!" the May queen yelped nasally, and the audience applauded. Eileen spoiled the death scene but brought life to an otherwise dull performance. Roberta, understanding Eileen's pique, enjoyed the incident, but her mother was snorting mad.

"The idea!" she gasped, corralling father in the church lobby. "The *very* idea! I've always denied that preachers' children were different from others, but now I'm not so sure."

"There was a snarl in her hair, likely," father replied.

Another of Eileen's duties was to perform occasionally in church with the young people's choir. On one choral appearance Eileen was to sing with her inseparable companion, Thelma Eaton, a duet, *The Lord Is My Shepherd*. The number was in the middle of an anthem immediately following a contralto solo. But the contralto was nervous and so tremulous that Eileen and Thelma began to giggle. Having begun this silly business, they completely lost control of themselves. At their cue to sing no voices sounded. They were choking.

The organist poked her head anxiously around the console to locate the trouble, and Eileen, seeing her pained countenance, snorted out loud. At this, father reared back in his pulpit seat and had a look, which provoked Thelma into an outrageous titter. Quickly the organist skipped the duet and proceeded to the ensemble, sung by twenty earnest voices.

After church a member with whom Eileen had previously collided caught her by the wrist.

"Not so fast, young lady, not so fast," he said. "You're a sinful child, and if your father can't chastise

[69]

you, I'll do it myself." Whereupon he proceeded to lay her out with words phrased, no doubt, during father's sermon.

Eileen reached home in tears, which father misinterpreted as induced by mortification. But she put him right, explaining her encounter.

Father jumped to the telephone, and the church member's dinner was cold before father finished with him. Any correction his daughter needed, he said, would be administered at home. There were enough busybodies criticizing the pastor's children without having anyone lay hands on one of them. And, furthermore, if ever he heard of such contumacious conduct in future, he'd show somebody what the "laying on of hands" could be like.

After that he ate his dinner agreeably. By mince-pie time he was in such a jovial mood that Eileen dared to mention again her desire for bobbed hair. She felt self-conscious, she said, being the only long-haired girl in the choir.

Father debated this silently, cocking his head to the right for pro arguments, to the left for cons. Finally his head remained slightly to starboard, and he smiled.

"All right," he announced, "I hadn't thought of it that way."

Eileen leaped up and kissed his forehead, but the demonstration was premature.

"That's lovely, dear," mother told Eileen. "You and I will *both* have our hair cut tomorrow."

Father choked. "You'll *what?*"

"I said we'd both go. I've wanted my hair short for a long time. We're very happy you see things our way."

"Oh, no," father backtracked, "oh, no! I said Eileen. That didn't apply to *you,* Hope."

"Why not?" asked mother. "If it's all right for your daughter, it must be all right for me. The principle is the same."

"Oh, no, it's not." Father began to sweat. "Imagine the preacher's wife with hair as short as a Boy Scout's britches."

"How many women in church have long hair?" mother went on.

"Why—" He named a dozen. They were all at least sixty years old.

"So you are classing me with the old ladies," mother replied indignantly. "We won't be old, and we won't be dowdy, will we, Eilie?"

Seeing the feminine side of the house gang up on him, father swallowed half a glass of water and arose hastily.

"Not on your life!" he said. "I'd never hear the end of it. Nobody gets her hair cut around here, nobody."

He retired to his fortress, the study. Mother patted Eileen's hand and smiled, but said nothing.

For weeks father resolutely held his ground, but he was a hunted man. He played more golf, found more sick people to call on, preached more old sermons during this period than in any other time I can remember. When he did come home, he entered stealthily through the front door instead of by the back way for his customary chat with mother in the kitchen.

Things being as they were, he was not informed that Eileen had decided to give a party. Her friends had entertained her countless times. Now she must reciprocate. Long talks with mother, easy now that father was so much away from home, resulted in a heroic decision.

Park Hill's idea of a party was a bridge game. And mother, in her belligerent mood, decided there would also be one in the parsonage, where there had never been a deck of anything but flinch cards.

Gaily Eileen invited fifteen of her friends, bought prizes and decorations, and placed an order at Baur's confectionery for ice cream, cakes, and candies. She could not bring herself to buy the cards, but compromised by borrowing several packs from neighbors.

The house was cleaned and dusted for the great event. Eileen washed and ironed her bedroom curtains. I waxed the stairway and hall. Fraser polished the silver. Baur's deliveryman left a big freezer on the back step, two large baskets in the kitchen.

Then father came home to lunch an hour late.

"What's all the doings?" he asked good-naturedly, but hurt. He liked to be in on all the secrets.

"You'll have to get your lunch somewhere else, Will," mother told him. "It's past one o'clock. We've all eaten, and I can't mess up the kitchen now. Eileen's giving a party."

"Well, well," father said, as though pleased, "I'll get myself a bite of something. I won't be in the way."

"If you do, you'll wash your own dishes," mother admonished, speeding upstairs to put on her best dress. The girls would be arriving in half an hour.

Father fried an egg and some bacon, sang a hymn softly as he scoured his frying pan and put away the salt cellar.

Eileen began opening the Baur's boxes. The cupcakes, white frosted and decorated with red hearts, spades, diamonds, and clubs, caught his eye.

"What's this?" he asked.

"Just the refreshments," Eileen answered, putting the cakes on plates.

"Aren't those playing card symbols?"

"Yes."

Father began to catch on.

Swiftly he bolted into the living room shouting, "Hope!" But it was the only word he spoke, for there, neatly set up, were four borrowed card tables, with bridge tallies and two decks of cards on each. A plate of spicy candies in reds, greens, and whites added brightness to the already glittering scene.

Sedately mother descended the stairs.

"Yes, Will? Did you call me?"

He was transfixed, staring. If he had seen highball glasses and ash trays he could not have been more shocked.

"What—" he asked feebly—"what's this? Card playing?"

"Just a girls' party," mother smiled. "Please run along now. It will all be over by four o'clock."

"By four—by thunder, it won't. It won't even begin in this house." He was articulate enough now.

"I gave my consent."

"But not I mine!"

"Nobody asked you," said mother.

"Nobody—" He paused, up to his neck in deep water. "I won't have it!"

"But the girls were invited to a bridge game. Of course they'll have to play."

"You invi—you mean you actually sent out invitations, *inviting* people to make a—make a card room out of the parsonage?"

"Eileen asked a few of her friends in. Now please let's not have any more fuss."

"I daresay they're playing for money."

"For prizes."

"Exactly, for prizes. And prizes cost money. Gambling in my own house!"

Father now was in a real temper, the kind he came home with from official board meetings. Mother knew he would not surrender. On a matter of principle father did not retreat.

"Perhaps," she said quietly, "you have some other suggestion?"

"It's not my problem to think up parties for children."

"You'd rather embarrass your wife and daughter before a houseful of guests and have the story all over town before night?"

That cooled him off. Scandal there must not be.

"Take them downtown to a picture show."

"In the Ford?"

"On the streetcar."

"I really think you mean that," she said. "I'm sorry for you."

That set him off again, but he steadied when a girl in party dress stepped from a chauffeur-driven car and ran up the steps. Eileen, who had been trembling just inside the kitchen door, ran to greet her friend and sidetrack her upstairs.

"You see," mother whispered. "You want your daughter to take girls like that on the streetcar."

"All right," father yielded, "we'll find other means."

Quickly he telephoned four of his best friends and asked dulcetly if they would drive his daughter's party downtown.

"And theater tickets for twenty people?" asked mother when he had finished. "Who'll pay for them?"

I had never seen mother angry before. Her wrath was icy, although her voice had not raised so much as a half tone.

Ruefully father dug into his pocket and extracted the only bill therein, a ten-spot, booty of a wedding the previous day.

By the time the next guest reached the parsonage, not a trace of the bridge party remained in the living room. The carefully laid tables, the bright candies, the cards, all were hidden behind dining-room doors.

Fraser and I watched the guests bundle into automobiles for the trip downtown. They were happy at the change in plans. So, too, was Eileen, who would not have dared suggest a theater party because of the expense.

The movie was over at five, and even if mother and Eileen had gone to Baur's afterward for sodas, they should have been home by six. It was nearly seven when we saw them coming down the street from the trolley line.

"Well," father greeted them from the porch, "so you came home on the streetc—" That was as far as he got.

Mother and Eileen both had bobbed hair.

"Holy mackerel!" father gasped. "What's happened

[75]

to your hair?" They looked a little funny in hats meant
for their former estate, and they were both self-conscious.

"We had it cut—after the party," mother said firmly
and walked into the house, Eileen following her.

Father was a defeated man. He went to the living
room and staggered into his leather chair, as mother
went up to her room to give him plenty of time to
think over what had happened. She wanted him to

have a good soaking. When at last she came down and entered the kitchen, she did so without a word except to call me to remove the party debris from the dining room and set the table.

Presently she summoned the family to dinner. Father proceeded to his chair. There, staring up at him, was a dish of ice cream and two beautiful white cupcakes from which some ornamentation appeared to have been removed. Beside his teacup was a plate of gay red, green, and white candies.

"Your supper," mother announced. "We can't let all this food go to waste."

Miserably father sat down, we after him. He dabbled at the ice cream, sadly broke a cupcake in half, and inspected its chocolate interior.

When he seemed about to say something, mother headed him off.

"Eileen and I were going to pay this out of our party budget," she said, tucking the bill from Baur's into his hand, "but we used the money for our haircuts. You'll have to pay it, Will."

Father did not say a word.

CHAPTER EIGHT

In the fall the Boy Scouts did not encourage my re-enrollment. That was all right with me, for I was busy with the Stumblers Club.

When the Two Gun Club dropped the white-masked bandit and eliminated the girls from its games, the girls organized a club of their own, named D.W.M. They were mighty secretive about these initials, but Walter wormed their meaning from Arline. They meant Down With Men.

Strangely enough, the members numbered six, an exact duplicate of our group. They were my "girl," Betty Havenor; Walter's "girl," Arline Trowbridge; fat little Agnes Angell, who developed a crush on Steve after he played the violin in church; Sally Phipps, who could wrap tongue-tied Chris Torcher around her finger with her long thread of words; and Mary and Frances Byron. Frances was only eleven, and the girls didn't want to include her, but when she eavesdropped on the club secrets and threatened to tell them to everybody she knew, they let her in.

After school Walter and I began to meet oftener on Betty's front porch and less often in the tree house. The lure was dancing. We didn't want the other members of the Two Gun Club to know. We had no doubt what Shorty, especially, would say if he caught us ankling around the Havenor living room, sometimes in the arms of Betty's mother, responding to such commands as "Don't look at your feet!" and "Don't saw with your arms!"

Soon, however, Shorty was there. He didn't want to be left out of anything that was going on, even sissy stuff. One afternoon he dropped in on the excuse of borrowing Betty's Ancient History and remained for a dancing lesson. Before long all the Two Gunners were there except Chris; he was practicing with the football team.

Such activity became a problem to Mrs. Havenor. Betty's father liked his evening meal on time. Night after night he came home from the bank to find his favorite chair pushed into a corner behind a noisy Victrola and his dinner not even started. Eventually Mrs. Havenor had to "take steps."

We moved to the Byron house, which had a large basement recreation room. Mrs. Byron suggested the creation of the Stumblers Club, which would meet at her house every Friday night. That was fine, we thought. Even Chris Torcher could attend then.

Mrs. Byron was an ambitious, bossy woman, who had her dimpled elbows in many organizations, including one section of the Woman's Club of which she was chairman. She had decided to divert the vigor of the twelve children to a purpose of her own. The project was a youthful sextette from *Floradora,* complete with 1890 costuming. The Woman's Club would sponsor it, with Mrs. Byron at the piano and her two red-haired daughters prominently in the chorus.

She broached her scheme to us after the club's Friday-night activities were established. Immediately everyone approved except me. So far as my parents knew, my Friday activities were concerned with bobbing for apples and guessing games. Any public hoofing on my part was likely to cause a greater rumpus than Eileen's bridge party.

Without much elaboration I told mother that Mrs. Byron wanted the twelve of us to be in some doings that entailed a song. Since mother was proud of my singing and did not question a Woman's Club recreational project for children, she consented. She was too busy at the moment with a church Christmas pageant to give the matter serious thought.

Two weeks later, when she discovered that I would need tail coat, a double-breasted vest, a high hat, spats, and a cane, she became anxious, but it was too late for me to withdraw. Rehearsals had begun.

These rehearsals, held in the Byron game room, would have shattered my father. The girls lined up and went through a parasol-dance routine, after which the six boys, simulating a hop step, dodged onto the scene and began a coquettish song:

> BOYS: *Tell me, pretty maiden, are*
> *There any more at home like you?*
>
> GIRLS: *There are a few, Kind Sir*
> *But simple girls, and proper, too.*
>
> BOYS: *Then tell me, pretty maiden, what*
> *These very pretty girlies do?*

And so on. The interchange became a dance for the twelve of us, which ended with a swishing of skirts and twirling of canes from the game room into the coal cellar.

One afternoon our rehearsal progressed so well that Mrs. Byron invited us to relax over milk and cake. Soon she had us in a huddle around her while she described a spiritualistic séance she had attended the night before. She told us how a spirit had entered the darkened room, knocked over the table and set it up again, and answered extremely personal questions with a rap or a double rap. Then had come a "revelation." In a corner of the ceiling, illuminated by an eerie yellow light, appeared a silver dagger, dripping blood.

At that point we all decided it was time to go home.

The February avenues were dark, the streetcar a welcome contact with the material world. But the bloody dagger pursued me down the black street from the trolley to the door, and I entered the house trembling. If life after death included such bloodcurdling stuff, why had I never heard of it? Why had father concealed this aspect? Did father's heaven, which he said was all kindness, happiness, and compassion, contain such threats and bleedings?

Over dinner I asked father to square his Hereafter with Mrs. Byron's. As my stammering question unfolded, the pork chop he was cutting scooted from his plate to the tablecloth.

"Great Scott!" he shouted. "Where in the world did you get hold of such nonsense?"

A thorough inquisition followed. He fumed, he fussed. He walked up and down the dining room until it became too small for his temper, then opened the folding doors to include the living room. Hands tucked under his belt, shoulders hunched down, jaw buried in chest, he paced, listened, and boiled. When I came to the dripping dagger, he could stand no more.

"Stop it! Stop it! Such utter asinine nonsense I never heard. Bloody daggers, indeed! Who is this fool woman, anyway?"

I told him.

He retired to the telephone and was gone a long time.

"Well," he gasped on his return, "I saved you from that anyway. Why didn't you tell me you were being made into a chorus boy?"

"A what?"

"A—well, never mind. It's ended anyhow. You're not to go back there again. Is that perfectly clear?"

"But—"

"I know how you feel, sonny," he went on, conciliatingly, "but you can't get mixed up in a stage show. I know you had permission, but your mother and I had no idea what was going on."

He stomped from the house and walked up and down the lawn. After I had finished drying the dinner dishes and had retired to my bedroom to study, he came to me.

"Here's a book," he said, "on psychic research. That's the scientific name for this bloody-dagger business. When you get time, read it. And now—" He sat down on my bed, his great hands covering his knees.

"The trouble is that we let you play in another neighborhood, where we couldn't keep an eye on what's going on. I'm not blaming you at all, son. The fault is mine and mother's. There are fine boys and girls right around here. You stay away from Colorado Boulevard."

With that he walked out, taking with him the tree house, the Stumblers Club, the Bluebird Theater, and Betty. I was happy to be relieved of the Floradora Sextette, but the rest were my life.

To make up for what he knew was hard, he bought me $7 worth of wireless equipment and a pair of earphones and let me drive the Ford to the grocery and to church. But every day I met Betty and Mary at school and sat in home room surrounded by the male contingent of the Stumblers Club. They all laughed, for their version of my retirement from the boulevard had come from Mrs. Byron.

After school I fidgeted at home, not knowing what to do with myself. Saturdays, particularly, were lonely. Juvenile life on that day centered at the Bluebird. And though the limitation on my activity was relaxed to permit theater attendance, I had no heart for it. There were too many memories.

I began to drift downtown on Saturday afternoons to Curtis Street, at that time the Little White Way of Denver, a glittering miniature of New York's Broadway. For two blocks, by day and by night, movie palaces on each side of the street flashed electric marquees. Just off Sixteenth Street, on Curtis, was the sumptuous palace known as Baur's, where often I inspected the windows, trying to imagine what kind of existence might include insatiable quantities of chocolates, fresh pistachio nuts, and caramels.

Sometimes I stood quite near the door to catch the creamy aroma that ebbed around exiting customers and to admire the horseshoe-shaped ivory-colored counters, the bright mirrors in frescoed frames, the showcases crowded with party favors and sweets and racks of dainties. I would watch Mr. Baarch, the superintendent, promenade the main aisle, nodding to rich dowagers who came in for a beribboned box or an afternoon tea, and sometimes I was Mr. Baarch, nodding to the ladies. I would gladly have worked at Baur's for nothing to be part of that glitter, and I was very envious of the boy about my own age who strutted importantly amid the candies, teased the black-costumed counter girls, and flipped caramels into his jaws with contemptuous nonchalance. I knew that he earned the princely sum of $7 a week, a fortune equal to twenty weeks of my recently enlarged allowance.

School had just ended for another year when I read in the newspaper that on the following Saturday the attraction at the Isis Theater would be *The Count of Monte Cristo*. Years earlier I had swallowed the book and, like a ruminant animal, remasticated it many times. I particularly admired Caderousse, who died with a poniard in his throat while swilling ale in an inn of low repute. Caderousse had become part of my world, along with D'Artagnan, Tarzan, and Tom Swift. With keen anticipation I set out on the streetcar with exactly enough money for my adventure, 10 cents and two tramway tokens.

On Curtis Street I paid my 10 cents and entered the theater.

The screen toward which I turned so eagerly, however, displayed no gay swordsmen in plumed hats, no handsome count with the jewels of an inexhaustible cavern at his disposal, no vengeance meted out to the wicked. It pictured an old lady with heavy, tear-stained eyes and weary body, scrubbing the porch of a building over which hung a sign: "County Home for the Aged." She looked out over the hill from time to time and sighed, then resumed her work. A fiery matron stepped from the door during one of the heroine's reveries and goaded her into more active labor. Subtitle: "You ain't so high and mighty now. Oh, you looked fine in your carriage and your silk dresses, all right. But you're alone now, and you'll earn your keep, same's everyone else." The old lady scrubbed, mixing her tears with the soapy water beneath her brush.

Into this tear jerker drove a carriage, and a handsome man stepped out. "Mother!" he cried. "My son!" responded she, leaving her brush. The grim matron retired in defeat, and the son carried off his mother in the carriage.

Sobs heaved through the house as the intermission lights came up.

Well, I thought, that's the bunk, people crying all over the place. But that's just the short feature. Now we'll get the newsreel and the comedy, and then we'll have something.

But after the launching of a new ship, the pictures of fat-bellied baseball players, and an endless automobile race, there was no comedy. Instead the orchestra played the overture to the main feature, Sibelius' *Valse Triste*— a little sad, I thought, for *Monte Cristo*.

The lights went down, the organist sought his pedals, and I sat forward in my seat. This was it!

But it was not. *Over the Hill*, said the title, and the

woman who lately had scrubbed the porch now sat in a comfortable living room with two blond boys. With a shudder of unbelief I sought an usher.

"What theater is this?" I whispered.

"The Isis."

"I thought you were showing *The Count of Monte Cristo.*"

The usher glanced with pain at the silver screen.

"I wish we were, kid," he said sadly, "I wish we were. It's next door at the Iris."

In my excitement I had misread the ad in the paper, confused the two theaters which unfortunately were situated side by side. And there I was, without a penny in my pocket and a whole afternoon before me.

I tried to get interested in *Over the Hill,* but it was no use. The little blond boys grew up. The sissy one went to prison to conceal the heinous fact that his father was a horse thief, and the rich one allowed his mother to be dragged, in agony and humiliation, to the county poor farm, accompanied by sobs from the audience that all but drowned the mighty Wurlitzer.

This was girls' stuff, and I, who had hurried downtown early to see *Monte Cristo* through twice, wandered dejectedly to the street.

I stared at the pictures displayed outside the Iris. There was Edmund Dantes, there Caderousse, there the gorgeous Mercedes, and the wicked old king's procurer, Villefort. There, also, was the box office, a grim, forbidding guard before the door.

I wandered over to the Olympic to admire the Bill Hart advertising and to the Tabor, which showed a Douglas MacLean feature. Then I found myself in front of Baur's, staring at a sign that poked neatly out of a paper doily: BOY WANTED.

Gone was *Monte Cristo*. Gone, too, I noticed, the Baur's stock boy who joshed the salesgirls. Mr. Baarch was not visible either. But there was the sign, and there was I.

It was not easy to walk into Baur's, the sweetmeat palace of the West, and confront those floorwalkers and salesgirls and the cashier who sat like an eagle in a big ivory cage.

Fright confounded me as I put my hand on the door. What if they had hired somebody else? What if I was too small? Perhaps I should go around to the back. I recalled newsreel scenes of factory gates with a big sign pointing to an employment window in the rear.

Quickly I ran around to the alley but found only a freight elevator laden with ice cream freezers and a screen door placarded KEEP OUT.

Out front again, I pressed my nose against the window glass and searched the store for an office. Off to the right was a paneled door with a sign over it: PRESIDENT.

At that moment a customer opened the door. I scooted in after her and down a side aisle to the paneled door, falling inside over a desk so large that it occupied the entire room except for a fat man who had squeezed himself into a swivel chair. On the walls were many photographs of Shriners in their fezzes at conventions; the pictures were inscribed in large white letters Buffalo, 1917; Cleveland, 1918; Long Beach, 1919. At them I stared, not daring to greet the president. He broke the silence.

"Well, young man, you're in a mighty hurry."

"Yes, sir," I answered and turned tensely toward him. One glance at his face, and I was at ease. It was not like any I had seen before, though reminiscent of the pictures of Canaanites in my illustrated Bible.

"I can't offer you a chair," he apologized, leaning back and steadying himself with a hand on which shone an enormous diamond. "No room for visitors. When people can't sit down, they don't stay long."

I started to retreat, but he arrested me. "Don't run away. You don't take up much room. If your mother is buying something, I'm sure she'll find you here."

"No," I mumbled, "that's not it. She's—I—"

"That's all right, sonny," the big man said hurriedly. "I understand. I didn't have a mother when I was growing up, either. A boy becomes a man sooner without a mother."

"But—"

"What did you want to see me about?"

"About that sign in the window."

Mr. Jacobs had not heard of any such placard. He did not allow posters in Baur's windows except during the annual Red Cross drive and the Y.M.C.A. campaign. Would I be good enough to show it to him?

We walked importantly up the main aisle. A floor-walker ran to hold open the door for us—for Mr. Jacobs, the president, and for me. The sign was still there.

"I didn't know we needed a boy," he said, embarrassed. "Carl, what's this notice for?"

"Mr. Baarch put it up, sir," the floorwalker answered. "We can't find a boy anywhere."

Like a parade the president, the floorwalker, and I

marched to the tearoom, where Mr. Baarch was talking to three ladies.

"This lad is applying for a job," the president said, and Mr. Baarch explained that by accident Baur's name and number had been omitted from the new directory. Steady customers would know Baur's number anyway, but not the tourists who took home the "best in the West." A boy was needed to bicycle around town pasting Baur's labels in the telephone books at pay stations, drugstores, hotels, and apartment houses.

"Well," Mr. Jacobs said, turning to me, "You have a job, my boy."

"And you mean I get $7 a week?"

The startled president and manager jumped in unison.

"What gave you that idea? We hadn't had in mind paying that—"

"That's what your other boy gets."

"This orphan has an eye for business," Mr. Jacobs laughed, patting me on the shoulder. "He'll get on."

I began that afternoon. Mr. Baarch provided me with a great many gummed labels, and I went to work. Logically, since I was downtown, that was the place to start. From the lower end of the business district I progressed uptown, taking each cross street until it became residential, then working back again. It was fun. But about five o'clock, while waiting in a hotel to ask the manager if he would put a label in the telephone directory of each room, the parsonage tapped me on the shoulder.

What would father say? How would he like the idea of my running all over town, going into all kinds of soft-drink parlors, cigar stores, billiard halls, and others dens of iniquity? How would he like having his son ranging the town unsupervised, unaccompanied, going to work like other men, to be gone all day?

It was almost six before my negotiations with the hotel manager ended, and I was overdue at home to peel the potatoes for supper. An immediate appearance or an explanation was mandatory. Twice around the block I walked, carefully phrasing a specious argument, memorizing neat sentences. At a free phone I put in a call. Father answered. But on hearing his great, melodious voice I became tongue-tied.

"Hello," he repeated several times and disconnected. All I had done was to swallow.

Again I telephoned.

"Father? It's me."

"Where are you? Your mother's frantic."

"I'm downtown."

"Well, come home at once."

"I can't. I have a job."

A great silence. "Where?"

"At Baur's—their name was left out of the telephone book, and I'm pasting it in."

Silence again. Then "When will you be home?"

"I don't know exactly. Later on."

"Is it just for today?"

"Oh, no, sir. Quite a while. Maybe all summer."

"What are you getting for it?"

"Seven dollars."

"A month?"

"No, sir, a week."

"Holy smoke," said father. "You are not required to work on Sunday?"

"No, sir."

"Well—come straight home when you're through."

Elated, but still wondering about father, I resumed my work. He hadn't really said I might keep on working. He just said to come straight home. Maybe if I waited until he had gone to bed—that was it. Just stay out until he was in bed. He always retired at nine-thirty on Saturdays.

I visited hotels, cigar stores, pay stations. At half past nine I was about to enter one more place when I saw a streetcar approaching. It was too tempting to be ignored. My legs ached. My arms were dead from carrying a big cloth sack heavy with labels.

"He's asleep, he's asleep," the rails rang. "He's asleep. He's asleep—"

But he was very wide awake.

Although it was after ten, the porch light was on, and father and mother were in the porch swing.

"You poor child!" mother called, as father came down to the two blue spruces to help me with the sack. "Have you eaten?"

"No. I—"

"Then come and eat. We can talk over dinner."

Food had been kept warm in the oven. The gravy was dry on the Swiss steak, and the potatoes and green beans were leathery, but I enjoyed them. Across the table, keen and appreciative, was father, and near by, anxiously listening, was mother. Father made me repeat twice how I had walked into the president's office to get a job he knew nothing about. As I retold the story, he chuckled.

"If you do a good job," he said, "you may even work into a job after school and Saturdays next fall. You may even ease into a regular position there when you are older—if you don't become a preacher, of course."

Oddly, he asked no questions about the store or its management. I did not know that after my telephone call he had immediately communicated with Mr. Fink, the store's tax expert and a church member, to assure himself that I would have no evil associates.

Wearily I arose and began carrying my plate, glass, and silver toward the kitchen. But mother intervened.

"Oh, no, son," she said. "When a boy is earning money outside the house, he does not have to do any chores inside."

And with that she took the dishes from me.

CHAPTER NINE

SEVERAL weeks passed, and my contact with Baur's luscious candy counters remained almost as far away as though I was not on the pay roll. Except on Saturday afternoon I did not so much as enter the store. Then I would visit the sweetmeat sanctuary with a city map on which I had charted in red crayon my week's itinerary. On a bicycle rented from a neighborhood friend I canvassed the city systematically, searching for telephone books.

When I reported, Mr. Baarch would scour the map skeptically, make a few notes with a gold fountain pen on the back of an envelope, and send me to the cashier for seven silver dollars in a bank envelope.

No other attention was paid to me until one morning Mr. Baarch telephoned just as I was leaving the house.

"I want you to come into the office today at ten o'clock," he said.

"Yes, sir."

What did he want? Maybe he had had enough. Maybe he had decided nothing was accomplished. Maybe there had been a complaint.

Up popped the memory of an episode of the previous week that might have caused trouble. I was working Colfax Avenue, a rooming-house neighborhood. The drugstores and soft-drink emporiums were not sympathetic to label pasting. My little speech didn't work.

One clerk listened while I explained that Baur's name had been omitted from the telephone book and that I wished to rectify the error.

"Oh, yeah!" he reacted, and I was demoralized. In my world everyone was friendly. I had never heard of a cynic, never encountered an adult ruffian, and was too astonished to reply.

"Whadda ya mean bustin' in here like that?" the clerk continued. "Cancha see I'm busy?" There followed a picturesque damnation of aristocratic Baur's and of nuisances in general and me in particular.

My inclination was to retreat without a word, but anger gave me voice, and I responded hotly. This was a job. He had a job, too, and he didn't need to make mine so tough. I hadn't done anything to him.

He kicked me out of the store.

A similar experience awaited me at a pool hall, and when I reached a large corner drugstore crowded with customers I resorted to subterfuge.

"I'm from the telephone company," I said authoritatively. "A number has been left out of the phone book, and I'm supposed to paste in a sticker at the proper page."

The counterman looked doubtful.

"Lemme see it."

I displayed the small label, not daring to bring out the big one.

"Lemme see your identity card."

"My what?"

"Your identity card. Everybody who works for the

phone company has a card. I used to work for 'em myself, Buddy."

"They didn't give me one."

He walked toward the telephone, intending to check my story.

Whereon I departed in haste from that neighborhood. Not until I had reached my own suburb twenty blocks away did I pause, guiltily scouting for policemen before stopping my bike. The cops probably had a dragnet out by now. They'd check with Baur's. I would be caught in a misrepresentation, labeled an impostor.

Trembling, I sat on a curbstone to rest. The drugstore clerk appeared before me again, his dark sleek hair receding from his temples like the illustration of Mephistopheles in *The World's Great Operas;* his dark eyes made blacker by horn-rimmed spectacles resting on a stubborn, once-broken nose, and his heavy jaw unshaven. There he was, leaning over with an elbow on the counter as though he might take hold of me forcibly.

"Oh, yeah!" he said.

But now with the house of a church member as refuge across the street, I knew what to say and said it.

"Yeah! I'm pasting Baur's number in the book." He was tough, but I was calm, standing my ground, giving him stare for stare until he turned away. I knew what to do, then. Father always began a moral lecture the moment I averted my gaze.

"What kind of way is that to talk?" I queried the curbstone. "You'd be a lot happier if you didn't let yourself get upset. Don't you know that's the way you get indigestion, being mean about everything?"

As father might have done, I temporized with him until he was jovial, then I bought a soda pop and conversed with him as one fellow to another until he began telling me his troubles, to which I was sympathetic.

When we parted, he offered to put the label in his book for me and told me to say hello to Pete Pierce up at the corner drugstore.

Emboldened by the curbstone victory, I leaped on my bicycle and charged to the nearest store. I intended to swagger in, but my knees would not cooperate. Instead I slunk to the telephone booth without a glance right or left, terrified of challenge, inserted the stickers and fled. No one paid the least attention to me.

Now I was really emboldened. At the next stop I

strutted in as though I owned the place, slapped my labels in the books without so much as a gesture at the proprietor, and swaggered out again. By nightfall my demeanor was that of a process server. I did my job authoritatively, nodded a condescending "Good day," to the clerk, and departed with dignity.

Then Mr. Baarch phoned.

As I peddled downtown, I could hear him ask, "What's this about your saying you were from the telephone company?" That would start a thread of inquiry as long as a freight train. Mr. Baarch would discover the big apartment house I had ignored because of an ugly doorman and the state office building without a single sticker because I had been chased out by a guard. He would uncover all the failures and ignore the miles and miles of streets in which every phone booth was plastered and the stickers that, in a burst of genius, I had pasted on every garden wall and gate in the snooty neighborhoods.

When I entered the store, he was walking the main aisle, inspecting the showcases. For a long time he talked to a new salesclerk about her cleaning and dusting. He took a chamois and polished a counter, then stepped back to inspect his work. I was in the way, and he stumbled over my foot.

He glowered.

"Oh, you," he said, and I began to take a last look at the tempting racks of succulent candies, the great torte cakes, and finally, in lingering longing, the fresh pistachio nuts.

"We want you to work in the store for a month," he

said. "The stock boy is going on a vacation with his parents."

The words were as unbelievable as a silver dollar when a whipping was expected or as permission to stay home from Sunday school with a toothache. The gilt around the creamy mirrors cast off a rosy glow, the pistachio-nut case grew large and inviting. The rubber mat beneath my feet became firm ground, and the whole showroom of a sudden was turned into an exotic and alluring home, mine for a month.

"Yes, sir," I said. My eyes came to the level of Mr. Baarch's third vest button, and it was a long way up to his face. "I'll get my labels—they're on my bike in the alley."

"Never mind the labels. Get behind the candy counter and make yourself useful."

No command more exciting was ever spoken. Get behind the *candy* counter! My ears rang with the words. My feet tingled. Behind the counter I sped, into the holy of holies, and stood there bursting, waiting to be told what to do.

Months later I learned the reason for my promotion. For weeks Mr. Baarch and Mr. Jacobs had heard stories of a funny little fellow in knickerbockers, who said he was thirteen but looked nine, who invariably wore a white wash tie over a black shirt and on his head the remnant of a silk stocking converted into a skull cap to keep his hair in a flat pompadour. They had been joshed about the labels pasted on each step of the golf-club veranda when the steward refused to permit their insertion in the telephone book. To them was relayed what Mrs. Stubbs' butler had said and the difficulty an apartment-house manager had had getting rid of me. These stories and others cropped up at so many dinner parties that one day Mr. Jacobs remarked to his superintendent, "Your original purpose with those stickers isn't bringing in their cost, but the word-of-mouth advertising Baur's is getting is sensational."

Once or twice dowagers engaging Baur's catering service for a lawn party asked Mr. Jacobs if they could see the funny little boy who had plastered a commercial telephone number on their entrance gates. Mr. Jacobs decided that for a few weeks I would have some exhibition value.

I found myself that first day galloping around the store on errands. The candy girls, the bakery girls, the cashier, the floorwalker, or the pastry chef had only to utter "Boy," and I appeared. Duty took me all over the establishment: to the third floor to send down on the dumb-waiter tarts from the bakery, to the second floor to urge along the caramels for which an out-of-town customer was waiting, to the basement to scurry up a two-quart freezer of tutti-frutti ice cream. The call-bell system's peremptory bing-bing-pause-bing-bing-bing sent me two steps at a time to the switchboard on the balcony, and on nearly every trip I detoured for a furtive grab into the sacred compound of pistachio nuts.

Toward midafternoon I was munching a caramel while unloading two-pound assorted chocolate boxes from the dumb-waiter when Mr. Baarch passed. He spied my swollen jaw, and immediately I swallowed the great lump, choking on it.

"You don't need to do that," said Marie, who had

been sixteen years behind the counter at Baur's. I was able only to point toward the manager's back. Marie smiled. "You can eat all the candy you want," she explained. "They know you'll get sick of it in a week, and hate the sight of the stuff."

But they had never hired a preacher's son before. From morning until night I chewed, swallowed, crunched, and gulped from one tray to another until I had sampled every dainty in the place.

In a few days certain favorites had founded a sympathetic friendship with my palate, a comradeship that grew and became fixed, outrivaling that of Jonathan for David. I became loyal to fresh pistachio nuts, strawberry caramels, and butter melbas and spurned a hundred other delicacies.

Mr. Baarch never knew it, but I was seldom without a few pistachios in my right-hand trouser pocket, a few caramels or melbas in my left. Baur's provided its employees with a free lunch, and we could order from the luncheon menu, which cost patrons 65 cents a plate. But I was seldom hungry at two o'clock, except perhaps for a piece of seven-layer cake with ice cream generously sprinkled with purloined fresh pistachio nuts.

And I acquired a hero. Into one corner of the showroom was squeezed a cubbyhole, its walls lined with racks from which protruded the tips of colored pasteboards. This was the downtown box office for the suburban summer theater in Elitch's Gardens. To Elitch's in summer came Helen Menken, Nazimova, Paul Lukas, the Gishes, the Barrymores male and female, Fredric March and Florence Eldridge, and many others; stars from glamorous New York. The lesser casting was done among western youngsters whose heads were turned toward Broadway after successes in college. Kenneth Vandenberg, a tall, sleek, theatrical young man was the assistant ticket seller. He knew all about the backstage of half-naked women and divorced persons, of smoking, drinking, and other kinds of loose morals. The manager of the downtown office was a Mr. Collins, but he was not easily approached.

As summer progressed, I discovered how much candy, cake, nuts, and ice cream normally were sold each day and early in the morning stocked the counter accordingly. By working diligently I could accomplish half a day's labor in three hours. Then, from eleven to twelve, I hung around the ticket office, coaxing stories from Kenneth. He had little to do during that period, since Mr. Collins personally handled the fashionable late-morning carriage trade.

Kenneth had little to say until he learned that the stage, in my father's opinion, was a "thing of the devil." Then he went to work to confirm father's thesis, for such stories as he told me of the goings on backstage curled the cowlick on the back of my head. But I listened. Fascinated by this new, iniquitous world, I became Kenneth Vandenberg's shadow and burned to see with my own eyes these stars, these dressing rooms, these people who never went to church.

No member of our family ever had seen a legitimate production. Over his newspaper father clucked from time to time at the antics of Broadway, accusing not the individuals but the tawdry world in which they lived. The stage, the brothel, the race track were identically tainted. Much as I hungered to visit backstage

[101]

with Kenneth at Elitch's, I dared not accept his invitation.

Eventually Mr. Collins noticed the *tête-à-tête* at his back and in an idle moment discovered what father thought of his malicious calling.

Mr. Collins was indignant. The theatrical world was as fine as any and every bit the equal, in morality and influence, of the church. Only an ignorant man could condemn the theater. Oh, no, I refuted him, father was no ignoramus.

All right then, he was narrow. Let him visit the theater to see what went on. Let him go this very week. Let him take a look at *The Two Orphans* and meet its sweet stars, Dorothy and Lillian Gish. He *dared* father to go to the theater and take the family.

I reported this conversation at home, with cautious omissions. Eileen was enthusiastic, father unstirred.

"The devil has ways of making his will attractive," he said, glancing at Eileen's bobbed hair, and resumed his Emerson essays.

"But he *dared* you, father!"

"Any cowardly fool can accept a dare. Courage is needed to ignore one."

"But—maybe he's right, father. You don't *know*."

Patiently father put down his book and took off his glasses. The whole family, even Fraser, was listening now.

"Were you ever bitten by a rattlesnake?"

"No, sir."

"But you know what would happen if you were."

"Naturally."

"Then let's not discuss the matter."

But mother wanted to go.

"Do you know how much those tickets cost?" she asked. "Two dollars and twenty cents. Mrs. Stubbs had a theater party there last week. The Bramley boys swim at Elitch's, and Dr. Bramley is a member of your own board."

"We won't discuss it."

"But, Will, I want to go."

Again father put down his book.

"All right then," he said, "you go. But don't include me."

I whooped, Eileen clapped, and next day I reported the conversation to Mr. Collins. It was his turn not to be impressed.

"I asked your father to take the family," he said. "If he won't go, nobody goes."

This was exceedingly disappointing to mother and Eileen. But father was pleased.

A few weeks later Elitch's had a very special attraction, a sensational play called *Excess Baggage*.

"A man slides on a tightwire all the way from the balcony to the stage," I said, having heard about it from Kenneth.

"You can see much the same thing at a good clean baseball game," father replied. "Hank Morfy slid into second yesterday, one of the most beautiful things I ever saw on a diamond."

This remark, of course, I took back to Mr. Collins, and he, still smarting, wrote father a note.

"This play," it said, "is about that sinful world you hold in such low esteem. It's a melodrama about show business, and show people. If you were trying to con-

vert me (and incidentally ask Dr. Caldwell at Mont-
view Presbyterian Church whether I'm the Devil's dis-
ciple), you'd want me to give you a hearing. Here is
the goods about my profession. I invite you to see it."

Father would not go. But he invited mother and
Eileen to view the Saturday matinée and gave them
money for tickets. Mr. Collins, in turn, provided box
seats.

Eileen, particularly, was fascinated. She went through
Elitch's Gardens' gaudy gate for the first time, heard
the roaring rattle of the roller coaster, drew in the
aroma of frying hamburgers, lingered awhile near the
great fresh-air ballroom, where even in the afternoon
there were 200 dancers, and ogled the paintings of
famous theatrical folk in the theater lobby.

Mother liked the play. The earthy, human heartaches
of a theatrical troupe were the problems she lived with
all the time. When she returned home, she told us so
over dinner.

"There wasn't an objectionable moment in it."

"Is that so?" said father.

"Indeed. And the slide down the wire was breath-
taking."

"The fellow," Eileen interrupted, eyes sparkling, "got
right out on the railing of the box next to ours, and
slid *standing up* clear down to the stage."

"Indeed?"

"Yes, indeed," she flared. "And it was a lot more exciting than any old slide into second base that you talk
so much about."

"Sure," I backstopped her. "Hank Morfy ain't in it
with this guy."

Father reached for a second cup of tea and turned on me. "Have you seen it, too?"

"No—but Kenneth says so. I told him what you said."

"Hm-m-m."

"And I must say," mother said, "I could write a much saltier play from our parsonage experiences."

"Hope! Let's have none of that, please."

"But why, Will? Let's face it. We mustn't hide our heads in the sand."

"The man who slides better than Hank Morfy is good, is he?"

"He's perfectly marvelous," Eileen exclaimed.

"Hm-m."

Excess Baggage was held over for a second week. On Wednesday I went as usual to chat with Kenneth Vandenberg at eleven o'clock, and Mr. Collins called to me.

"Your old man's quite a fellow."

"My old—what's that?"

"He came out to the show last night."

"*My* father?"

"Your father."

"Gosh. Did he stay for the *whole thing?*"

"Did he *stay?* Why, he stuck around until the actors finished dressing after the show. I thought I'd never get rid of him."

"Are you sure it was *my* father?"

"I certainly am. He wouldn't leave until he had met the fellow who could slide better than Hank Morfy."

Eileen was particularly grateful for this triumph over the Elitch taboo. Now she could attend theater parties with other girls on her promise not to dance there, and

I could go with Kenneth Vandenberg any evening that he invited me.

By the time school resumed, I had entrenched myself at Baur's. For work after school and on Saturday I was to be paid the same large sum that I had received over the summer, $7 per week.

There was no difficulty until Baur's asked me to work on the Sunday immediately preceding Christmas. Father wouldn't hear of it.

"Isn't it enough," he asked, "that Christmas should have surrendered completely to materialism, without its encroaching on Sunday too? You'd think Christ's birthday was an invention of the merchants. Or have you forgotten that Christmas is a religious festival?"

We were in the living room, he in his leather chair, I standing before him. He had been interlineating a book with pen notations, probably a denial of the writer's philosophy and a justification of his own. He did not stop writing.

"No, I haven't," I answered, "but since everybody *buys* presents now, someone has to sell them."

"The question is whether *you* are going to work on the Sabbath." He seemed to be inviting a debate.

"There are lots of people who work all week, same as I do," I said, "who never have a chance to do their Christmas shopping. You can take time out during the day. But you're an exception. I know that, because I work."

"So do I," father intruded calmly.

"Yes, but not—in a store or an office. All those people have to buy Christmas presents for their friends. Candy is the most important thing at Christmas."

"How's that?"

"Well, most important after church, I mean. It would be terrible if people couldn't give candy just because they didn't have a chance to buy it. And you *can't* send people out to select your Christmas gifts for you. It's part of Christmas to choose them yourself."

He paused in his writing.

"You really believe that?"

"Yes, sir."

"And you can square it with your conscience?"

"Yes, sir."

"All right. If that's what you believe, go ahead. I suppose people have to make a living all kinds of ways these days. It's a hard admission that the Sabbath must yield."

"But it's to give people a happier Christmas, father."

"If it's what you believe, go ahead," he said. "It's your decision."

From that time on decisions were easier for the whole family. If Eileen could square bridge playing with her conscience, she played it (but prudently, and if she won a prize she did not bring it home). Since Joe, of the purple trousers and red Packard, was still not tolerated by father, Eileen met him at another girl's house for double dates.

My own estate was handsome. I had a wireless set in operation and had completed my wooden automobile, called a "chug." Moreover, I was a working man, with money to take Betty or Dorothy to the movies (the early evening show) and the right to drive the Ford to Epworth League meetings on Sunday night. To top all this, father took me downtown to buy me my first long-trousered suit, with my own money, and a bicycle, with his. A week later he pushed home a bicycle for Fraser.

Relieved of the financial responsibility for one young-ster, who now could even buy his own clothes, mother increased the allowances of Eileen and Fraser. My brother profited most. At the age of seven, Fraser's spending money was 25 cents a week, although at his age Eileen and I had grubbed through on a dime. And I was twice his age before I got a bicycle. Since I was relieved of home chores, Eileen and Fraser had oppor-tunity to earn extra money, too, mowing the lawn, washing the car, and tidying the attic.

Our cup, as the Psalm said, was running over.

But this was too good to last.

In April father was invited to a parish in Iowa.

CHAPTER TEN

WHILE father deliberated whether to go or stay, none of the family had any idea what he was thinking. Lest selfish considerations influence him, he kept to himself.

Usually we could sense his mood from the blessing he invoked upon the evening meal. When he was in good spirits and saw a particularly delicious dinner before him, his prayer was long and enthusiastic. When he was weary, the grace was short. When he was fretful, he asked divine support for his patience as well as his appetite. And when he was burdened with a problem no one but himself could solve, he quoted from the Psalms, without interpolation.

For a week we had Psalms, and then one night he returned to form.

"Give us, O Lord," he intoned, "Thy strength, for that which we absorb from this table is not alone enough for us—"

The prayer for strength. Fraser cast me a cautious signal across the centerpiece that Eileen intercepted and confirmed with a quick pursing of her lips. Father had made up his mind and was marshaling his courage to speak to us.

Mother helped him.

"When do we go?" she asked abruptly.

"After the twenty-fourth," he said.

"Two weeks!" mother exclaimed. "Can't we wait until school's out? The children will never pass new school requirements with only a month of the term remaining."

"It's urgent— We *have* to go."

"Then can't the children and I remain here until June? It would only be a few weeks."

Father's glance traveled from floor to ceiling and all around the room before he dared to face mother's eyes.

"You know we can't do that, Hope," he said.

Families that have lived all their lives in one house or in one town ought to pack their belongings just once and set up again in Sheboygan or Kankakee, or somewhere just for the experience. Then they could appreciate a home with roots to it.

Some of my most bitter memories are of toys that were left behind when we moved. In Clarion, Iowa, when I was three, there remained on the vacated porch a little cart with a long handle. It was not much of a cart, but it was my only gift from my grandfather, and I had watched him whittle it from a board.

"We can't take it," father said regretfully. "There isn't room."

In Fort Dodge we abandoned a coaster wagon, the only one I ever owned with disk wheels. Father had given it to me for Christmas after an artful campaign on my part, and when we moved it was only eight months old. It was taken to the freight yard but did not reach Omaha, and when I inquired about it, father said, "It wouldn't go in the car, son. We had to leave it. I'll get you a new one." But the new one had wire wheels.

In Omaha it was a sled, a dandy, the longest one in the neighborhood; and Eileen's English doll buggy; and a huge box of building blocks that a neighbor had given to Fraser.

Abandoned at Sioux City was a tremendous bobsled on which I had spent half a winter's labor and all my money. The college boys and girls often asked me to bring it out onto the hill. Dismantled was a telegraph set strung between our house and Dick Packer's, a block away, over which we held staccato conversations in the dead of night, furtively muffling the metallic impulses against the sharp ears of our parents, who thought we were asleep. Jettisoned was an antique white-enameled chair with a red-plush seat given Eileen by a rich old lady. Lost also was the great orchard of Whitney crab apples and Jonathans and plums, the fruit of which during the war I had sold to the corner grocer for prodigious sums that filled book after book of War Saving Stamps.

Now we were on the move again, and I knew what would happen. My big "chug," to which I was about to add a one-cylinder gasoline engine would be the biggest casualty. My wireless could be taken with us, but not the fine aerial that stretched from my bedroom window to the Steinberg roof two hundred feet away. The two new bicycles would be carried along, for they were a substantial investment, but what of all the ingenious devices Eileen had put into her room to make it livable: the built-in shelves, the five-and-ten-cent-store whatnots on the walls, the apple crates chintzed into a vanity dresser? And what of Fraser's vast assembly of electric-railroad equipment, with which I also played?

[111]

In those days the household moved by railroad freight. The accumulation of sixteen years of house-keeping filled an entire boxcar and more, and the surplus had to be thrown away. Into dresser drawers and down among father's books in hastily cased boxes, Eileen, Fraser, and I smuggled and sandwiched much of the "trash" we were told to leave behind, cooperating desperately against the awful cubic limitations of a freight car.

Through the last week I continued to work at Baur's but delayed notifying Mr. Baarch that I was leaving until it could be postponed no longer. Father had pointed out the necessity of giving my employer time to secure a successor. When there were only three days left, I saw Mr. Baarch smiling over an unusually large order. The auspicious moment had arrived.

"I'm leaving at the end of the week, sir," I began, chin quivering.

"What's the matter, son?" he asked. "The work too hard?"

"No, sir. I wonder if you'd give me a letter of recommendation?"

The manager looked down from his full height. He seemed displeased, as he said, "You'll have to ask the president about that." And turning, he walked up the main aisle.

That could mean only one thing. He must have discovered I was not an orphan. If so, Mr. Jacobs would know too.

Saturday afternoon arrived before I marshaled sufficient courage to face Mr. Jacobs in his little office; and I would have avoided the scene entirely except that father insisted I carry away a commendatory letter with me.

About four o'clock I saw the familiar green light emerging from the presidential cubicle and stepped to the door. Mr. Jacobs was adding figures. He did not exactly mistrust office equipment, but he liked to check totals for himself on his fingers.

"Come in, come in," he said.

"Yes, sir." I stood uneasily at his enormous desk. "This is my last day, and I wonder if you would recommend me for another job."

Mr. Jacobs stopped counting and asked, "You haven't found a better job than Baur's?"

"No, sir," I said. "I'm leaving town."

"Well, we'll be sorry to see you go. But I guess all boys have to move up in the world. You're going to get an education, is that it?"

"Well, you might say—"

"Come, come, you don't need to be modest with me, boy. You're a hard worker. I like hard workers." He promised to see me later and went back to his fingers.

Now I was more anxious than before. He had not promised me the letter. During my last three hours I kept both ears cocked for a summons to the president's office, but nothing happened.

At seven o'clock he was waiting at his paneled door when my work ended. Smiling jovially, he handed me my pay.

"We've included a little bonus," he whispered confidentially. "It may come in handy."

"Thank you, sir."

"I'm sorry to lose you, my boy. I've watched you with a good deal of interest."

"Thank you, sir," and then, furtively feeling the bulge of pistachios in my left trousers pocket, I added, "I won't find many places to work as good as Baur's."

Mr. Jacobs beamed and walked me up the main aisle. Everyone in the store saw this final triumph. As we approached the front door, he reached to the counter and pulled off a *de luxe* five-pound assortment and handed it to me.

"Thank you, sir," I said, taking a quick last look at the Louis XV décor, the racks of caramels, and the pistachio-nut bin and breathing deeply a last whiff of the creamy aroma that was as much a part of Baur's as the "Est. 1872" on every candy box. I murmured "Good-by" and hurried out, the five-pound box tightly under my arm.

Turning into the alley, I looked in the pay envelope with its seven silver dollars of wages. Added were two twenty-dollar bills. Misty-eyed, I opened the letter of recommendation and read:

"To Whom It May Concern: The bearer of this letter, Hartzell Spence, has been in my employ for three years as stock and counter boy. He has given good and intelligent service. I hope any prospective employer who contemplates hiring him will not be influenced adversely by the fact that this lad, an orphan, has no father to help him with life's battles. He is capable of fighting them by himself."

I did not show the letter to father. Instead I produced my enormous wealth.

"Look," I shouted, "forty bucks extra."

Father looked.

"And what about the letter of recommendation?" I did not reply. He was about to reprove me for forgetting it when he caught sight again of the twenty-dollar bills.

"Well, you can't eat a letter, I suppose," he sighed.

We lived the final Sunday in Denver surrounded by packing boxes, which overflowed the bare, echoing rooms onto the yard and porches. But after church, on our way back to the parsonage, mother made an announcement.

"Will, I'm not going to ride across Nebraska in that rickety old Ford. You take the boys if you want to. Eileen and I are going by train."

When we had moved from Sioux City to Denver, the five of us had eaten Nebraska dust for two days, while father, mounted like a jumping jack on the driver's seat of the touring car, burned the dirt road with the grim eyes of an Old Testament prophet. Each bump sent mother soaring to the canvas top and down again with a terrific jolt, and we children, jostled by each bump, sang songs to keep up our morale.

"How's that?" father asked.

Mother planted her feet solidly on the sidewalk at his side.

"I said Eileen and I are going on the train."

"But, mother—"

"If Riverton wants you as badly as you say, it can afford two railway fares."

She took Eileen by the hand, and they led the way home. I fell back to fortify father. Head down, deeply

hurt, he didn't notice my support, but I knew what
he was thinking. Never had the five of us been separated in any momentous undertaking. That three of us
should go on ahead without mother was unthinkable.
Who would feed us that first night in the new parsonage? Who put up the beds? Who find in that debris of
moving exactly what we needed first? Who act as buffer
between us and the great onslaught of bosomy women
who would besiege our new home?

Mother must have had identical thoughts, for she
was smiling as she spread our dinner on packing boxes
—three plates on one for father, Fraser, and me; and
two on another for Eileen and herself.

"I have it all arranged," she said quietly. "Eileen
and I will stay with the Bramleys until Thursday. That
will get us to Riverton on Friday afternoon. You and
the boys will be on the road four or five days. We'll arrive together."

"Hope! What is this?" Father's voice was soft, the
hands that reached for her clumsy.

Her shoulders squared, and she faced up to him, she
who weighed only ten pounds more than one third her
husband. "Will. I just cannot face a ride in that awful
car all the way across two states."

"What's the matter with Old Maud?" father bridled.

"Nothing, except that Eileen and I aren't going all
that distance in it."

Mother was close to tears, and so was Eileen through
sympathy. Even Fraser, who never worried about anything, nibbled at a slice of bread and looked up with
wide hurt. eyes as though he had been slapped.

Father reached out and touched mother's shoulders

[116]

bound volumes

Educ. -back issues V.1-3 - V.
Feb. 1971 - 1972
Feb. 1971 - 1972
issing issues
an. - Dec. 1971
yrs. Fall 1970 -1971
eplacement March, April 1970
        "   issues
        "   May 1969
        "   January 1969
n. - Dec. 1971
. - Dec. 1971
. - Dec. 1971
. 1971-1972
eplacement issues
, 1971-1972
V. 3
    - Dec. 1971
    renewal

β
5+3α

awkwardly. "You're perfectly right, mother. I—I should have thought of it myself."

The next day, as the packers moved our belongings to the railroad siding, father chafed and fretted to be off. Early in the morning Eileen and mother went to the Bramley home, after which father set to work as though he could not bear to stop and think. At the siding he checked the car loading patiently but quickly. It was highly important that our goods be dispatched on a train leaving that day so that we could set up a bed in the new parsonage on our arrival and thus avoid hotel expense. Satisfied that all was in order and that the freight was sealed, he wiped his brow.

"All right," he said, "let's go!" And away we went, the three of us in the front seat. The rear seat was jammed with a trunk and suitcases.

That night father popped Fraser and me into bed at McCook, Neb., immediately after dinner and at dawn routed us out again. On and on we pushed, but by nightfall were still west of Omaha. Father insisted on stretching this leg of the journey across the Missouri River into Council Bluffs, Iowa.

Of Council Bluffs we saw no more than we had of McCook: the inside of a hotel room, a plate of Cream of Wheat, and a gasoline filling station. Then on again, scarcely looking up from the gravel to renew acquaintance with the pleasant Iowa landscape, which for most of our lives had been home.

About five o'clock we rolled past a large railroad shop and pitched headlong into Riverton's freight yards. Our household goods had been on a siding for several hours. Father took a bed, a mattress, and the bundle of bedding that he had loaded last of all, just inside the freight car door.

"I must have the rest first thing in the morning," father repeated until the freight agent took his pipe from his mouth and responded sharply, "You'll get it, parson. Keep your shirt on."

Assured then, father relaxed and smiled.

"Three days from Denver to Riverton," he gloated. "That's traveling. Barney Oldfield couldn't do better."

We were surprised at so handsome a parsonage. A substantial brick house, it stood on a corner at the crest of a hill, surrounded by large maples and the homes of stable citizens.

"And," father said, bringing in the bedding, trunk, and suitcases from the Ford, "hardwood floors, a separate room for each of you youngsters, a *new* gas stove, and a good roof." He was proud of the place, but I was happy mother wasn't there. The house was filthy dirty.

By nightfall, however, the attic and basement floors were visible, and the following morning a van backed up to the house with our goods.

Father, coat and vest off, his gray suspenders flagrant over his white shirt, ordered the furniture to be left on the front porch and set to work with feverish diligence. As fast as Fraser and I finished mopping out a room, father was in it, laying carpet and opening crates with a great screech of hammer.

Toward eleven o'clock Fraser and I emerged from the future living room for a moment's rest. A tall young man with a beard blacker than father's sat leisurely on the porch rail, grinning at the confusion.

Father almost set a box of books on his toes. The tall man moved a few inches and spoke.

"You the new preacher?"

Immediately father became professional and introduced himself, conscious at last of his inelegant attire as the stranger continued, "Thought you must be. No hired man ever worked that hard."

"And you're from the country," father responded. "No city man ever spared words as you do."

The visitor was a reporter for one of the local papers. In a few sentences Mr. Schlotzhauer and father were friends, and in five minutes the two of them were carrying a chiffonier upstairs.

The spectacle of the newsman at manual labor attracted two of the neighbors. Father soon had them at work, and it wasn't long until all the heavy hauling was done. Some of the rooms Fraser and I had not yet scrubbed, but that made no difference to father. He got help while he could.

Relaxing then and puffing a little, the newcomers smiled a little foolishly, aware that they had been taken in.

"Well, gentlemen," father said, "I really should offer you all a cool glass of something, but we haven't had time yet to get ice or even lemons for lemonade. And now you must excuse me. Come again."

He picked up a few books that had been overlooked and carried them indoors. The interview with the press had ended.

By three o'clock the house was clean and settled, and father emerged from his bedroom bathed, shaved, and once more elegant. At 3:17 we were at the depot to greet mother and Eileen. Father was immensely pleased with himself.

Mother was suspicious but said nothing. Even when escorted, as by a wedding usher, into her new home and conducted from shining room to shining room, she ignored father's pointed pleas for praise.

For this moment he had trailed dust across three states and worked himself haggard and now, like a Shakespearean actor, he wanted a round of applause at the final curtain. Mother merely smiled.

"And the dishes," he hinted broadly. "The pots and pans are washed and put away in the kitchen."

This was so obvious that mother laughed and took off her hat. "You are dears, all of you," she said, "and hungry, too, aren't you?"

Her work had begun again.

Before the week end we children were in school. Eileen took naturally to high school, but I, accustomed to junior high, found difficulty getting accustomed to high school ways, and Fraser, impaled on a new curriculum, was lost. Mother made two trips to consult his teacher before she could convince the authorities that he was not a backward child.

But she could not talk up for me. The course of study prescribed for the third year of junior high in Denver did not fit Riverton's schedule for first-year high school. Nothing I had done all year was of any account. Riverton insisted that I begin high school again in the autumn.

Father took the news stoically.

"Well, kids are graduating from high school too immature these days anyway," he said, "and what you learned in Denver can't hurt you, even if the school ma'ams won't accept it. I'll be hanged if we'll send you to school for another month if you've nothing to learn."

"Yes, *sir!*" I agreed.

"Maybe," he said, "you can rustle yourself a summer job somewhere."

On Saturday I applied at the basket factory on the riverbank, and was immediately employed at the task of putting handles on baskets for 4 cents a dozen. Two hours of labor convinced me that by working like a beaver I could earn $1.60 a day.

On Sunday we were presented to the church. It was a cold-looking congregation, and the choir was a sorry lot. Father, seated in the pulpit, winked at me as usual during the processional. And the four of us in the pews, aliens in an Ellis Island of unfamiliar faces, drew together closely against the eyes that were scrutinizing us in every part of the house, including the balcony.

We must be on our good behavior. We must listen attentively, though we had heard this particular sermon before. We must not twitch or scratch or fidget, and we must roundly sing out the hymns without looking at the book. By these trivia is the pastor's family judged.

It was father's custom to call us to the altar on the first Sunday, just before the offertory, to receive us as members. In this way he served notice that any who desired to join the church must come forward for all to see.

At the call for new members we arose from our pew.

This was embarrassing, for everyone who had not previously identified us gaped now. Head erect, mother stepped out boldly, Eileen beside her, Fraser and I behind.

Nobody had warned us about a cold air register in the middle of the aisle. Over it I stumbled and fell with a profane thump. People in the balconies leaned over to titter, and folks in aisle seats put hymnals to their faces.

I expected father to be grim when finally I reached the altar, but smilingly he introduced us.

"My wife, my daughter, Eileen; the little one is Fraser, and the clumsy one is Hartzell; he's at the awkward age."

CHAPTER ELEVEN

*T*HE BASKET factory was not at all like Sunday school.

While working at Baur's I had been in contact with highly skilled technicians who considered themselves artists: cooks, pastry chefs, candy creators, and ice cream molders, and with dignified floor walkers and counter girls, who had been at Baur's for years and were as well known to Mr. Jacobs as his own family. It was an old-fashioned establishment with an old-fashioned *esprit de corps*.

At the basket factory there was none of that. The plant had three floors and an annex, flanked by warehouses on the up- and down-river sides. Salesmen whom the craftsmen never saw sent orders for baskets in carload lots. A semiexistent management issued orders from the annex. Pulp rafted down river from Wisconsin and Minnesota was soaked, stripped, and sliced into fine fiber lengths, which shot upstairs, warmly steaming, for cutting and dyeing on the second floor. This wood, heavy and smelling like rotting potatoes, was trucked to the weavers on the top story. Here at pattern tables that could be adjusted to any size and shape stood four long lines of women who wove with wide, sweeping hip and shoulder motions and nervous fingers. An automatic machine then ate the weaving and expelled it shaped and stapled with a strong wooden border, complete except for handles.

At the end of the line, my mouth full of tacks, I sat surrounded by handles already warped to shape. I thrust a handle into each basket, nailed it down and, when I had a dozen, baled them with wire. I was paid 4 cents for each set of one dozen baskets.

Some of the women had drunkard husbands, a species with whom I had never come in contact. Some had exceedingly amorous beaux, whose techniques were elaborated to girls with less imaginative lovers. At home all had want and privation. If because of a machinery breakdown or for any other reason there was momentary stoppage of the assembly line, the anxiety was great; every idle moment meant less than the $2.03-a-day quota toward which each worker strove.

Closest in line to me was a middle-aged scrawny woman, whose conversation was paced to the tempo of her labor. Sometimes singing, sometimes laughing, always smiling, her fingers, hips, and shoulders always busy, she communicated the episodes of her life to those about her. The details were not on the parsonage-approved list for adolescents.

Tillie's husband had been a wiper at the C. B. & Q. Railroad yards before the big strike, but for the last three years had made an occupation of looking for another job. Tillie supported him and a son in high school and, so talk said, an Irishman who came up out of the willow patch along the riverbank to meet her sometimes after work. Her loud tongue was respected. Nobody talked back to her. Tillie had sail and style in a brave, dilapidated way. She wore her hair high on her strong forehead; her skirts were long, where every other girl's were extremely short; and she wore a corset to work. She taught me a good deal that I'm sure my mother didn't know.

"The old man got drunk again last night," Tillie confided to Augusta one morning, laughing as she flipped another strand into her weaving. "He beat the jesus out of me."

"Yeah? Why didn't you let him have it then, Tillie? Gettin' old?"

"Gettin' old, hell, Augusta. He likes his liquor better."

A laugh all around.

"Why don't you go to work on Jack, Tillie?" Augusta jibed. "He looks ripe for plucking."

Whereat I became exceedingly busy, for I was Jack. When I had reported to Clancy, the foreman on our floor, he looked at the name on my timecard and laughed.

"How do you pronounce it?"

I told him.

"Well, we got too much to do to call anybody by pretty names, sonny. When I shout 'Jack,' you jump."

"Yes, sir."

"And don't *sir* me, sonny. The name is Clancy, and if it's good enough for my old mother, it's good enough for you."

A laugh from the assembly line.

"*You* got a mother, Clancy? That's a good one. Clancy never had a mother. He was born solo."

"All right, ladies, all right," the foreman said. "You tend your weaving, I'll tend mine."

"You got to answer back to these mugs," Tillie had said to me after my first reprimand from Clancy. "They get hell from the guys in the annex, and they pass it on to you. The old army game it is, and you got to give 'em hell right back. You get *respect* that way."

"Respect?"

"Sure, respect. I been here twelve years. Every meek sister in the place has been fired, but here I am. The boss sends word they've got to maintain discipline, so somebody gets fired; but they only fire those who won't make a stink about it. Meekness never got anybody anywhere."

Evidently she had not heard of a certain sermon on the Mount.

In little chips the parsonage lacquer fell from me. But I was timid, and the flybelt commotion of screeching machinery on the lower floors terrified me so much that at noon I did not take my lunch box into the yard with the men. Instead I ate upstairs with the girls.

After a week the boys on the second floor began to notice the newcomer who sneaked upstairs in the morning and down again at night, who did not board the big bus that transported employees into town, but climbed 212 steps to the top of the bluff, where the aristocrats lived. They got the idea that I lived "up on the hill," which of course was true.

I had finished my lunch one day and had resumed work when a deputation of seven lads called on me. They were big boys who had quit their schooling at the legal post-truant age of sixteen. Their overalls had the professional appearance of usage; mine were shiny new.

[127]

Even when they gathered in a semicircle around me, I did not realize that something unusual was astir.

"Is this him?" one asked.

"That's him."

"Hey, you," thumping my shoulder, "get up."

"Yes?"

"You stole my bike."

"Me?"

"Yes, you. It was out by Warehouse Three, and you snitched it last night. Pete saw you."

"Oh, no, I didn't take any bike."

The largest boy shouldered to me and looked down my nose. "Are you calling me a liar, bud?"

"No, I'm not calling anybody a liar. I didn't steal any bike, that's all." With that I sat down and began again to handle tack. I was angry but cautious.

"*I* said you stole that bike."

"*I* said I didn't."

"Then that makes me a liar. I'll show you who's a liar." With strong fists he yanked at my overalls and lifted me to my feet.

"Yah, yah, yah. Who's a liar now?" the other boys shouted. The big fellow let go of me with his right hand, drew it back, and swung. The fist caught my shoulder and spun me around.

The girls meanwhile had stopped eating. When the blow fell, Tillie leaped up and seized the big knife, razor sharp, which she used to trim her baskets. With a screech she sailed into the ring that surrounded me, but I scarcely saw her. I was doing some swinging of my own, and I had the advantage, for my hammer was in my hand. The big boy, stepping back quickly before

[128]

the hammer, backed into a vat full of blue dye and flopped over into it with a tremendous splash. A roar went up.

Clancy, returning from lunch, arrived to see the violation of his precious dye. The gang scattered, diving down the stairway with ducked heads, one of them dripping a lurid trail behind him, his face and hair the color of his overalls.

"The idea!" Tillie wailed. "Picking on a kid half their size! That's like those rowdies, but don't you worry, Jack. You just keep that hammer handy, and don't forget how to swing it."

I lugged the hammer home with me each night for a week. But nothing happened. The second floor had decided to leave me alone, after a warning that if ever I showed up on Oak Street there would be trouble. But I had never heard of Oak Street. The incident provoked curiosity about me, and I was careful not to let them know I was a preacher's son. Tell anyone the details of your life, and he is interested; tell him again, and he has had enough and lets you alone. But tell him nothing, and he will pry until he discovers what you are hiding.

The girls surmised that I didn't amount to much; otherwise I'd be in school. However, my amazement at their common speech, my lack of understanding of their home lives convinced them that I was a queer bird. This was accentuated when one of the girls described how on the previous night her "old man" had been jugged for lifting a box of cigars. Everyone was amused except me.

"You mean," I gasped, "your father's in jail?"

"Sure, Jack," the girl, a skinny-legged, high-chested blond named Mary, answered debonairly. "But he'll only get ten days."

"You mean he was *stealing?*"

Mary chewed hard at a pulp fiber and surveyed me.

"Where were you born, kid?" she asked. "He just snitched a box of cigars. It's only ten days. You don't call that *stealing.*"

Never before had I been so close to crime. Arrested for stealing, and there was his own daughter, working close to me!

I was thrilled, and they sensed it. None of their world was excited about an altercation with the law; it was their football or basketball game, their amusement, and the man who got caught was just the fellow who pulled a boner during the game and ran the wrong way with the ball. Ten days in jail were a lark, like a vacation among the Wisconsin Lakes. Because I did not understand, they were suspicious of me.

They speculated on whether I might be a relative of Mr. Teagle, the factory owner, but Mr. Teagle's nephews would be at school during May. Besides I was poor. Nobody but a poor boy would slave daily to put handles on forty dozen baskets, his fingers stained from the drying dyes, lips cracked from tack scratches. My shoes were better quality than most, but somebody could have given them to me; I wore cotton shirts instead of denim, without patches, but there was nothing conclusive in that. Didn't I *walk* home every night, although the bus went right by the gate?

Two of my late adversaries struck up a curiosity-inspired acquaintance, but it didn't last. They couldn't trail me without walking up those 212 steps. For a week or more sly questions and jibes greeted me wherever I went in the factory, and daily I became more terrified at revealing my identity.

What would they say if they knew I was a preacher's son? Would they modify their language, as lusty men did in father's presence? Would they stop telling those fascinating stories about what Joe said to Charlie and how Ethel handled the fellow from the furniture factory that night in the city park? Now on the hem of their world, I would be scissored entirely out of it as the preacher's son you couldn't tell stories to or talk naturally in front of. A windbreak had been up all my life, sheltering me from people.

Meanwhile at home we became adjusted to a new environment. The Epworth League immediately claimed Eileen and me, but we didn't much like it, for the group that had been young ten years ago continued to dominate the organization, as though clinging grimly to their youth. Father tipped off the president that I played the flute, and I was invited to perform. In reality, father was cautiously leading up to my playing the offertory in church as a relief from the choir.

Always embarrassed to be pushed into the limelight where my own age group could comment that the preacher's son was showing off again, I was also in deadly fear that someone from the basket factory might see me. It would be bad enough to have my identity discovered, without having the added stigma of playing a musical instrument.

Hastily scanning the assembly as I arose to play, I saw no familiar face but noticed a very pretty girl. She was about my age and seemed to like flute playing. We sparred visually as I performed. After the service I was introduced to her. Brown haired, a little on the gangly tall side, she was named Mildred. She played the piano, she said, and would like to accompany me sometime.

Pushing the invitation, I suggested that there was no time like the present, to which she modestly agreed, and we started to walk toward her house.

I was not familiar with the neighborhood. North Hill, where we lived, geographically ended at North Street. Then the prairie leveled for a long flat run out of town. Beyond North Street the thoroughfares, oak shaded, were darker. I glanced at a curb marker so that I could find my way back. It was Oak Street.

Oak Street, home of the basket-factory toughs, where I had been warned that trespass meant murder.

Keeping quite close to Mildred, I walked the rest of the way to her house. No alien face appeared; no suspicious whistle sounded. Mildred's family received me cordially and listened to the music from the book of solos I had brought with me. I was fed hot chocolate and butter cookies and returned home unmolested.

During the next week the second-floor boys seemed to have forgotten me. They had found a new diversion: someone had called on Pete's girl while he had spent the week end fishing the Mississippi. He did not take kindly to the unknown interloper who had cut in on him while he was away.

"I'll get him," Pete said. "I'll get him," but the razzing went on all week.

On Sunday night Mildred again was at Epworth League, as was I. We stepped from the church together and kept right on walking. Mildred was a sophomore in the high school I would attend in the fall, and as we strolled she described the school life that soon I would know. It was a warm night, and children were playing on the streets, but we were too busy with each other to notice them. We did not even observe that a large crowd seemed to be playing under a lamp on Oak Street almost directly in front of Mildred's house.

But we did see Pete step from behind a tree into our path.

"Now I've got you," he said tensely and waited for his rival to step into the light. I was the last person he expected to see.

"You!" He couldn't believe it. He didn't know whether to laugh or bluster or threaten. But his aides were not in doubt.

"That guy! Yah-a-h. Oh, boy!"

I found it prudent to run. Mildred also ran, onto her porch to summon her father. Prepared for my flight, the gang cut me off, backing me against a tree. They did not strike, because Pete intended to finish his rival himself. Those were orders. The gang was responsible only if I got away.

Pete swaggered up and poked his face into mine.

"So you're the guy who's going with my girl."

No answer seemed required; so I offered none.

"Won't talk, hey? Scared, hey?"

There was no use denying an obvious fact. Surrounded by Pete's friends except for a narrow avenue blocked by Pete's shoulders, I stood helpless. But the thought hit me that if Pete had been surprised, he

wasn't the only one. Our mutual predicament seemed funny, and I smiled. That was a mistake.

"Oh, you think it's funny? We'll show you what's funny. What's a matter, can't you talk?"

"What good's talk?"

"You'd better talk fast and plenty, wise guy. What're you doing on Oak Street?"

"That's my business."

"Your business! Hey, gang, did you hear that!" Everyone laughed, but there was no mirth in it.

"I own this street. Nobody comes on it without my say-so."

"Says you."

"Says me, and I'm telling you."

Pete was strutting up and down, but his guard wasn't up. Maybe he was like the packing-house toughs in Omaha, who had to pick on you four at a time. I remembered how they had waylaid me after school because I wore shoes before the weather turned cold and had a suit coat instead of a sweater and a Mackinaw instead of an old cut-down overcoat. I could see them again, waiting for me at the corner, always four of them. Attack hard had been my strategy then; charge through them and get away.

On the porch Mildred and her parents were watching. She was biting her nails, begging her father to interfere. He started down the steps toward us. Pete saw him too, turned half around for a better look at the new foe.

At that moment, using the tree as a springboard, I charged, head down, into Pete. Hit in the stomach, he grunted, spun around. I raced down the avenue of silent figures, but I did not escape. Someone projected a foot and tripped me. Two boys sat on me until Pete arrived.

Goaded by humiliation, he shouted, "Get up!"

I arose and attacked again. He had not expected such a quick strike, and I passed him and sprinted down the street. Someone, however, was faster than I.

This time, when Pete caught up, he swung on me with cold, sober fury, catching me on the cheek with a flaming jab. The crowd howled. He swung again, onto my cheek bone, continued to flay my head and face until I put both hands before my eyes to ease the shock.

Breathless, Pete paused.

"That'll teach you not to walk with Mildred," he said and walked away. Some little boys jeered, and one pushed me over the back of another who had knelt behind me.

Down North Street I retreated, aching and bruised and bitter, bitter not that I had been whipped, but because I had been dumped by the little boys, with Mildred watching from her front porch. She might even have sympathized with me, being picked on by a bully— but the little boys, that was too much. I imagined how next day she would see Pete and smile at him, and he would swagger in front of her. And at work what would he do?

There was only one consolation. They still didn't know I was a preacher's son.

CHAPTER TWELVE

*N*EXT day, however, when I appeared at the factory gates, the boys were waiting for me. Mildred's sister had disclosed my secret.

"Yah, yah, preacher's son," they shouted, while the older men grinned. "Preacher's son, yah, yah, preacher's son."

The chant followed me into the building and up the stairs, I concealing my blackened eyes, bruised cheeks, and burning blushes.

"That's all right, Jack," Tillie said gently. "Don't let it get you. It takes their fun away if you don't let it get you."

The trouble was it had got me.

"Go out in the yard this noon," Tillie advised. "Show 'em you can take it."

The opening whistle blew. She hurried to her piecework and I to mine. Boys found excuses to parade to the third floor and laugh. Clancy watched them come and go. They would carry materials to the storeroom, pass me with arms full, deposit their load, and take a whispered crack on their return.

"Boy, what a shiner! Oh, my!"

"Who hung that on you, sister?"

"See you in church, black eyes."

Tillie was disappointed that I did not answer. Once she thumped me on the shoulder.

"Talk back," she said ferociously. "Remember what I said about respect."

At noon I did not know what to do. The girls had said very little, although usually their Monday chatter was an animated recital of week-end excitements. Now I must choose whether to have lunch with them, probably in silence, or go into the yard to eat alone. I decided to eat alone.

Behind the factory was a great stack of pulpwood, from which the Mississippi stretched away up and downstream. The view was beautiful: tree-clustered islands, neat farms on the Illinois bank, a big bridge downstream. The current inquired among the pulpwood logs with pleasant, industrious chatter, and a warm breeze rubbed the warehouse shadows. Here I had opened my lunch box when Pete ambled around the corner.

"Hi, bud."

Cautiously I put aside a sandwich, ready for trouble.

"Hi, yourself," I said.

"What's the matter? Too good to eat with the rest of us?"

Too good? Why, I'd have given anything just to sit among them. But you didn't join Pete's gang that easily. You had to be one of them, not an outsider.

"I'd like to eat with you," I said.

"Then come on."

Pete helped me pick up my lunch and led the way back into the yard. They were going to razz me again, I figured. Then they would leave me alone.

The second-floor boys were sprawled along a lean shadow, their backs against the building. Pete and I sat down among them. I busied myself with my lunch. As long as everyone was eating, I was safe.

"Getting hot," somebody said, looking at me.

"It's awful hot on the third floor," I said.

"Boy, you wait 'til summer. That tin roof just soaks up the sun. Last year it was 110 degrees up there one day."

"We gave him more heat than that last night," Pete said. His voice was friendly, and I gulped my egg sandwich and laughed.

"You sure did," I admitted.

After that they included me in the conversation, and I felt better. The lunch went on. Somebody had wrecked a car over the week end. An eyewitness volunteered minute details. Pete's brother had lost his boat when it hit a snag in the river.

I could understand this. They weren't so tough. I just hadn't known them, that's all. I began to relax. Pete noticed it and threw up a barrier.

"What do you do on Sundays, Jack, go to church?"

"That's about all," I said, at once miserable again.

"Can't you go fishing?" someone asked.

I had been afraid of a question like that. "No," I said.

"Can you go to the movies?"

"No."

"Just church?"

"I take a spin in the car usually," I answered. I had to say something to offset their contempt.

"What kind?"

"Ford."

"You drive?"

"Sure."

"You weren't driving last night."

They laughed, but Pete stopped them quickly.

"Couldn't you go fishing if somebody wanted you to?" he asked, incredulous.

"Not on Sunday."

"That's tough," Pete consoled me, and the others nodded. They were my betters. If I couldn't go fishing on a blue-sky Sunday, I was nobody. They could afford to be friends.

When the whistle blew, they were at ease, and so was I.

After lunch the girls who had seen me in the yard recovered their voices.

"Hey, Parson," Mary called, "does your pa have any pull with the cops?"

"Not that I know of. We're new in town. Why?"

"Nothing, except I thought maybe he could get my old man out of hock."

"I thought he only got ten days."

There had been a slip somewhere, Mary explained. The old man had been pulled too often. She didn't understand exactly. He was what the law called a "habitual criminal" and might get a tough rap. They might even send him down the river to the penitentiary.

"Why don't you see your pastor?" I asked innocently.

Looms became idle. Everyone looked at Mary and at me.

"*My* pastor?"

"Sure."

"I don't go to church."

"Not even on Christmas and Easter?"

"No."

This was beyond belief. Everybody went to church once in a while. Everyone had a pastor to go to in time of trouble. That's what the preacher was for. He didn't just orate on Sundays and take up missionary collections. His job was to help people.

"Could you come to our house after dinner?" I suggested. "Father might have an idea."

"Oh, I couldn't bother you."

"Why not? That's what father's for."

She thought a moment, afraid of the reaction of her coworkers. Tillie, quick and sensitive, resumed her work furiously.

"I'll go with you, Mary," Tillie said. "A little religion wouldn't hurt me any."

And the looms and the preacher's son's hammer became busy again. We had all lost a great deal of time.

That night at dinner I explained the situation to father, and he was pleased.

"That's fine, son," he said. "I'm always glad to listen to your problems and those of your friends. I'd be mighty disappointed if you didn't come to me when something's on your mind."

He was fascinated with Tillie. She approached him humbly, but not mutely, clad in her best skirt and navy-blue-silk blouse. She was sprucer, younger, less brittle in her finery than at work, and self-conscious of her duty.

"Preacher Spence," she plunged, "we shouldn't bother you."

"What do you mean, *bother?*" father responded. "Come in. I'm proud to meet Hartzell's friends."

"Whose? Oh, Jack. Gosh, you threw me for a minute! You're supposed to wind up before you pitch curves, mister. The kid's 'Jack' to us."

Father snorted a little, then escorted his awkward guests into the living room and seated them. He pretended to be busy with a little chore long enough for them to appraise the rugs, drapes, and the arrangement of the furniture. Finally, when they relaxed, settling into the mohair davenport on which at first they had leaned gingerly forward, he began to talk, directing his questions at Tillie, the stronger vessel. Their personalities reached out and fingered each other, feeling for common denominators.

I was surprised at father. He seemed to know the Tillies of this world very well. They talked shop, and father might have passed for a slightly dignified shop foreman, he knew so well the terminology, if not the crudities, of factory speech. Before long Tillie was relating the saga of Humboldt O'Brien, Mary's father. He had been wrestler, railroad freightman, teamster, cigar maker, magazine distributor, vacuum-cleaner repairman, cabinet maker. He was agile with his hands, too adroit, in fact, for he could pick a pocket or a lock as easily as he could wrap a cigar, and he was just naturally tempted to take advantage of opportunities that presented themselves.

Several times he had been arrested, but that was nothing, a little fun, a diversion from the humdrum.

Humboldt O'Brien was a happy and fun-loving fellow, kind to his family. If anything, said Tillie, glancing at Mary for nodded confirmation, he might be described as a good man, a man with a heart of gold. He'd give you the shirt off his back. Everybody loved him. He was weak, yes, but a criminal? Not Humboldt.

Father had known a number of men, he said, who fitted the pattern of Humboldt O'Brien, good men, good providers, good fathers; industrious, thrifty, clean. The only thing wrong was that their lives lacked direction. They could not segregate the evil influences from the good or perhaps were unaware what influence was evil. Given a driving force, they could walk heads up with any man living. The trouble with Humboldt was that lack of drive. He would like to meet Humboldt O'Brien and talk to him.

Promising nothing except the interview, he reassured Mary and said good-by to Tillie as jokingly as though she was his wealthy aunt.

The details of this experience, relayed to the third floor, made material for profound discussion. Tillie's succinct description of father would have pleased him. "He's my old man on a Saturday night when he's all slicked up for a brawl, a real gentleman."

And this story of my father helped me in the yard. At noon Pete's gang was definitely interested in the preacher and listened to me respectfully.

Next day Mary added to the story. Father had seen Humboldt O'Brien. He had walked into the jail with as much ease as though he'd been there before and had picked Humboldt out of a crowd of four in the bull pen.

"I must have known your father in Fort Dodge," he had said. "Name of Sam, a railroad conductor."

He was wrong, but unabashed. Humboldt disapproved of the interview, afraid he'd have too hard a job living down the stigma of a visit from a preacher. But father did no praying; he cracked jokes.

Then he went to the O'Brien home to see Mary's mother. To her he suggested but not firmly, that Mary's younger sisters ought to be in Sunday school. They were missing an experience that might make them lovelier women, even if they never joined a church.

Mrs. O'Brien took the hint. Next Sunday as I was ducking in the vestry door I heard a low voice.

"Jack!"

There was Mary, with her sisters. "You take 'em," she begged. "I got 'em this far."

The girls were clean and well ironed and wore blue hair ribbons. They were pretty with dark hair and freckles and big mischievous eyes. They enrolled in the junior department, and father beamed. But Mary remained across the street, watching the door from the steps of a funeral parlor until her sisters reappeared.

Next day father went to the county attorney and asked about the case of Humboldt O'Brien, two of whose daughters were in his Sunday school. Later in the week, when O'Brien appeared in court, father joined the spectators. The prosecutor suggested that influences were at work in Humboldt's life that might be taken into consideration. His daughters were in Sunday school. He was thoroughly aware of the seriousness of his long succession of misdemeanors. Perhaps sixty days in jail would cure him, but another offense would send him to the penitentiary. O'Brien went back to jail, two months short of freedom. He expected the preacher to make another call, but father did not go near him.

"I've got the kids," he said at home. "Get the kids, and they will get the parents."

On the third floor of the factory Tillie sheepishly suggested that the miracle of intercession had occurred and that it might have been the answer to prayer.

The assembly line could not accept this.

"How do you know?" the women asked Tillie. "He called on the D.A., didn't he? He's got drag, that's what."

"Nobody's dragging that D.A.," Tillie suggested, "not all by himself. Besides, I wasn't referring to him."

The looms quieted. Everybody stared at Tillie. She alone continued to work, her eyes hawking the wood fibers that sped through her hands into the shell of a bushel-sized basket.

"Ho-*ly!*" somebody said.

"Well," Tillie admitted self-consciously, "maybe that wasn't it, but it didn't do any harm. And that Mr. Spence, is *he* handsome."

That noon in the yard I was invited to eat with the men as well as the second-floor boys. I was even allowed to watch the blackjack game patronized chiefly by the foremen. I had become a hero, for *my* old man had *influence.*

CHAPTER THIRTEEN

*T*HE SUMMER was half over before something happened that led father to investigate my working environment. By that time I was having fun.

One scorching day the humidity sludged out of the river bottom and competed for man's discomfort against a beating, baking sun. Under the factory's tin roof the temperature was more than 100 degrees Fahrenheit. Welcome was the whistle that let us into the outdoor shade for an hour at noon. The second-floor boys saw I was fagged out.

"You need something to bolster you up," Pete said and pulled a plug of chewing tobacco from his pocket, enthusiastically describing its medicinal wonders. It gave a man the lift he needed against the long afternoon. All I had to do was put a slug of it in my cheek and chaw on it occasionally.

Tobacco was sinful. But so was the heat. I decided to counteract one curse with the other and speculatively bit into the bitter plug. It didn't taste too bad.

The whistle blew. Upstairs I resumed my labors, interspersing them with experimental mastication of the alien weed. Nobody had told me not to swallow the tobacco juice. I washed it down generously with ice water.

By two o'clock I was not feeling too brisk. By half

past two I was ill, yet determined not to be beaten down by the heat, of which everyone complained and which everyone obviously was fighting. I hung on. About three o'clock Tillie rushed over and jerked up my head.

"For Heaven's sake, Jack," she shouted, "your face is purple."

That was all I needed. A few minutes later I was enroute home, sicker than I had ever been in my life.

Meeting me on the porch, father did not need to be told the particulars. What was required was accomplished, with the aid of a physician and a stomach pump. Father remained with me through the ordeal. But as soon as he was assured that I was not going to die, he began to ask questions. True to character, he berated himself for subjecting me to an environment in which fifteen- and sixteen-year-olds carried chewing tobacco in their trouser pockets.

"I had no idea," he kept repeating. Next day he did not forbid my return to work. Instead he was outside the gates in the Ford at five o'clock. Pete and another boy from Oak Street known as "Cappie" were with me. Father invited us all to climb into the car, ascertained the Oak Street address, and drove up the road, his head tilted to intercept the conversation in the back seat. It was enlightening.

"Jesus, this is the nuts, hey, Jack?" Pete offered.

"Yeah," I admitted woefully. I knew what father was doing.

"Imagine *my* pa giving me a lift," Cappie laughed.

"He can't lift his — off a bed," Pete said.

The car began to move along a little faster.

"Not unless the old lady's on it," Cappie said.

From there on the conversation became unprintable. Pete and Cappie were showing off, playing a game called "shocking the preacher." The more frantically I signaled them to hush, the louder became their speech. They would let go a foul expression, cock their heads, shake with silent, uproarious laughter, then bubble over with another remark which topped its predecessor. Never in the factory yard had I heard such talk.

The car was racing up the hill now, wide open, as though the noise might drown the profanity. Father's ears were red, his jaws set, his eyebrows down like Moses' on his return from Sinai. Still far from Oak Street he had had enough. He yanked the car to the side of the street and stopped.

"Where did you boys learn such filthy talk?" he roared, swinging around to confront them with brimstone eyes.

They had not expected such a belligerent reaction to their game. Frightened and mute, they scrambled over the door to the curb. Their eyes focused on a street corner several blocks away, and their bodies confirmed with speedy feet what the eyes transmitted to the brain. Father watched them go. He was trembling. I was alone in the rear seat, very much alone.

"They aren't like that, father," I said timidly. "They were just trying to shock you."

"Shock me!" His jaw muscles twitched. "Well, they did it."

We drove slowly home. He did not appear for dinner, but remained in the quiet refuge of his study, to which he had gone immediately. About nine o'clock he summoned me. His hair was grooved where his big hand had run through it; his expression was bewildered. He pointed to a chair. I sat. He was silent a long time. Twice he opened his mouth, only to clamp his jaws again. When finally he spoke, it was quietly.

"I have never had such an experience in my life." It was a declarative sentence, requiring no reply. "I cannot believe there is such filth in the world."

Rising, he jammed his hands into the top of his trousers and walked to the window.

"Even if that's the way they always talk, which it isn't," I began gently, trying to tap a wedge into his turmoil, "I'd have to get used to it sometime. I can't live in the parsonage forever."

He stepped back, his face ashen.

"You—what?"

"I can't live in the parsonage forever. Sooner or later I'll have to earn my way."

A swivel chair creaked as he lowered himself into it.

"It's monstrous."

"But they were just shocking you, father."

"Why should they want to shock me? I was only taking them home."

"It's because you're a preacher, father."

"I'm just a man, like any other, son."

I smiled grimly, and he noticed.

"Isn't that so?" he asked, begging for confirmation.

"No." It was all I could say.

We stared at each other. I wanted to explain how he was set apart, and his family too. In the eyes of the factory world we were goody-goody, forbidden to fish on Sunday, forbidden to see movies on Sunday, forbidden to dance, forbidden the emotional and physical release that factory workers need to replenish their minds and bodies for another week of piecework under a hot tin roof. How could I tell him that Pete was trying to do me a favor, sandpapering off a little of the parsonage polish, letting a little living in?

Father did not believe in that kind of living. A man could be a Christian and still have fun. He had often said so. But rubbing against a girl while dancing wasn't fun; it was sin. Not going to church on Sunday to thank God for his bounty was sin. Sunday fishing would be all right if the excursion started *after* church, but it never did; it began at dawn, robbing the Lord of his day. Vile talk was not living, ever; it was reeking, vulgar indecency, like spitting on a carpet.

"Let me hear what you have to say."

"They don't talk like that," I said. "That's every nasty thing they have heard in their whole lives, thrown out at once. They're good boys, father. They work hard. They play hard too. But they're not hard themselves. Maybe a little coarse, and maybe you'd be too if you had to work where they do—and live where they do. They laugh at me because I can't do lots of things they do. This was their way of laughing at you."

"I never thought a son of mine would ever have to hear such things."

"It's the first time I've heard them—most of them."

"And it's the last," he said. "First chewing tobacco, now this. Well, that's all anyway."

He had made a decision and felt better. He even tried to smile.

"I don't think you'd better go back to the basket factory."

To my mind that was no solution, and I said so.

"It will prevent your hearing things like that."

"Oh, no, it won't, father. I even hear them in Sunday school."

He leaped up, shocked to the roots of his life.

"Son!"

"But it's true, father. The boys in Sunday school talk like the boys in the basket factory."

"Impossible!"

"Of course they do. I don't mean they talk like what you heard in the car, but I've tried to tell you Pete and Cappie aren't like that really."

"Well, they think it, or they couldn't speak it. You won't go back."

"Then why should I go to Sunday school?"

"Next you'll tell me the boys chew tobacco in Sunday school." Father was not yet quite master of himself.

"But, father—"

He walked to the door and opened it.

"Son," he said, "I'm doing my best to control my temper. I want you to make your own decisions. There are a lot of things in the world I'm not supposed to know, but I'm not such a fool as I look. You are only fifteen. If you were older, experiences like these would bounce off of you. I don't want you to have them yet, that's all. Do me a favor, and don't go back to the factory."

"But how will I make a living?"

This remark punctured the inflation of his anger. He laughed happily.

"I think your old dad can provide for you a few more years."

"But I want to earn some money. I don't like to scrub floors."

He was still smiling. "Maybe you can rustle up something else. But please—for me—no more factory."

The following morning I sprawled on the porch, attempting to read a book, after canvassing the town unsuccessfully for a new job. Father spotted me when he came downstairs from his study to try out a sermon thesis on mother. To his cheerful greeting I made no response. He looked through the open living-room window for a moment, then came out to me.

"What's the matter, son?"

"Nothing to do."

"You ought to be glad on a hot day like this to be able to loaf. Look at me; I've two sermons to write and not an idea in my head."

"Try Mark 7:15," I said.

My sarcasm annoyed him. Quickly he retreated to look up the verse, then returned emphatically to the porch and drew up a chair beside me.

"You know your Bible better than I thought," he said, "but you've got to give up this notion without any bitterness. There must be boys in this neighborhood to play with."

"I don't know a soul in town—except at church, and this isn't Sunday."

"Well, son, that's your problem. I'm having to make friends too. This isn't a very good town for it; you have to work at it."

"I'd rather work for twelve bucks a week."

He looked me up and down and said, "We're both tired. Let's go fishing."

That was more like it. Father didn't often take time out to play.

We chartered a rowboat with an outboard motor and went to an island up the river. He had been there before, I discovered, with a man who owned a fishing shack, Billy Burbank. In the shack were fishing lines, bait, and cooking utensils. We sat for a long time on the dock, trying to tempt catfish.

And father, relaxing in the sunlight, began a monologue.

[There was nothing like fishing to compose a man's mind.] Emerson had said that when he put out on a river in a rowboat the first stroke of the oars pulled him away from society, and the knapsack of custom fell from him, and that was true. A man who was fishing could spit when he wanted to spit, and a quiet river was the most patient listener he knew anything about. When you wanted to give a church deacon a good cussing out, the place to do it was on a riverbank. Furthermore, fishing taught you to relax. Society was so high geared that there was no relaxation in it any more. A man had to go fishing to get time to think. The present generation had developed such tension that it couldn't even fish properly; it had succumbed to the nervous disease of fly casting, which wasn't fishing at all, but a mania in which the body, taut as a piano wire, exhausted itself.

Now take catfishing—

On he went, working hard at the job of comradeship. But all this energetic business set him more apart.

A man fishing with another talks a little and fishes a little and shares a great deal of silent comradeship, each appreciating the other. But when father was with other men, they listened while he talked; they followed where he led, always on their toes lest they offend him or say or do anything of which he would not approve. He did not realize this. He led; he talked; he accepted the respect, unconscious of any impact except that of his own personality on another.

Now he talked to me as he talked to other men, but for all his effort he was still just a little in the pulpit; he had a catechism in his hand.

We returned to town without a fish. At the dock he told the boatman I was to have the outboard any time I liked. This meant that, now he had shown the way, I could amuse myself alone.

He became more liberal also with the car. Any time I wanted it, he gave it up and walked about his parish calls. On Sunday evening he encouraged me to drive to Epworth League, suggesting I might take a spin with a young lady after the service.

When I returned to the basket factory to draw my last pay, father offered the car, and I picked up Pete and the gang.

"What's the matter?" Pete asked. "What'd you quit so sudden for?"

"Father thinks I've worked enough for this summer," I answered casually. "We been going fishing up at Big Island."

"Fishing! On Sunday?"

"Pretty near every other day. He's rented a shack up there. I stayed overnight once."

"You did?"

"Sure. The old man had to come back to town, but I stayed. Next time you hear an Evinrude, look out on the river. Might be me."

"And you aren't coming back to work?"

"No. The old man says he'll support me. I'm going to high school this fall."

They thought this over as they stepped down from the car at Oak Street.

"Not bad," Pete said.

"Not bad a-tall," I said. "Be seein' you around."

"Yah," Pete said. "See you in church."

I winced. The barrier was up again.

Returning home, I noticed immediately that something was wrong. Windows were wide open. Through them came the unmistakable sounds of a dance record on the phonograph and, unless I was crazy, there seemed to be dancing figures profaning the parsonage living room.

I went up the front steps two at a time. There, sure enough, were a dozen or more girls dancing together, Eileen among them.

Where was mother? Where was father? Saturday afternoon, of all times, when he was supposed to be putting the finishing touches on his sermons.

So busy had I been at the basket factory, so absorbed in my work, that I had not paid much attention to Eileen. True, I had been chased out of the living room several evenings when boys had called on her. She had talked a lot about Bob somebody or other, but the natural barrier between a nearly seventeen-year-old girl

and a fifteen-year-old brother is very wide, particularly if there is a beau on the porch. We had not been very close to each other that summer. And now there was dancing in the parsonage!

Eileen ignored my frantic gestures, gave me unmistakable signals to get out and leave her alone. Horrified, I watched for a moment as the girls jumped about the floor, from which the carpeting had been rolled away. Eileen was having a wonderful time, and she was extremely proficient at dancing. Watching her, I wondered why I had never discovered this before; she could teach me plenty. There she was, executing a step which a girl named Valeen had tried to show me a week before, and failing had labeled me a "dummy."

[156]

But wonder was not so strong as fear. Obviously father was not in the house. If he came in, sparks would fly, and I hated to think what might happen. The least I could do was stand sentinel and warn of his approach.

I went to the porch. Striding up the street a block away came father.

Immediately I burst back into the house and stopped the dance.

"Father's coming," I shouted. "Get the rug down; hide the records."

The girls paused, glanced curiously at Eileen and at me as I unrolled the rug. Eileen stormed over to me.

"What's the big idea?" She was furious.

"It's father. Quick, he's coming up the walk."

"Pooh," she snorted. "What of it?" She turned the phonograph on again and resumed her dance.

Okay, I thought. If she wants to get the dickens, that's her problem, but I won't be here. I ducked up the stairs and peeped through the banisters as father came in.

He stood a moment, watching. Eileen danced on, her face very red. Father nodded and smiled to such of the girls as he recognized, then left them alone.

That was too much. Tiptoeing down the back stairs, I found mother in the kitchen, making sandwiches.

"What's going on?" I asked, shocked still further.

"Eileen's giving a party."

"I know—but dancing!"

"It's all right, dear," mother replied. "Father agreed, if they don't dance with boys."

Now my humiliation was complete. I had made a

fool of Eileen before her friends. I had played a beautiful role of meddling brother, and if I knew Eileen
there would be reverberations.

There were. As soon as the last of the girls had gone,
she flamed into the kitchen. With mother to lean on,
she began to cry. She was never so embarrassed in her
life. Just when she had convinced these girls that she
was no different from them, I had to come along and
spoil it. She'd never live it down. Wasn't it hard enough
to be a preacher's daughter without having to put up
with a brother?

I retreated to the back porch and sat on the top step.
Father found me there. He had an uncanny knack for
searching out people who were in trouble.

"So you've been driven out too, have you?" he asked,
sitting beside me. "What's the matter, son?"

"Nothing, sir."

"This is too nice an afternoon to be sitting on the
back porch."

"I'm all right."

But I wasn't. Soon he had the story of the rug un-
rolling.

"It's hard to know *what* to do," he admitted.

"It sure is."

He thought a moment. Then, "I guess dancing is all
right, *if* you do it at home. I don't approve of it, you
understand, and I wouldn't consider your dancing in
public or at a place like the golf club. But in the home,
if you can reconcile it with your conscience, I won't
object."

"You won't?"

"No."

I jumped up and started for the door.

"Where are you going?"

"To phone Valeen," I said. "Maybe she'll give me a dancing lesson tonight."

CHAPTER FOURTEEN

*E*ILEEN's dancing party brought to my attention the fact that not only Eileen but Fraser had been in trouble.

I had noticed mother's preoccupation with Fraser but had not paid much attention to it. Now I began to see mother's handiwork, like lace, the pattern of which is not discernible until much of the work is done, in Fraser's as well as in Eileen's reorientation.

We had not been in Riverton a week before mother received a telephone call from the principal of the school in which Fraser had enrolled. He was unresponsive and sullen, would not make the acquaintance of his classmates, or answer to his name in class. He did not even respond to a roll call.

Mother visited his school, and that night after Fraser had gone to bed she described the visit. Her first judgment was that Fraser, frightened by the upheaval that had transferred him to a new school near the end of a term, could not adjust his seven-year-old outlook to new prescriptions. Soon she realized that his trouble was more deeply grown. Therefore she begged the teacher to let Fraser remain in class until she could discover what was wrong and thus could plan intelligently for his future.

For several weeks she explored Fraser's tightly locked mind. His laughter, his jesting spirit, his quick retorts,

his tendency to practical jokes were no longer noticeable.

One Saturday afternoon I sought mother in her sewing room to ask her to mend a frayed shirt cuff and
found her in pursuit of Fraser's difficulty. Quickly she
motioned for me to be silent. She had just discovered
that Fraser hated his Denver teacher.

"Why, dear?" she queried him.

"She didn't like me."

"What did you do to make her dislike you?"

She hadn't let him have any fun. She was even angry
when he painted black whiskers on the faces in his
reader. He smiled. So did mother.

"What else didn't she like?"

"The glue in Esther's inkwell."

"Who was Esther?"

She was the little girl who sat in front of him. Miss
Burman had reprimanded her for spilling ink. Fraser
had filled her bottle with something that wouldn't
spill, and when she dipped her pen in it a long string
of sticky stuff came out of the bottle and got in her
hands and hair.

"What did Miss Burman do?"

"She put me in the back of the room away from
everyone else."

There he had remained for the rest of the year.
When he volunteered to recite, she had ignored him.
When obviously he did not understand, she had called
on him to talk. He had been accused of every prank,
even though now he was in no mood for foolery. When
she discovered that he was leaving town and would no

longer be in her class, she had snapped at him before all the children.

"She said I was stupid, mummy," Fraser wailed. "She said any teacher would just be wasting time on me. Do you believe that, mummy?"

"Of course not, dear," mother answered, confident now that she had probed the depths of his spiritual isolation. "You remember how you found the hidden button at Howard Bramley's party when nobody else could find it?"

"Yes."

"You learned the Twenty-third Psalm faster than anyone in your Sunday school class."

"Yes."

"You were the only one of all the children who could explain to Mrs. Ferguson what 'doxology' meant."

Fraser began to relax.

"You were just a naughty boy, son," mother went on. "Teachers don't like to have their textbooks marked up and glue put in the inkwells. That's not funny."

"Oh, yes it was, mother."

"Well, maybe it was to you, but not to the teacher. What would father say if you drew pictures in his Bible or put glue in the hymnbooks?"

Fraser's eyes gleamed with mischief, the first flash of impishness since our arrival in Riverton. Mother too smiled.

By the end of June Fraser passed an intelligence test that determined his advance to the third grade. At about that time he also found a kindred spirit.

He was returning from the grocery one noon when he was greeted by a mangy, feeble, but very tail-waggy puppy. It was the first Rivertonian of any breed to nod in his direction. Fraser put down his bundles to stroke the puppy's head. Having sampled affection, the dog followed Fraser home. But the house in which we lived belonged to the church; we were merely its stewards. There could be no dog scratches on the hardwood floors, no bone holes in the lawn.

The pup did not understand this. He had been petted, and from that moment Fraser was his master. Even when abandoned on the back porch, he waited patiently for Fraser to reappear, then swarmed on him with love and devotion. Naturally, they began to play.

The puppy slept the first night in the basement but the next day was invited to the front porch. There father found him. Father also found a hole in the front lawn and immediately associated the two. Fraser tamped down top soil and grass seed, but in an hour there was another hole. By evening there were others, and very little remained of a geranium bed.

Such destruction of church property could not be tolerated. Father pointed this out reluctantly during dinner. The puppy must go. But where? A pup as ingenious as Hugo wouldn't let himself be lost, after sampling friendship and raw hamburger. He was a dog of singular loyalty; there was no doubt about it. Even father almost succumbed to his inquisitively cocked head, his frantic, clumsy desperation to pad his short legs at Fraser's heels.

Mother was frightened lest the disappointment of separation from his pet reemphasize Fraser's maladjustment. She watched the tears drip from his cheeks to his plate, arose, and called him and me aside.

First invoking Fraser's loyalty to father, she then suggested that when school began the puppy would be very lonely. Fraser would be gone all day. It was unfair to the animal not to give it love and care. What a growing little puppy like Hugo needed was an association with other dogs, with whom he could play happily. There was a place called the dog pound where little strays like Hugo could find a good home. Fraser wanted Hugo to be happy, didn't he?

Solemnly he nodded.

"Well then, suppose you and Hartzell take Hugo to a good comfortable home. Would that be all right?"

This nod had tears in it, but it was affirmative.

Quietly I led Fraser and the pup from the house, down the hill to the city pound. There, yipping in pens, obviously having a great time playing together, were many dogs.

Fraser watched Hugo run among them and nuzzle them, saw his comrade pushed aside.

"I can't." He began to cry again.

"Yes, you can, Fra."

"But look, they don't like him."

"He'll get acquainted soon. He has a bone now. See how much fun he's having with the bone?"

Fraser looked. Hugo, on his haunches, was growling and gnawing at a sizable ham hock.

"Now, you see?" I encouraged him.

"Yes."

"Shall we go?"

"I guess."

During the rest of the summer mother encouraged Fraser to see almost every movie that came to town.

Often he left the house immediately after lunch, returning just in time for dinner, and nothing was said when he overspent his allowance. In the evening he would go to the phonograph, play over and over again his supply of records.

At bedtime he would undress, climb into bed, and amuse himself by singing the recordings to which he had listened. Night after night the parsonage about eight o'clock rang with a clear boy soprano voice singing:

I've come to see Miss Jennia Jones,
Miss Jennia Jones, Miss Jennia Jones,
And how is she today?

No matter how hard father was trying to concentrate on a sermon, he did not once still this recitative. He would wait patiently until the song ebbed into a mumble, and died away altogether, before resuming his writing.

Usually when we moved to a new town, father jumped into community life immediately; we children discovered neighborhood playmates within a few days; and mother, after many months of trial and error, sifted a few more or less intimate associations out of a large church membership.

Riverton, however, was a settled community. Its traditions had become patternized, like the gestures of a Chinese actor. It had its ways, and we had ours. For three years in Denver we had been adjusting our almost unalterable life to the liberality of a big western city. Now, after the joviality of the West, we faced an entirely different culture, a bitterly unfriendly one.

After a few rebuffs on near-by play lots, Fraser began to spend much of his time on the front porch.

One Sunday afternoon mother encouraged him to take a walk with Eileen. We were all on the porch that day, driven outdoors by clammy humidity. They were not yet out of sight when mother turned to father.

"Will, they're the loneliest youngsters I've ever seen."

Father, whose children meant very little to him a few hours before a sermon, merely grunted.

"They'll make friends," he said.

A few minutes later Eileen and Fraser returned and resumed their boredom on the porch railing.

"Well, Eilie," mother asked brightly, "have you nothing to do?"

For answer Eileen spilled tears and retired to her room. Mother did not take up her reading for a long time.

The next night when I returned from work, Eileen was again on the porch. A moment later mother joined her with a sack of peas and a pan and enlisted Eileen's and my aid in shelling them. The conversation worked around, by degrees, to the subject of entertainment. During the last month of school and the first weeks of vacation, several girls with cars had called regularly for Eileen, but this had ceased recently.

"By the way," mother asked, "what's happened to Helen, Catherine, and Neil? I don't see them any more."

"You probably won't either," Eileen answered.

"Why not?"

"They got tired of my not being able to do anything."

"What do you mean?"

"We always end up somewhere I can't go. You can't just ride around town all afternoon. I'm a wet blanket. So they've stopped calling for me. If I could drive *our* car," Eileen went on, "then I'd be in a position to say where we were going to go."

Mother did not pursue that one. Father was afraid to give Eileen the car. Girls who drove were likely to be what he termed "wild." Eileen argued that the hand on the wheel determines where the machine will go and where it will stop. But father would not agree.

A few boys had called on Eileen, but only one persevered. The rest wearied of dates with a girl who could not dance or go anywhere except to the movies.

More and more Eileen had remained on the front porch, with Fraser beside her, until finally mother had another talk with father, and the decision was made to relax the prohibition on dancing sufficiently so that Eileen might have a party for girls only.

This was to be Eileen's bid for acceptance. I had spoiled it by warning of father's approach. The effect Eileen had hoped to create—that she could dance even at home—was blasted, and the guests afterward talked not of Eileen's emancipation, but of her brother's fear that she be caught in a surreptitious act.

But Eileen did not hold her grudge against me long. Soon we were sharing a secret. She had developed a crush.

One evening in Epworth League a rustle of her sleeve attracted her attention. A note was being passed from the row behind. Always happy for any diversion from a pious lecture, Eileen took the note, glanced around. Directly behind her was Fred Dunning, a boy she had noticed casually at school. He was not a Methodist, which made him the more glamorous.

The note, on the back of an envelope, concerned the curls on Eileen's neck. Quickly Eileen answered. For twenty minutes they carried on a conversation that exhausted both sides of the envelope and spread onto the fly leaf of a hymnal.

The correspondence led to a friendship. Fred owned a boat, which he invited Eileen to inspect. Before long they were cruising among the islands. Eileen learned a little navigation, a little astronomy, a great deal about Ol' Man River, catfish, snakes, and the treatment of boats and trotlines, all of which she relayed to me and later to mother.

Mother was delighted, prepared savory lunches for them. Her heart overflowed when Eileen asked Fraser to go along on her outings. Fred did not object to the inclusion of a little brother. To him Eileen was just another sailor. His interest was primarily in his boat, and Fraser asked flattering questions about marine lore, in answering which Fred could display to Eileen his knowledge of things both nautical and masculine. He wouldn't have protested had Eileen brought along a Chinese missionary, provided the fellow wanted to learn about marine engines.

Mother was beginning to think that her labors, and her prayers, had been answered, when father stormed into the house.

"What's this I hear about Eileen?"

"What on earth could you possibly have heard about her?" mother asked. A girl on as slow a train as her daughter couldn't possibly be on the main line of scandal.

"I hear she's traipsing all over the river and up among the islands alone with a grown man."

"A grown man, indeed! Fred is just through high school."

"Well, in this town that's as adult as they ever get."

"Besides, she isn't alone. Fraser is with them."

"So they're out now, are they?"

"Yes. They go several times a week."

"Hm-m-m," said father. "I've had it rubbed in to me today that in Riverton nice girls don't gad about the river. Girls who do are tomboys or worse—"

"Well," mother replied, "I think our daughter's happiness at this moment is more important than such nonsensical gossip. If you hear any more, you just mention that Fraser is with them."

But Fred's father could not ignore the talk. He was in the insurance business. The river outings ended without explanation.

Eileen resumed her chair on the porch with Fraser, and now I, having left the basket factory, was with them.

Mother was driven again to action.

"Will," she said, tackling father in the presence of all of us, "the children need a vacation."

"I can't be expected to keep them amused, Hope," father answered. "I've work to do."

"You don't understand, Will. They don't know anybody; there's nothing for them to do. We've got to take them away from here until school starts."

"Hm-m-m," he said. That meant he was thinking fast.

"All right," he concurred. "Billy Burbank says we can have his river cabin any time we want it."

The vacation was arranged for the last two weeks in August. We would return to town coincidentally with the reopening of school, when there would be work aplenty for all the family. The arrangement pleased me, for it was the cabin father and I had visited, and my fishing equipment was already there.

As our overladen boat chugged up to the Burbank dock the next Monday morning and we could see a little cottage squatting on stilts in a mosquito-saturated clearing, father turned off the Evinrude motor and scrambled over children and baggage into the boat's prow. The current, which sucked swiftly around the tip of the island, caught us and heaved us back into the channel.

Stumbling aft, father wrapped a string around the starter and pulled. There was no response. Evidently the Evinrude had decided that its day's work was done. Briskly we drifted downstream while father yanked and fussed at the motor without getting anywhere.

"What the mischief is the matter with this fool thing?" he sputtered. Successively he worked off his hat, coat, and vest, but even the sight of a disrobing clergyman did not intimidate the Evinrude.

The boat drifted halfway back to Riverton. Mother crouched with Fraser on a center seat, and I was forward, out of the fury. It was not a good moment for mirth, but Eileen giggled.

"All right," father snapped, "you try it then, if it's so funny."

Calmly Eileen primed the motor, which father in his excitement had forgotten to do, pulled the starter cord, and the engine responded. But she refused to relinquish the tiller.

"I'll take her in," she said.

When again we reached the dock, father gave the orders.

"Bring the bow in, Eileen, but don't turn off the engine until I have a good hold on the piling."

Leaning far out of the boat, father made a grab at the pier. He grasped it, all right, but again misjudged the current. Down river we roared without father. He was hanging to the dock, his legs in the water. A most unecclesiastical rip was spread the breadth of his trousers.

Even mother joined the laughter. Eileen and I quickly brought the boat to a landing. Happily we went ashore.

Having lost the seat of his pants on arrival, father was unable to recover his dignity. Morning devotions were abandoned. Father let his beard grow. His shoes soon lost their shine. The old shirts he had brought became tattered by encounters with underbrush.

For two weeks he hunted snakes with us, fished, swam, introduced us to a game that could be carried on indefinitely. We were pioneers in the western wilderness. Our speech took on the drawl of the Kentucky scouts who first had explored that territory. We bargained with (and strangely made no attempt to convert) imaginary Indians. When we needed food, father went to town, returning with gay yarns of adventure.

As a result we ate better than at home, for he needed a chicken to go with his story of shooting a pheasant on the prairie, and a very large steak to substantiate an encounter with buffalo. The fish were biting well too.

Eileen was a little mature for this nonsense and occasionally refused to play the role of an Indian squaw or Nancy, the ol' hoss thief's daughter. She preferred being a Chickahominy princess.

Mother sat on the porch, safe from the mosquitoes, and watched the fun. Her idea of an outing was a de luxe hotel, where everything would be done for her. The river camp, quite appropriately named Rustic Rest by its owner, was no vacation for her. But she did not complain, not even at having to cook on a miserable two-burner oil stove.

By Labor Day we were tanned, itchy with poison ivy, and eager to return to town. Riverton, sitting on the hills overlooking the river, had taken on a different appearance. We children were pointed toward the school year ahead. We were ready for what the autumn would bring.

CHAPTER FIFTEEN

*B*Y THE third day of school I was jubilant. The school principal was a Methodist and taught in our Sunday school. The superintendent of schools was a member of father's official board. The registrar, music supervisor, and dramatics coach were well known to me and treated me as a personage. Anything I wanted was mine; I was Dr. Spence's son.

The school work was easy, first because of father's enormous library and second because of the extra year I had studied in Denver. In English, glancing down the list of required reading for the first semester, I noted no book I had not already read. In Latin I had begun to read Caesar in Denver and was 128 pages ahead of this class. In history I found myself in the Holy Roman Empire, which was old stuff.

The school paper was run by another minister's son, and so I joined the staff promptly. The chorus had few trained voices; as a veteran choir singer I found myself, with Eileen, immediately in the front row. The orchestra had no flute; the director was happy to enroll me.

Mother and father thankfully blessed these many activities, without keeping too close an eye on me. Restrictions that had pinned me to the Methodist Discipline toppled without even an argument. Not only I, but Eileen and Fraser as well, could attend school parties, act in school plays, do anything that did not clash with a fundamental, if only we were happy.

Father's one concern was lest our absorption in affairs scholastic cause us to forget our church. To prevent this he ordered Eileen and me to ready a flute-piano number for the Sunday offertory. As usual, he had a dual purpose. If we did not disgrace the muse of music (we couldn't possibly be worse than the choir), he would invite other church young people to provide offertory instrumental music.

In the congregation, as usual, was the school principal, Mr. Haskins. Since the school year was too young to have developed musicians for competitions, he had no musical numbers on hand for his assemblies. Before him in church he saw one ready made. Two days later Eileen and I performed in assembly, which enhanced our position at school. I was invited promptly to bring my piccolo into the high school band.

This would seem to have been enough. And it was for Eileen, who belonged to two societies and the chorus and wanted a little time for social life. But I found another opening. One afternoon I discovered in the auditorium some boys trying out before the dramatic coach, Mr. Martin, for the privilege of representing the school in extemporaneous speaking.

I, who had stood before dozens of church audiences, listened awhile. The speakers were uneasy, and their discourses lacked coherence and organization. When Mr. Martin asked if there were any other candidates, I stepped forward. It did not occur to me that the contestants, all upper classmen, had spent many hours

[174]

preparing for this contest and that I, a newcomer and a freshman, was precocious and definitely out of order in competing against them. Mr. Martin explained the rules. From a group of slips containing topics I was to draw one for an eight-minute speech, quoting only reputable authorities, such as *The Literary Digest*.

The subject I drew was mother love. There seemed to me no connection between mother love and *The Literary Digest*, so I was compelled to cite other references.

Here parsonage training backed me up. Father always began a discourse by defining his subject. Lord Byron had said something about mother love. I quoted it. Shakespeare had said considerable. I quoted what I could remember. Then I went back into a few of father's better sermons on the text "Greater love hath no man" and became emotional about the Spartan courage, sacrifice, and tenderness of mothers. The audience was unmoved. Five minutes passed, and I realized that I needed a conclusion. Facts were useless unless coordinated. Again I drew on a sermon. Faith, hope, and love, and the greatest of these is love. Mother love embraced all. And with another citation, this time from Emerson, I flourished from the stage. I had won. But there was no applause.

The extemporaneous contest against other schools was at Clinton, Iowa. Enroute, Mr. Martin gave me a pep talk on my responsibilities as representative of Riverton, of the stiff opposition I would get from senior boys and girls of eight cities. As we entered an auditorium packed with townspeople and Clinton students, an autumn storm began to rage.

Seven dignified boys in razor-pressed trousers and a meek-looking girl with stringy brown hair and a red silk dress joined me for an explanation of the rules. We would draw numbers to determine our speaking position, then be locked in separate rooms. Five minutes before speech time a referee would appear, let us draw one title from among fifty subjects, and a few moments later we would be summoned to speak.

My draw placed me sixth among the nine speakers. For a half hour I gnawed my fingernails, watching the thundershower outside. The referee appeared. I drew a slip from his hand. It read Mussolini.

Here was a subject about which I knew very little. Mussolini was an Italian. A month previously he had gathered together a horde of malcontents or something, in black shirts, and chased the government out of Rome, after which he had set himself up as leader of a new order, the fascist state. That was all I remembered.

Father's sermons were no good to me now. There was no parallel to Mussolini from Genesis to Revelation, or at least father wasn't there to point it out, and Emerson died the year before Mussolini was born.

On stage I had just started to speak when lightning struck near by, putting out the house lights. I kept on talking, but I had nothing to say. I placed eighth out of the nine contestants and probably would have been ninth except that the judges gave me liberal allowance for the sudden darkness.

The winner was the girl from Fairfield, Iowa. Her subject, ironically, was mother love. I inquired into her background, but she was not a minister's daughter.

Bounding into school prominence was great stuff, but

it had one severe drawback: insufficient funds. My allowance of $1.25 a week had to cover five lunches in the school cafeteria. This left nothing for parties, society dues, play and operetta tickets, and a large-eyed freshman named Betty.

Father was no help at all.

"If I get a wedding between now and Friday, you can have the fee," he promised one evening. "Right now I have 70 cents in my pocket, and I'll split it with you and Eileen." Thirty-five cents didn't go very far, and the most Eileen and I could count on from a wedding was a dollar each. If there was a five-dollar wedding, mother discovered a need for at least three dollars of it.

Then I met John Donnelly. A year older than I, John answered the telephone every evening at the office of the *Gazette,* one of two daily newspapers in Riverton. Folks whose paper had blown away telephoned for a replacement, and the pool halls about town inquired for baseball and football scores and results of horse races, which came in on the AP ticker too late for inclusion in the paper. John also carried a large paper route. As some days he could not complete this duty in time to reach the telephone by six o'clock, he was about to be fired. I became his assistant.

This was the beginning of a grandiose enterprise in finance capital. By spring we had added enough collateral activities to form a corporation. It was the Donnelly & Spence Co.

Pooled were the telephone service, the paper route, a carrier route of the morning newspaper, the *Courier,* which I had acquired during the winter, a magazine

[177]

subscription concession, and an Essay Production Company, which very much on the quiet, wrote book reports, themes, characterizations, and essays for high school students at 10 cents a page.

Our joint income was around $12 a week, but this was not enough. We applied to both local papers, John to one I to the other, with the suggestion that we report school news for $2.50 a week each. The proposals were accepted.

My job as a reporter on the school paper was to keep news from the dailies until the *Panther* was distributed each Monday afternoon. John's task, for the *Gazette,* was to beat both the school sheet and the *Courier;* my province, for the *Courier,* to scoop both the *Panther* and the *Gazette.*

John and I solved the problem by dividing the news. Certain events, such as sports, could not be kept from the daily press. Certain other highly marketable news, who would be May-fête queen, who editor of the *Annual,* must be held for the *Panther.* In the four months that our arrangement lasted, there was not a single complaint from any of the three publications, although we noticed that after a few weeks the sports editor of the *Gazette* resumed his own round of high school athletics.

My only personal conflict came during the month of April, when the Clisthonian Debating Society gave its annual play in the school auditorium. Amateur theatricals were highly developed in Riverton, which had its drama league, eight high school productions, and a generous share of road shows. Being in the cast of any of them was a distinction. The Clisthonian show was particularly funny, since the boys took female as well as male roles.

The play that year was *Officer 666,* in which a log-witted detective is confronted with the theft of Gainsborough's *Blue Boy* from a private collection. There were numerous incongruities, chief among them our prop for *Blue Boy,* a ten-cent store print fifteen by twenty inches, which drew laughter from the crowd. Another was that the Methodist preacher's son was the suave, white-tied villain of the piece. It was a role to please anybody, and I, in borrowed tailcoat, thought myself a very dashing figure.

In reviewing the play for the *Courier,* however, what could I say about myself? I could not very well say, in a review everyone in town would know I wrote, that my acting was one of the high spots of the performance. Modesty had to be maintained in public. The editor suggested that a newspaperman had many things to learn, among them self-effacement. I wrote the review, mentioning myself only as one of the cast, and emphasizing the antics of the female lead, who, forgetting he was in petticoats and not in trousers, hitched up his skirts when he sat down.

John Donnelly, writing for the *Gazette,* evened the score. He praised me with burning partisan loyalty, then wrote a letter to the editor of the *Courier* for publication in the *Letters* column, applauding my modesty in refraining from personal mention in my own review.

So the corporation worked out very well.

Father watched these activities and my swelling bank account admiringly. His only anxiety occurred when I took over the *Courier* newspaper delivery, and had to work for three hours on Sunday morning.

"Do you *have* to do this thing on Sunday?"

"Of course," I said. "Sunday has the biggest paper of all."

"Yes," he responded, "I guess it does," and gave his consent after I promised to return in time for Sunday school and church.

Up to that time John had always answered the telephone at the *Gazette* on Sunday afternoons. We had assumed that father would block any such activity on my part. After a few Sunday mornings of paper delivery I told father that John's family was going into the country for the week end and I was substituting for him at the phone that Sunday afternoon. Father did not like the idea, but he was so proud of the corporation, even carrying in his pocket a sheet of our letterhead stationery, that he could not very well deny me this transient Sunday attention to corporate duties.

After that I was at the *Gazette* almost every Sunday, planning business enterprises. Arrival of the summer would end our reporting of school news and liquidate the Essay Production Company. We needed other ideas.

In those days house-to-house canvassing had not been developed into a nuisance. Housewives were still curious when their doorbells rang. Soliciting subscriptions to magazines had convinced us that there was a lot of money in women's pockets. We reasoned that since we were beating at doorbells anyway, we could as well sell half a dozen articles as one. But what articles?

A round of inquiries on our handsome letterhead brought numerous possibilities, but we settled on two:

[180]

a knife sharpener that solved forever the blunt-utensil problem in the kitchen and retailed at 50 cents with a 30-cent profit to the seller and an aluminum gadget that flicked off milk-bottle tops with a simple twist of the wrist, purchasable at 3 cents, salable at 15 cents or two for a quarter.

To get the best price we must buy in gross lots, and that required capital. I had a $600-savings account, and John had amassed $226.84, but our fathers refused to let us touch these assets. Cautious suggestions at home that the corporation be loaned $800 were not well received.

We went to a bank.

"Come in, boys," President Edwards called from the doorway as we were announced. His wavy white hair and pin-stripe blue suit fitted my idea of a banker, but his purple bow tie and soft broadcloth shirt seemed a little too Y.M.C.A. for a capitalist.

We sat in blue-leather chairs, the cushions of which deflated under us. Mr. Edwards carried his dignity to a swivel chair behind his desk and looked across at us, his hands touching at the finger tips. The nails, I noticed, were professionally manicured, and on his left hand flashed a Knights of Columbus ring adorned with diamonds.

"Well, gentlemen," he asked, "to what do I owe this distinguished visit? You wish to open an account?"

We did not tell him our savings were in another bank. Instead John said, "We want to borrow capital to finance a business."

Mr. Edwards wiped amusement from his eyes with one rub of his eyelids and sat back to listen. Then he studied our correspondence files and checked our books.

"Why don't you get the money from your parents?" he said at last.

We explained why this was impossible. John's father was in the postal service; mine was the Methodist preacher. Where would they get $800?

Mr. Edwards gleamed. Would they put their signatures to a note?

They most emphatically would not.

The banker pondered. The state banking department did not permit loans on the security of two energetic faces, he said. He himself believed that the best investment a man could make was in the younger generation, but he could not evade the law.

We did not argue. The law was something our corporation knew nothing about. Thanking him, we started out.

"However," he went on, "there is another possibility."

He waited for us to return to our seats.

"When a corporation needs additional financing and has reached the limit of its borrowing capacity, it can sell some of its stock. Who owns your stock?"

"We do," we said, "500 shares each."

"Exactly," the banker went on. "Suppose you offer some of it to outside investors. From your books it would appear that you are earning about 45 cents per share annually. If you declared a 5-cent quarterly dividend and put the remainder in surplus, in time you would have enough money to repurchase your securities. Meanwhile anyone who held the stock at $2 per share would have a good investment. I might be interested in—say, four hundred shares myself."

Although I had trouble with mathematics in school, I could add this up to $800.

"It's a deal," I shouted exultantly.

The banker concurred.

"There's another point I'd like to raise," he said delicately, "merely because it's good banking practice. When a banker takes a substantial interest in a new corporation, he likes to be represented on the board of directors."

"You mean we ought to elect you to our board?"

"Something like that might be advisable."

"What does it cost?" John wanted to know.

"Usually directors are reimbursed for their expense of attending meetings," he answered.

"How would 25 cents a meeting be?"

Mr. Edwards nodded.

"Ample under the circumstances," he said.

We called a directors' meeting on the spot. John and I surrendered 200 shares each to the corporation. It then sold the stock to Mr. Edwards. We also elected him vice president of the company, vice chairman of the board, and gave him a typewritten share certificate signed by both of us.

The board then voted to John and me a salary from the corporation out of gross income. We had $800 working capital. Orders were sent for knife sharpeners and bottle openers and, at the suggestion of our new director, we specified in the orders, "two percent, ten days," thus saving considerable money.

The next Saturday a letter arrived from the Handy-Cap Milk Bottle Opener & Cover Co., Newark, N. J., which we did not have time to read. It was necessary that we make collections from house to house on our paper routes in the morning, and there was a track meet in the afternoon.

Sunday afternoon we opened the letter while answering the *Gazette's* telephone. The Handy-Cap Company offered, through no less than a vice president, to make the Donnelly & Spence Co. the sole distributor in Iowa of its milk-bottle openers provided we take four gross per month. A sample lot of two dozen which we had bought earlier and tested had sold rapidly. Housewives bought as many as four at once. That they would continue to purchase at the rate of sixty to eighty a day, we did not doubt. But four gross a month were a lot of bottle caps.

"Look," John said. "Why not line up boys in every big town in Iowa to sell our gadgets house to house? We could ship to the boys, cash in advance, for 5 cents each; they would make a handsome profit, and so would we."

The idea was so staggering that we talked a little too long about it. We were framing a telegram to the Handy-Cap Company, accepting the offer, when mother telephoned.

"It's time for Epworth League," she said.

Glowingly I started to tell her of our great new scheme. Sharply she suggested I go to League meeting, then come straight home.

When I arrived, she was waiting.

"I will not have you transacting business on the Sabbath," she said.

"But gee, we were only sending a telegram."

"It makes no difference. Your father and I allowed

you to carry papers on Sunday because you had contracted to carry out a week-long assignment, and it did not interfere with your home or church activities. Now you are down at that *Gazette* office every Sunday afternoon, and you almost missed League meeting. If father hadn't telephoned from the church asking where you were, you wouldn't have given it a thought. Would you?"

"Well, I did forget, but—"

"Exactly. You would forget your church for a matter of business."

Father added a few phrases to the subject later. Corporation or no corporation, I was not to go near the *Gazette* on Sunday. That was the law.

The telegram was sent the following morning, and the next report to the board of directors carried the following sentence: "Because of increased business the management decided, on May 12, to employ a part time worker on Sunday afternoons from three to six at 25 cents per hour."

Lining up workers in neighboring towns was easy. By mail we asked every Methodist preacher in the state to suggest a wide-awake boy who wanted to earn summer money. When school adjourned, we had sixteen outlets in addition to ourselves. On our paper routes John and I called weekly at nearly 450 houses. There were hundreds of other homes in which I was recognized as the preacher's son. John had lived in Riverton all his life and knew his end of the town thoroughly.

The milk-bottle openers sold so rapidly that we were over our quota the first month. The knife sharpeners did not go so well but were profitable. As long as our stock was outstanding, we worked like demons. But as soon as the surplus more than equaled the redemption value of Mr. Edwards' parcel, we began to feel too executive for manual labor.

Why should we work when those kids out of town were earning us $30 a week? We deserved a little fun. Every corporation executive took time out for recreation; why shouldn't we?

On one pretext or another we found reasons to slight our house-to-house endeavors. First the circus came to town. That took all day. Then John and I were appointed delegates to an older boys' conference by our Sunday school. The substitutes who managed our many activities during the three days of our absence did very well, indeed. Early the following week I had a particularly lucrative morning and checked at noon with John, to discover that he had not been at work.

"It's too hot," he said.

To get even I did not work the next morning. That evening, when over the baseball scores we opened the mail, we discovered that the heat and the lethargy were widespread. Our sixteen salesmen were not functioning well.

The next day we sent them blistering letters. Five of them resigned. The following week two decided to accompany their parents on vacations. All returned their unsold goods, demanding reimbursement.

The corporation faced a crisis. Stock on hand numbered 3,000 Handy-Caps, with four gross arriving immediately as our quota for August. We discussed the situation over ice cream cones. The solution was painfully plain. John and I would have to go back to work.

We drew up a long resolution outlining our obligations to the firm and concluding:

"Be it further resolved: that the disability of one member of the firm shall in no way hinder the other from carrying out his duties to the fullest extent and that on such rare occasions as the above schedule is temporarily abrogated by mutual consent the time must be made up somehow.

"It is further resolved that: having cut our fingers too many times while demonstrating the Non-Slip Safety Knife Sharpener, and the bandages on our hands being detrimental to convincing sales arguments for the above, this item shall be dropped from our line and stock disposed of, at a loss if necessary."

Business picked up for a week. Then two more salesmen resigned.

"I think," John said, "that we'd better call a directors' meeting and pay off Mr. Edwards while we're still solvent."

The banker attended our meeting in style, as he had previously. The directors' room was the circulation manager's desk at the *Gazette*. Promptly at seven-thirty in the evening he drew up in his chauffeur-driven Lincoln, stepped from the car, slapped his cane over his right arm, doffed his black Homburg and gray gloves, adjusted his bow tie, and paraded to our cubbyhole.

"Gentlemen, good evening," he said, waiting for Chairman Donnelly to take a seat behind the telephones before he himself sat down. He leaned forward in his hard chair, resting on his cane.

"I received notice of the meeting. It is not exactly on schedule."

"No, sir, it's an emergency session."

"An extra dividend, I hope," Mr. Edwards said, smiling first at John, then at me.

"We are now able to retire our outstanding stock indebtedness from surplus," John went on, "and honestly, Mr. Edwards, we think you'd better get out before we go broke."

"So," said the vice chairman, "I'm sure the shareholders won't be afraid to ride out a little crisis with you. What's the difficulty?"

We explained. We also pointed out that school would begin soon and that our activity might end then. We thought of liquidating our assets and putting the profits in a savings account.

Mr. Edwards agreed. We repurchased his stock for $2.01 a share, which gave him a $4 profit in addition to the $20 in dividends he had already drawn and the 75 cents for attending three directors' meetings.

The banker was affable.

"I can't give you your stock certificate tonight," he said. "It's hanging on the wall in my office. But I'll see you get it first thing in the morning. This has been a very pleasant business association, and I hope you'll remember me next time you are offering a sound investment. I'm always in the market for a money-maker."

He shook hands all around and departed. Then John had another of his ideas.

"I'll tell you what," he exclaimed. "We don't *need* to bust up when school starts. I'll make a swing around the state and line up new salesmen to work after school and Saturday all winter."

[188]

"On whose money?" I asked.

"Why, company money. We've got $200."

"But it's time for a dividend."

"We can pass it. Every company passes a dividend now and then."

"But I need the dough," I said. "It's twenty bucks and I want it."

Actually, I didn't want John to have fun spending money all over Iowa while I remained at home to carry two paper routes, answer telephones every evening (except Sunday), and resume my house-to-house selling rounds which were getting tedious. We had worked all the good territory in town by now.

The corporation was deadlocked. Since retirement of our partner, each of us owned 500 shares. Neither could outvote the other.

"Okay," I said finally, "let's just quit. I'll take half the dough in the treasury and half of the unsold stock; you do the same. We'll split the September shipment of Handy-Caps when they get here. If we get out and hump, we can wind up the summer with $500 each."

But John's eyes were on July, when our salesmen did all the work and we cleaned up.

He proposed that I take all the cash, the morning paper route, and 1,000 Handy-Caps and leave him with assets that had a retail value of $600.

"I can make a hundred a month out of this all winter," he said.

"Okay," I answered. "I've had enough."

But here father stepped in. If I resigned from the corporation, said father, my name went along with me.

There would be no corporation with Spence in the title without a Spence in the management.

John agreed to operate as the Donnelly Specialty Co., if father would pay for new stationery. We had 500 sheets of the old letterhead on hand. Father concurred.

I hauled my carton of Handy-Caps home in Old Maud and deposited them in the basement. They were worth $250, but I never sold them. I was tired. I had not even had a date since before school ended. The corporation had taken every moment of my time. But I had made $289 in nine weeks and still had the *Courier* route, which yielded about $3.50 a week.

When father was sure I had emerged from the corporation with a profit, he was greatly relieved.

"You know, of course," he said, "that if you had failed, Mr. Donnelly and I would have been responsible. You're both minors, and a man is responsible for his son's debts."

"Gee, father," I said, "why didn't you tell me?"

"Mr. Donnelly and I had a talk about it," he admitted. "We knew you'd come out all right."

"Thanks, sir," I said.

"But I want you to know," he went on, "there will be a little matter of taxes involved in your summer's work. I could have used your losses for a deduction, but I'm hanged if I'm going to be responsible for your profits. They're *your* problem."

CHAPTER SIXTEEN

MEANWHILE Eileen was preparing for college, and father delayed from day to day a decision on her school.

The selection was difficult. In the first place it must be a Methodist institution. As father was a doctor of divinity from and a trustee of Morningside College and an endowment committee member of Iowa Wesleyan College, there were two logical matriculations for his daughter. Not only logical, each was almost mandatory; for if he sent his daughter elsewhere, what was Iowa Methodism maintaining colleges for?

Eileen herself preferred the University of Iowa unless, of course, father would consider Methodism's Northwestern University in exciting Chicago or Methodism's University of Southern California out near the movie stars.

Father really had in mind only one school, Ohio Wesleyan University, from which had sprung more bishops, more missionaries, more preachers than any other in the land. It was 750 miles away from Riverton, but it didn't have the humbug of sorority houses; sorority girls lived in dormitories with nonaffiliated women. For a long time Eileen opposed this choice; she didn't want to be a missionary.

But by midsummer she didn't care where she went, she told me, so long as it was far away. There would still be chapel service every morning no matter where she was sent, but no Sunday school. And if occasionally she opened a sleepy eye on Sunday morning and discovered she couldn't get to church—well, she would charge that off against all the days she had heard father preach both morning and evening. And no more Epworth League! The world was an exciting temptation, and she meant to be tempted a little.

Ohio Wesleyan was chosen eventually, and when Eileen left in August, she was excited over the journey and a trunk and four suitcases full of new clothes. Father was proud and worried, mother prayerful, Fraser in tears as we put her on the train. And I was envious.

Home to a quiet house, to a dining-room table set for four. It wasn't right, somehow; it was as though we were on the move again, to a strange town, in which we would have to learn to live all over again.

Father, who had squinted a little at the station and pretended a gaiety he did not feel, broke down over his blessing of the noonday meal. He had to alter the grace now to include a benediction on one of us who was away. It was almost more than he could do.

"Place, O Lord, Thy blessing upon this house—" He paused. Mother, with only Fraser on her left now, kept her eyes tightly closed. "—and Thy hand upon that one who now—must rely solely on Thy understanding wisdom. Guide her and keep her, O Father, that she may walk humbly in Thy sight. And bless this food to our use and us to Thy service, in Jesus' name, Amen."

Almost before we could open our eyes he rose from the table.

"Excuse me," he said, wiping away tears with his napkin. "I'm not hungry."

Mother's appetite failed too. Fraser and I cleared the table and washed the dishes, and a silence settled over the house. I was no longer envious. I missed Eileen.

When she had graduated from high school, the exercises had been held in the football stadium, graduates and dignitaries occupying a temporary stand erected on the fifty-yard line. Eileen was in a gray cap and gown, and father, mother, Fraser, and I were present not so much to cheer her as to bolster her morale.

After the ceremony father said, "Well, Eilie, I guess you're mighty proud today."

"What for?" she asked. "I should be graduating from East Denver."

In Denver were all her real classmates; in Riverton she had spent only a year. I knew how she felt as the young people filed past Mr. Haskins for their diplomas. They were mere names to me, and they must be to her. They weren't the kids we had grown up with.

We had both missed our Denver friends, and now that she was on her way to Ohio I was more than ever alone. For a while I had forgotten this loneliness in school activities and in the corporation. Now it returned again.

I telephoned Betty. But she was not sympathetic toward men who spent all their time operating corporations. She let me know that she had not enjoyed being dropped precipitantly at the beginning of the summer in favor of a corporation.

"I'm busy," she said pointedly.

I called Valeen. She was going on a picnic.

[193]

I called Mary Edith. She was sorry, but Charlie kept her pretty busy. I didn't even know to which Charlie she referred.

This was serious. Maybe I'd better call Ed Rimer and find out what had been going on. Even he was cool.

"Where you been?" he asked. "I haven't seen you all summer. I can't talk now; I'm getting up a picnic." But in a moment he called back. "You got your car?"

"I can get it."

"Okay. Get yourself a date. We're going out to grandpa's woods."

"Who's we?"

"All of us. We need another car."

So that was it. I hung up thoughtfully.

A book father had been reading lay face down where he had left it. Carefully turning down the page he had reached, I began reading *Pickwick Papers*. Mr. Winkle had shot Mr. Tupman instead of a rook while learning the complicated routine of English gentlemen's hunting before the telephone rang again.

"Come on, we're waiting," Ed Rimer said.

"Waiting? Oh, that. I'm not going."

"But you've got to."

"Why?"

"Because we've bought the ice cream. Pa won't let me take it in our car, and Kay can't in hers. We need your car to haul the freezer."

"But I haven't a date."

"Well, come on anyway."

I went. It was the first of many picnics to which I carried the ice cream. The Rimer car, the Doughty car, the Gurstine car were substantial vehicles. An ice cream freezer is no respecter of property; it leaks over everything, and salt water leaves marks. Old Maud soon became the ice cream truck for the entire juvenile population of North Hill. A few watermarks made no impression on her.

Betty and Valeen welcomed me distantly. But Helen, a fuzzy-haired, plump-legged, witty newcomer to Riverton, was not neglecting any opportunity, even one cast off by her more substantial sisters. She needed a stimulus for her sixteen-year-old ego. So did I. When the girls found that Helen and I were having a very good time of it, they thawed. After all, school would start soon and there would be parties. Boys were scarce on North Hill. Even a preacher's son who had to be home at midnight was an asset. They might not need me themselves, but there always seemed to be an extra girl at the last moment.

After the picnic father complained a little about the car. I had to wash the back seat, where the ice cream had been. But he could tell from the gusto with which I attacked the job that the picnic had been a success. While I scrubbed Maud, he sat on the coping and asked me about the afternoon. At one point he laughed aloud.

"You can't neglect the ladies," he said. "You've got to work on them all the time. You've got to telephone them even when you haven't anything to talk about and compliment them even on an old hat. Bob used to call your sister on the phone so often I couldn't get near it, but you didn't hear her complain."

That evening I telephoned Betty. What was she doing?

"Nothing."

"Swell picnic, wasn't it?"

"Uh huh."

"That was a good cake your mother baked."

"I'll tell her."

"Getting ready for school?"

"Gee, yes. Aren't you?"

"Sort of, I guess. But it's a lot of work—"

And so on, until I was wrung dry.

"Well, I got to be going," I said at last.

"So soon?"

"Got some work to do. 'By." I hung up. Father, reading in his big chair, had not turned a page. There was a watermelon-long grin on his face.

"Now, she'll wonder what I called her for," I complained.

"Exactly, my boy, exactly," he said and began to read again.

School started. Now I was a sophomore, an associate editor of the *Panther,* and, because I was a year older than most sophomores and a preacher's son, I was elected a class officer. I was again in band and orchestra and chorus, and my studies were no more difficult than they had been before. Having decided against another try at extemporaneous speaking, I looked around for something else to do, and found it.

I became cheerleader. There was a thrill in grappling with 800 vigorous throats and merging them in unison, of awakening a lethargic mass into a thunderbolt, of coaxing school spirit from a shivering, sleet-swept school populace whose team was being violently kicked around down on the field. I forgot who I was when I stepped out before the crowd, self-hypnotized into a personification of a mass of waving pennants. Eileen commented by mail on my new activity.

"I'm glad I'm not there to see it," she said. "You were funny enough as the villain in that play last year, when your mustache fell off while you were grappling with our hero. Remember? But if you must be a cheerleader, you should see ours. He shaves his head before every football game and comes out on the field with a big *W* painted all over the top of his head. The team isn't so hot this year, but Eddie, who plays right end, is divine. He serenaded me last night. Imagine! Just when I was taking a bath. Why is it things always happen to us at the wrong time?"

Father fussed. He did not dare to read my correspondence without permission, since our rule always had been that the property of one member of the family, even open letters and boxes of candy, was inviolate; but he was like a hungry child from the time he recognized Eileen's handwriting until I handed over her letter to him.

"Now who do you suppose this Eddie person is? Hope, has Eileen said anything about an Eddie?"

"No, dear."

"Well, he plays football, and he serenaded her. Disgusting exhibition."

"You played football, dear, and you serenaded me. Don't you remember how you and Ted Moore and—"

He retired to his study to write Eileen. We knew it was a lecture by the number of times his rapid typing halted while he changed from black ribbon to red and

[197]

back again. When he really wanted to emphasize something, he put it in red.

I wrote, too, reporting that the position of cheerleader had definite advantages. For one thing, I had made a hit with Betty. I was invited to most of the parties, not to as many as the football captain, but enough. In fact, if I looked sharp and hinted, I could go almost anywhere I liked. And, I wrote, underlining the words, I seemed to be eligible now to the strict society of North Hill. The ice cream truck and the cheerleading had put me over.

When Eileen came home for the Christmas holidays, she didn't look a bit sinful. From her appearance as she stepped from the train, I concluded that she had been to Sunday school regularly all fall.

Father beamed as she brought him messages from half a dozen professors and a bishop, and as she described the campus, her dormitory, and her instructors. She was completely happy for the first time in her life, and father knew it. For an hour he pursued her about the house, asking questions, listening to her conversations with mother, Fraser, and me, afraid lest he'd miss a word, searchingly examining her face to be sure that she was not masking anything.

She was changed. What was not apparent in her eyes —they were still Epworth League, charter member— sneaked out of her hands and feet—they were College. The habit of biting her left thumbnail nervously whenever father spoke was gone. She was sure of herself, quick to express an opinion, and her speech was saturated with colloquialisms that father chuckled over and repeated under his breath until he had them mastered. Then he began firing them back at her with the enthusiasm of a sophomore. This encouraged her to tell more than she intended: of theater parties in towns adjacent to the campus, of fraternity parties and what went on there, of sorority cat fights, and of the pranks played on freshmen.

Father decided that she was still a good girl. He had no doubt of it, actually; but he was uneasy over the abbreviation of her skirt, which had been taken up since she had left home, and her familiarity with a few of the worldly pleasures.

Toward midafternoon three girls called to take Eileen Christmas shopping. Two were home from Stevens College, one from Illinois University. All of them, father observed, were wearing fur coats.

Eileen had scarcely returned when father greeted her.

"Those other girls," he said, "were wearing fur coats. Is that what *all* the girls have?"

"Yes," Eileen answered cautiously.

"Do they wear them at Ohio Wesleyan?"

"Oh, yes. Ohio Wesleyan isn't an *ordinary* school, father."

"Of course not," he replied. "That's why I sent you there."

For Christmas she received a fur coat. Father let her pick it out so that there would be no mistake.

The big social night was shortly before Christmas, with three important parties. Eileen's age group had been invited to Charlotte Forrest's house, which had a ballroom large enough for 100 couples. Hostess to my friends was Anita Dillingham's grandfather, who once a year opened his mansard attic to the younger generation. Fraser's schoolmates were to dance at the Hotel Riverton under the sponsorship of Edward and Charles Pauley.

We had not expected invitations to these affairs. You had to have three generations in Riverton cemetery to consort with the Forrests, Dillinghams, and Pauleys, and although father, in a year, had stowed a few aristocrats away in their family vaults with proper dignity, this was not proximity enough. My cheerleading and Eileen's attendance at an eastern school had put us over. And Fraser was Ed Pauley's best friend.

Seeing his children scurry about the house dressing for these dances, father was a little dismayed, but not displeased.

"Imagine it," he said to mother. "If anyone had told me twenty years ago that on Christmas, 1924, my whole family would be gallivanting off to dancing parties, I'd—" He stopped and smiled. "They're happy, anyway."

At half past seven I drove Fraser downtown and returned home to put adhesive tape carefully over all the holes in Maud's battered isinglass side curtains. Meanwhile Eileen had dressed herself in a burnt-orange taffeta evening dress with a flash of lemon-yellow facing. Her escort that evening was a very handsome junior from Harvard, who was spending the holidays at the Forrests'. Soon she would be swishing her full skirt up the big Forrest stairway, after leaving her new fur coat (given her before Christmas so that she could wear it this night) in the ladies' room.

At the incredible hour of nine o'clock I left in the

Ford to call for Betty, with a dispensation from mother that allowed me to stay out as late as the party lasted. As mother always waited up when we were out at night, this was a great concession.

Betty was dazzling in a new frock and elbow-length white-kid gloves, which complemented my new Oxford-gray suit. We parked Old Maud in front of the house and dashed through snowflakes to the door. Gentlemen to the right, ladies upstairs to the left.

While waiting for Betty, I noticed in a paneled living room off the foyer an old gentleman in a dinner jacket, puffing cigar smoke into a fireplace. The firelight had a monopoly on his face and shirt front and flicked golden pebbles onto the walnut panels above him.

"Good evening, sir," I said, for when the minister's family went to a party, we were careful not to neglect the host.

"Eh?" he said and coughed at his cigar. "Oh. The party's upstairs, young man, on the top floor."

"Yes, sir," I said and introduced myself to Grandpa Dillingham.

He liked to have a cigar, he said, to fortify himself for what went on upstairs. Usually nobody disturbed him.

If this was a hint, I did not take it. I expected Betty to come downstairs to speak to our host, but she did not appear. An orchestra was thumping out a heavy rhythm somewhere. Mr. Dillingham and I talked on and on. Finally he threw his cigar in the fire and arose.

"Don't you dance, young man?"

"Yes, sir."

"Then go upstairs. The ladies will never forgive you."

On the second floor there was no sign of Betty. A black-clad maid stood at the door of one of the rooms. I asked her whether Betty was there.

"All the young ladies went up long ago," she said.

At the head of the stairs I discovered the receiving line: Anita Dillingham, her father, and mother. Behind them, in a vast room the length of the house, tromped the dancers. Stretching away from the orchestra along the right wall was the self-conscious stag line; along the left, primly stiff in their straight-backed chairs, the unescorted little girls.

Betty was dancing. I tried to cut in, but she repulsed me. In her new dress Betty had no trouble getting dances. And the stag line was watching her.

Anybody with any brains, she told me when the music stopped, would have had sense enough to come upstairs. She was never so embarrassed in her life, standing there for a half hour waiting for me. If that's all I thought of her, I could just get my own dances; her program was full, and she flashed it before me.

I could see that she was telling the truth. But the next dance had been bestowed on a boy I knew I could lick. I took the pencil that hung from her program on a gold cord, scratched out his name, wrote mine in. Emboldened by this, I scratched out a few others farther down.

The music began, and her partner slid over from the punch bowl.

"Get away, brother," I said, nudging him aside.

"But this is my dance."

"Not any more," I said and whisked Betty away from trouble. She liked that. I didn't even have to apologize.

But for the next six dances Betty was gone from me. The long interval was unbearable. I danced with Anita, talked to her mother, then fiddled by the punch bowl until my sulking became noticeable. Beside me was Sidney Rapper, who had not brought a date and consequently could not get exchanges with any of the girls he liked.

We watched a fresh supply of punch arrive. Beside us, but not with us, were two twelve-year-old girls. They were giggling a little. After two glasses of punch they were laughing, one a bit hysterically.

Rapper watched them a moment.

"Looks as though they got hold of some firewater," he said.

"They haven't been *drinking?*" I asked, aghast.

"Looks like it," he said.

The hysteria turned to weeping in a moment, and both the girls ran for the stairs. We did not see them again, nor did we return to the punch bowl.

When I reached home, Eileen had not yet come in. Mother, of course, was still up.

"How'd Fraser do?" I asked, after describing my own party.

"Oh, the poor boy," mother exclaimed. "He went to sleep on a davenport in the anteroom and missed half the dance. The Pauleys found him just as they were ready to leave and brought him home."

Eileen, however, had a different story. She had been well received; her man had been attentive and a wonderful dancer. It made a difference, she said, being home from school. Nobody treated her like a minister's daughter.

On Christmas Eve we gathered around our tree as though Eileen had never been away. Electric lights now replaced the old candles, and father no longer needed to bring tubs of water from the basement as a safeguard against fire. Bob dropped in with a present for Eileen. I sneaked out for a half hour with a present for Betty. Neighbors called, but not in as great numbers as in other towns.

In the midst of our Christmas carols the telephone rang. Father listened a long time, then returned gravely to our little group.

"Hope, were you up when Hartzell came home from the Dillinghams?" he asked.

"Yes, indeed."

"Was anything wrong?"

"Why, no. He sat up with me for an hour, waiting to talk to Eileen."

"He was perfectly all right?"

"Yes, why?"

The story had gone around town, father explained, that Hartzell and Sidney Rapper, the grocer's son, had spiked the punch. Two of the poor girls at the party were ill.

Eileen scrutinized me with renewed interest.

"That's utterly ridiculous," mother said. "There was nothing wrong with Hartzell when he kissed me good night. Not a breath of suspicion."

"Well, then, we'll forget it," father replied. "I'm glad you waited up."

But Eileen did not forget. When I turned in early against my five-o'clock rising time, she joined me.

"I think I'll go with you in the morning," she said. "It must be fun to deliver papers on Christmas."

But she found no fun in being wakened next day nor in the icy wind that tugged us off the porch into the snow. She was sleepy, and not until we were a half mile from home did she remember what had really brought her out before dawn.

"Have you started drinking?" she asked.

"No."

"What about that story of father's?"

I told her all I knew. The two girls must have been sick from excitement. "If anybody had a right to get drunk on that punch," I said, "I'm it. I drank more than anybody else. Anyway, even if I wanted to, I wouldn't dare. It would hurt father."

She had no opportunity to ask other questions, for I opened a factory door and stomped inside with a booming "Merry Christmas!"

Jake Hawthorne, the night watchman, poked his head out of a coffin in which he had been resting and returned my greeting.

"Is this a casket factory?" Eileen gasped.

"Sure," I said. "The truck drops my papers off here every morning. If they're late arriving, I have a place to sleep." I pointed to a plush-lined casket.

"In that?"

"What's softer?"

We put the papers in my canvas bag and started out

again through the industrial west side into a dilapidated residential district, I folding papers into compact
squares as we walked and throwing them one after another in a long arc onto a subscriber's porch. In many
homes Christmas-tree lights sparkled from behind curtains.

"Have you had any fun?" I asked.

"I've never had so much fun in my life," Eileen exclaimed. "You can't imagine what it's like to do just as
you please."

"No, I can't," I admitted fervently. "What is it like?"

We were cutting across a city dump, stepping nimbly
over cans and crates half covered by the snow.

"It's just the same," Eileen said reflectively, "and yet
it isn't. I'm just a priss, I guess. The parsonage haunts
me. Every time I want to do something, I feel a hand
on my shoulder."

"That's Divine Guidance," I suggested.

"I thought of that. But why can't it guide me to
Columbus on Saturday night? Other girls go and sneak
up the fire escape when they come back after hours. It
doesn't do them any harm. But I'm held back by that
darned parsonage training."

"Yeah," I said, "I know what you mean."

CHAPTER SEVENTEEN

*T*HE GOSSIP around town about the Dillingham punch bowl inspired Anna Dawson to invite me to a supper party during Christmas week. Evidently she expected me to live up to my reputation.

Her mother, however, had other ideas. I had scarcely stepped inside the door when a sparkling-eyed, gray-haired woman with great diamond rings on her fingers strode to me.

"Young man, don't you try any tricks on me. I'll be watching." Then her face softened, and she beamed a welcome which suggested that, had we been alone, she might have offered me a snort herself.

Anna tried for the next five minutes to swing me into the party, but I was lodged in the corner of a sofa, listening to a life story.

Mrs. Dawson was married at the age of seventeen, in a field car along a railroad right of way, where her bridegroom was a maintenance superintendent. Her man John was ambitious and inventive, and a few gadgets he had created to speed his own work were accepted by railroaders generally. They did not live long in the boxcar. By the time their son was grown, they were able to send him to Harvard and to live themselves at the Algonquin Hotel in New York. But they had wearied of metropolitan life and moved West finally, to an Iowa farm.

"Mummy, let Hartzell go," Anna interrupted. "He's not interested in that stuff."

But I was, and in the story teller too. She was much more fun than the party, not at all what I had expected in a white-pillared mansion with a butler who, town gossips said, made champagne from the Dawson grapes and a cook who could put on the table a turkey so large that John Dawson had to stand up to carve.

By the time Anna began to entertain, the Dawsons had been all over the world. They had seen everything and done everything they wanted to. And now, amid her oriental rugs, surrounded by her Manx cats and Kerry Blue dogs, Mrs. Dawson wanted everyone to know that life had not always been luxurious.

"Yes, it's nice," she said as I admired her furnishings, "but don't forget I set up housekeeping in a freight yard." It was work that had built all this and furnished it, and she wanted me to realize it. She wasn't ashamed of her antecedents; rather she was proud of them. She was a little worried about children who concealed the lowly origins of their fathers and talked of beginning life where their parents had left off.

"Damn snobs," she called them. "This country is done when people get too proud to start at the bottom. John and I couldn't appreciate this without the other."

With some of the town's select Mrs. Dawson was not too popular, and now I knew why. She liked too well to let the wind whistle out of windbags, and that's why Anna went to a public school instead of having a tutor.

"I hope," she whispered, "that when my daughter

marries it will be to somebody without a bean. Yes, without a bean. If she sleeps with a man in a bed that creaks, then she'll get something that wealth can't destroy."

She told me that her husband, although retired, still invented gadgets. For instance, he had rigged a lock through the radio into his liquor storage in the basement. Only when the three radio dials were spun to the proper combination would the door in the basement open. He was not present tonight, or he would show me how it was done. Meanwhile the party guests were trying to find the combination themselves.

Mrs. Dawson kept one eye cocked on the dials, ready to defend her husband's stores if the secret was discovered. It was not.

Charades and other party pastimes were played until a Dresden piece crashed down from the fireplace mantel and broke. Mrs. Dawson merely sighed.

"I was sick of it anyway," she said, patting her suddenly tearful daughter on the shoulder and resuming our conversation. About ten o'clock the icebox was raided of its last strawberry. Mrs. Dawson was not perturbed.

"Anna can make her peace with cook tomorrow," she laughed, "and won't steal the breakfast fruit another time. Cook is not one to be trifled with." Her eyes gleamed, reminiscent of many battles, and I got the idea that the old lady when angry was not one to be trifled with either. I said as much, and she was delighted.

"My temper," she confirmed, rustling her jangling earrings, "is something you have to see to appreciate.

After one of my tantrums the cats don't come home for three days."

About half past ten, when I was thinking I should join the party, a car swung into the drive. The dogs went about their barking business of guarding the estate, the cats scampered to the cellar, and Anna, leaving her guests, screamed through the doorway into the arms of three people outside.

The arrivals were a relative of the family, her daughter, and a friend, all from Beardstown, Ill. They had promised to drive up for New Year's, but had not been expected until the morrow. Standing beside Mrs. Dawson, I was the first of the party guests to be introduced; but I met only one, really: a vixenish, coquettish, immediately flirtatious little blonde with a blue dress and an ermine (no less) coat. Her name was Eleanor.

Such a girl I had never seen. Apparently she had never encountered anything like me either, for I immediately amused her. She was Mrs. Dawson's niece, but that wasn't important. Nothing was important for about ten minutes except her eyelashes and what went on under them. When the party was resumed, I followed Eleanor around like a puppy.

She was fourteen but had lived her years feverishly. Her speech referred to places and things that to me were half imaginary. Eleanor was a personification of them, a child whose conception had been someone's whim and who had lived on whims all her short life. Incredulously, I learned that she was not compelled to go to Sunday school and had not been to church even on Christmas Sunday.

She was sin and I was putty. In fifteen minutes we

were by ourselves in the library, dancing to a phonograph.

"I should have met you a long, long time ago," she
cuddled.

A few things father had said about dancing recurred
to me, but only fleetingly.

"I'll say," I agreed.

"I think it's wonderful you picked out little me right
away. Here we are, best of friends."

"Yeah."

"Kiss me!"

"Uh?"

The music had stopped; the needle was scratching. I
backed off precipitantly.

"I got to—to change the record."

"Ne'mind the record; kiss me!"

The need seemed to be urgent. She clung to me, flut-
tered me with those eyelashes, rubbed her forehead on
my cheek and looked up, her lips slightly parted.

Kissing girls wasn't exactly in my line. That too was
a form of sin. Backing as far away as her tight-clenching
arms allowed, I pecked her on the cheek.

"No," she whispered scornfully, *"kiss* me!"

So I gave her the kind I gave Eileen. The phonograph scratches were getting louder and more imperative.

"You don't call *that* a kiss?"

"What's the matter with it?"

"Matter with—why, don't you know how to kiss anybody?"

"I thought I did all right."

Her arms dropped to her sides. Her eyes came out

from behind the long lashes in disdain and amusement. She giggled, strode to the phonograph, and put on another record.

We danced again.

"You're queer," she said.

"Why?"

"I don't know—you're just queer. You don't even hold a girl right."

"How'm I supposed to hold one?"

That was all she needed. She showed me. We danced more slowly; I was not paying attention to the rhythmic music, not paying much attention to anything. I could see blond curls tightly against my cheek, smell perfume, feel soft arms, but I didn't seem to be hearing much of anything.

"Now kiss me," she said. It was she who kissed me, and it took the wind out of me. We didn't kiss like that around our house. There was something about it I didn't understand. Perhaps another one would make me comprehend.

"Kiss me," I said, and she did. There it was again, a rushing around my head, a lightness of the feet as of being lifted up over great space, an abstractness akin to detachment from the body. And I was scared.

"That," I said, backing away, "is *kissing*."

Great laughter came through the doorway. The other guests had been eavesdropping. Trembling, I took the razzing and sat on a sofa. The party went on. The phonograph played other tunes. Everyone danced except me. Eleanor now coquetted with the other boys, coiled them about her, and I was angry. She had kissed me; yet she was flirting with somebody else. The next mo-

ment she ducked with her partner through a swinging door into the butler's pantry. Miserably I watched the door until she reappeared, her partner blushing and a little out of breath. At this I retired miserably, to join Mrs. Dawson in the library.

"Take off that lipstick," she whispered, her eyes very merry.

Embarrassed, I wiped it away and a few seconds later found an excuse to leave.

At home mother was waiting, wrapped warmly in

her blue-wool dressing gown. To conceal my confusion, I talked excitedly of Mrs. Dawson, her home, and her Manx cats until Eileen came in from her date. Then mother retired. As soon as her door had closed overhead, Eileen leaped to the davenport on which I was sprawled.

Cornelius, the Harvard boy, had asked her for a New Year's Eve date. Of all the girls the Forrest family had introduced him to, Eileen was the only one he had asked out again.

"Where will you go?" I asked. Maybe there was an idea in it for my own celebration. It would have to be good to please Eleanor.

"That's the trouble," Eileen whispered. "He'll probably want to take me to Dreamland. That's where everybody else will be."

"Would you go?"

This was like asking her whether she would sell beer at a church social. Of all the places of public entertainment in town, father railed most often against Dreamland, the American Legion's dance pavilion.

"I don't know," she answered, looking at me thoughtfully. "There'll be such a mob nobody would notice me. If you'll go, too, father can't object very much."

"All right," I said. "I will."

"Good," she approved, suddenly kissing me and jumping up.

"Say, Sis," I called after her, "what do you do when a boy kisses you?"

She swung about. "For Heaven's sake, why?"

"How can you kiss somebody without feeling silly?"

She returned slowly and sat down beside me.

"What happened?" We had been in league against restrictions for so long that we had no secrets from each other.

I told her about Eleanor and asked, "How does Bob kiss you?"

"What makes you think he does?"

"I've got eyes. You and Bob get along all right."

"You've been peeking," she flared, blushing.

"No, this is serious."

She pondered, as though wondering just how Bob *did* kiss her. Apparently not very effectively. "He just kisses me, that's all."

"How about that Harvard guy?"

"Oh!" Her eyes illuminated suddenly. "He just acts like he's got a right to it. Like this." She gathered me up off the davenport and kissed me hard.

"Yeah," I replied, when I could get my breath. "That's it. I see, now. You've got to get the upper hand."

Blushing furiously, Eileen was definitely going upstairs now.

"You be careful of that stuff," she warned. "It's dynamite."

In the morning, Eleanor telephoned to ask me to a New Year's Eve party. The festivities would start at the Dawson house and end at Dreamland.

"Swell," I consented jubilantly, "that is, if I can get the car. I'll call you back."

"Drive out here and tell me. Everybody's gone away and left poor little me all alone in this great big house."

"No, I can't right now. Later," I said. Father had already made known his need of the car.

"Not even for little tiny me?"

"I can't, honest. Not now. I would if I could."

"You don't love me," she pouted.

"What?" Nobody had ever been concerned about my love before. Father was sitting just six feet away in his leather chair.

"I said you don't love me."

"Yes, I do."

"Say it, then."

"Say what?"

"Say 'I love you,' like that."

"Oh, gee, Eleanor, I—"

"Tell me!"

"I can't now. Later. Look, I—"

"You tell me now, or you don't need to come out and see me again ever."

Interposing my shoulder between father and the telephone, cupping the mouthpiece in my hand, I mumbled the words she wanted and hung up quickly.

"Who was that?" asked father.

"Just a girl, father."

"Which one?"

"One named Eleanor. You don't know her."

"Is she in Sunday school?"

"No, sir. She's visiting the Dawsons, and she called to invite me to a New Year's Eve party."

Then the question of the car came up.

"You are taking this—this girl Eleanor, your love for whom you are communicating to the telephone operator?"

There are times when it is best not to reply, and this was one of them.

"I think," he went on, "you'd better not go. That's not the kind of crowd for you to be in."

"But, fa—"

"We won't discuss it."

"But please, father," and the argument began.

These arguments always had been serious, but friendly. He did not tolerate heat or anger in them. Sometimes my sister or I won them, in which case his punch was a moral lecture on the perils involved in our action, his prayer that we would conduct ourselves as Christians.

But this day I was desperate. I *had* to go to that party. The vision of Eleanor at the dance with somebody else, coaxing smiles and maybe even kisses from him, goaded me. My voice rose.

"You just do everything you can to spoil my fun."

That ended the argument.

"You are not to go," he said with cold finality. "You may have the car New Year's Eve to take Betty or any other wholesome girl I know, but you're not going out with—with some little chit of a fool who has you talking on the phone like a puppy."

"That's not fair!" I shouted.

Father rose to his pulpit dignity.

"Don't ever shout at me again," he said.

It was four in the afternoon before I had the courage to telephone the Dawson house, and I did not talk to Eleanor. I made my excuses to Anna, saying I could not go to Dreamland. That seemed the best alibi.

Then I called Betty. It was imperative that I get a

date. She had already accepted an invitation to the Dawson party.

The next noon I was still considering my predicament when father entered the house, his eyebrows heaving.

"Son!" he roared. Such a call could be only for me. Fraser never got into trouble. "Did you have the car this morning?"

"Yes, father, I went to Dawsons' for a few minutes to make my excuses to Eleanor, since I can't go out tonight."

"It's true, then," he said miserably.

"What, father?"

"The story I heard downtown. That the parsonage car was parked on a road west of town and you were pawing some girl."

"We parked for a minute, but it was on the main highway."

"I thought I told you to stay away from that girl."

"No, sir. You said I couldn't take her out tonight."

"You know very well what I meant. You were out there this morning."

"I kissed her, that's all."

At another time this admission would have knocked words back down his throat, but not now.

"Why do you suppose I denied you permission to go with her tonight? And what kind of way is that to treat a girl anyway? If you want to act like a lovesick calf, that's your privilege, but what are people going to say about the girl? Did you consider that?"

Gossip concerning Eleanor had not occurred to me.

"You are forbidden to drive the car for one month," he announced pontifically.

That night Eileen, excited over the prospect of defying the household even if I could not, left with Cornelius, and Fraser went to a house on the next street to a taffy pull. I went nowhere.

In the living room there was not even a radio to be turned on. We could not afford one. When father retired, I was staring out the window. On the pane was a vision of Eleanor dancing with someone else. And Betty dancing with someone else. At ten o'clock I went to bed.

In the morning the town shuddered with scandal. Somebody had taken liquor to Dreamland. One of the town's "best" boys had fallen on the dance floor. There had been other scenes. Riverton, upon discovering that its younger generation had let prohibition liquor get out of bounds, frantically phoned the parsonage for advice and to ascertain whether the preacher's family had been in on the disgrace.

Quickly I hurried to Eileen's room. She was asleep, a yellow down quilt pulled over her head.

"Psst," I whispered, "wake up. Were you at Dreamland?"

"Why?"

"There's hell to pay if you were. Listen!" The phone was ringing again.

"No, Mrs. Jordan," father said. "Yes, Mrs. Jordan. Well, I— If you— That's exactly what I—" He didn't seem to be getting far with his caller, and Eileen was irritated. Then father got his words in, and Eileen heard them.

[219]

"I can tell you this much," he was saying emphatically. "Whatever happened, no child of mine was there."

"Was where?" Eileen asked quickly.

"Dreamland last night."

"Oh," she scoffed, "we didn't go. His idea of New Year's Eve fun was scattering confetti from the balcony of the Palace Theater." Disgustedly she rolled over and resumed her sleep.

Father was gay all morning. He sat by the telephone with his book, annoyed when the summons was for another member of the family. He said nothing to us, but we knew that this act, this thunderous repetition of our innocence, was for our benefit. It was exactly as though he was saying, "You see, sometimes your dad is right. Sometimes he knows what he's talking about. Not often, but sometimes. Aren't you glad you weren't there?"

Then I heard something else.

"Who?" he was inquiring. "Mrs. Dawson?"

I sped up the back stairs so that father would not see me, ran to the study, and softly lifted the receiver from the extension phone.

"So *you* are Doctor Spence, the man who won't let his son attend my parties."

"Well, now, that's hardly—"

"Nonsense, Doctor. You can't fool an old lady like me. To be quite truthful, I didn't like their going to Dreamland myself and at the last moment kept them home. We had a nice party."

"Well, that *is* fine," father responded. "I'm glad someone in this town has some sense—"

"But I missed Hartzell."

"Missed him?"

"Yes. Of all the guests my daughter has here, he's the only one who has courtesy enough to sit with me for a few minutes."

"Is that so? I'm glad to know. He *is* a fine boy."

"How about letting me have him for dinner tonight? It's a farewell to my niece, and she asked for him."

"Oh, yes, I heard about her. She's *leaving*, you say? Why, I'm sure he'd be delighted."

Cautiously I replaced the receiver, tiptoed down the back stairs, and strolled into the living room. Father had just hung up the receiver.

"What do you think, Hope?" he called in the direction of the kitchen. "Mrs. Dawson says Hartzell is the only polite boy in town."

"Yes, dear," mother replied. She was basting the turkey and hadn't heard a word.

Jovially father tossed me the extra set of automobile keys that I had relinquished the day before.

"Who is this Mrs. Dawson?" he asked. "She sounds like a very understanding woman."

"She is, father," I said. "You ought to meet her. What did she want?"

Father grinned, for this had been a wonderful morning all around.

"You know as well as I do," he said. "You were listening the whole time on the upstairs phone."

CHAPTER EIGHTEEN

*E*ILEEN returned to school, but I scarcely saw her go; I was in such a fog over Eleanor.

For two successive week ends I returned directly home from basketball games instead of gathering with the "gang" in the basement playroom at Mary Edith's. Over my Latin lesson I dreamed of Eleanor; my English themes were character sketches of her. Then circumstances caused me to be put in detention. Any teacher could assign a pupil to one hour's afterschool incarceration in a special study hall for failure to recite or for infractions of rules. It was not the sort of place a minister's son was likely to frequent, but I was in for two weeks—the stiffest kind of sentence.

The disciplinarian was my geometry teacher. Stiff-backed, white-haired, and decorous, Miss Migram was a genuine old maid. No joke ever rocked her classes; no smile ever softened her face. Primness had built a high hedge around her personality, so that no one might see inside. She taught uninspiringly but thoroughly and was both dreaded and respected throughout the school.

During the noon hour she policed the halls for forty minutes, walking sedately up and down from the administration office past the front stairway to the Latin recitation room. She had only to appear, with arms folded, body rigid, eyes repelling flirtations, to command a mortuary silence.

The second noon after Christmas holidays I idled in the hall at the top of the main stairway with Sidney Rapper. Someone tossed him a glass Christmas-tree ornament filled with water. With a flip of the wrist he passed it on to me. I returned it, and again he juggled it back, this time so hard that it nearly broke in my hands. Impulsively I wound up, threw with all my might. Rapper laughed and jumped. The missile sailed over his shoulder directly at Miss Migram, who was bearing down on us. With an explosive pop the Christmas ball crashed at her feet, water splashing up from it. She yelped in dismay and lifted her black-silk skirt and purple petticoat in a most undignified leap.

Everyone in the hallway smothered laughter as Miss Migram surveyed the wreckage of her dress and the glass and water on the floor. I took the front steps four at a time and scampered into the snow.

But running away did not save me, for my geometry lesson immediately followed the lunch hour. Twenty minutes in the cold chilled me into a desire to make peace with her at once, but I could not face her accusing eyes. The bell called. Still I dallied. Finally, fully five minutes late, I slunk to my seat in her class.

Miss Migram was waiting.

"You will go to the principal's office," she ordered and resumed her discussion of a theorem.

Mr. Haskins was in a peculiar mood. He seemed to have been laughing violently. But he wiped his countenance clean as I entered and pondered for some moments. Twice laughter almost broke through again, but he controlled it and spoke,

"Miss Migram reported you."

"Yes, sir."

"She says you threw that thing deliberately. Did you?"

"Deliberately at Sidney Rapper, yes. Nobody would ever throw anything at Miss Migram."

"You will apologize to Miss Migram after class and explain that you were throwing at Sidney. She will give you what punishment you deserve for violating the rules of the hall." Miss Migram sentenced me to a fortnight of detention hall, assigning a great number of complicated geometry problems to keep me busy. But all I could think of, sitting in the deathlike quiet of a large room waiting for 4:20 p.m., was Eleanor, and the only work I accomplished was a daily letter to her.

My punishment had not quite ended when Eleanor wrote a rapturous letter. She was going to give a house party the following week, and I *must* come down. Enthusiastically I replied, special delivery, that no demon could keep me away, that I'd be there if I had to hitchhike.

But mother refused me permission to go. Usually I gained mother's benediction, then faced father with the statement that "Mother says it's all right." But persuasion and cajolery had no effect on her. As often as I broached the subject, she replied gently and economically with one word, "No." Finally she had had enough.

"Now, son," she said, "we aren't going to talk about this any more. I have said what I mean. Your father and I don't like this girl, and we definitely do not approve of house parties."

"But if father says I can go, can I?"

"No matter what your father says, my answer will be the same. If you go, it will be without my permission."

That made the venture impossible. The consequences of defiance in the face of such an edict were too legion for speculation. We children never knew what might have happened had we disobeyed our parents to such an extent, and they never had to reveal their ace in the hole. The manner in which they spoke was very much the way father, in his young days in the pulpit, had referred to the fire of hell. It was not something to walk into.

Gloomily I wrote Eleanor that I could not come. She did not answer. (Four years later I bumped into her in Estes Park, Colo. She gave me a quick but complete once-over and said before I had opportunity to greet her, "Let's not borrow on an old friendship," and hurried off.)

Little by little the flame for Eleanor died, but the anguish was a long time healing. Each day I looked on the telephone table for the letter that never arrived. At school, however, I still saw Betty. Passing me in the hall, she would smile as though she understood all my miseries, but she did not speak. I began to recover by admiring Betty's loyalty, her unspoken intimation that she was still around. Soon I was comparing her, and her friendly though unvoiced sympathy to the girls who taunted me about Eleanor, and the comparison set up Betty as a very special woman.

In the office of the *Panther* we worked side by side

at adjacent typewriters, I plugging out purportedly humorous feature stories, she rounding up news of girls' activities and bits of corridor gossip. We would lock eyes over our typewriters or catch the other's eyes through a mirror, she to smile shyly, I sheepishly. But no words. She was waiting, like a lady. If she had spoken my name just once, I would have come tumbling to her. But she didn't, not Betty. It was plain I would be received, but I had to go all the way alone.

The Clisthonian annual party was approaching, and I was determined to escort Betty. No one else would do now; Betty had become the symbol of all that is noble in woman. I was miserable for the way I had made a fool of myself with an out-of-town blonde. Perhaps I would have been more miserable had I known Betty had bet Marjorie Holcomb a new compact that she'd attend the Clisthonian party with me; but that was something I was not to hear about until later, from Marjorie.

Somehow I had to get Betty to speak to me. I remembered that the previous year Eileen and her Bob had had a furious quarrel. Eileen let him know that the parsonage porch was not large enough for the two of them. His fatal error had been to object because Eileen wanted to take Fraser along one Saturday when Bob invited her for a ride in a new car.

Angry words had passed between them, until finally he had returned to his new car alone and departed. A half hour later he passed the house slowly, with another girl. That had fixed him.

To make amends he sent a large and very showy bouquet of flowers, with a note which Eileen did not disclose to the rest of the family. The delight at receiving her *very first* flowers was unmistakable: spending money on flowers, which soon wilted, was the supreme gesture. Gifts were supposed to be practical things that could be worn or eaten. Eileen telephoned Bob immediately to thank him, and the rupture was mended.

I went downtown and spread the entire week's profit from my paper route on a bouquet of spring flowers shipped in from Chicago. The florist spent nearly a half hour arranging it and insisted on delivering it. I wanted to take it to Betty, but he said that wouldn't do. It was too obvious. I should send it nonchalantly with a card. Together we tore up half a dozen tender sentiments, then hit on what appeared to be just right:

"This beautiful spring day reminds me of you."

I hurried home, ready to rush to Betty's as soon as the phone rang. All afternoon I waited. Not a tinkle. The house was silent. Perhaps Betty was out playing golf. I telephoned the florist, who assured me that he had delivered the bouquet. Betty's mother had taken it at the door. During dinner the telephone rang, and I jumped at it; but it was Edward Pauley asking Fraser about an arithmetic problem. Shortly after dinner it rang again; Fraser was invited to George Carroll's for parchesi.

About nine o'clock father put aside Robert Frost's poems and began the ritual of retiring. He took off his glasses and wiped them clean, planted his feet firmly on the floor.

"You're not going out?"

"No, father."

"Wasn't there a basketball game tonight?"

"Yes, father."

"Are you ill?"

"No, sir. I'm just—not going out tonight."

He approached the davenport on which I was sprawled and looked down at me.

"What's the trouble?"

"Nothing, father. I'm just tired."

He squinted sharply at me. Having trained for medicine, he loved an excuse for diagnosis.

"Your eyes are yellow. Let me see your tongue— Hm-m. Well, get some sleep and lock the garage before you turn in."

"Yes, father."

I remained a long time in the living room. Fraser came in and went to bed. The telephone had not rung for hours. I gave up and followed Fraser upstairs.

Betty did not telephone on Sunday either. I spent the afternoon making posters for one of mother's church activities, my disappointment over spending so much money vainly on flowers compounded by resentment over Sunday school.

Not once during the year, I reflected while busy with freehand lettering, had my class been anything but a gossip pot. Instead of teaching, the instructor pried into the private lives of the twenty boys who sat under him.

I pondered for a while a scheme to release me from the indignity of that Sunday inquisition. The *Des Moines Register* was canvassing Riverton for a new distributor. The town consumed about 500 copies of the Des Moines Sunday edition, but the circulation department did not think this sufficient for a town of 26,000. I could earn about $15 a week, with an opportunity to collect bonuses for new subscriptions, if I became the *Register's* representative.

The only difficulty was that the papers arrived in great bundles at the railroad station about four o'clock on Sunday morning. I would be required to load them into a car, drop off quantities at every cigar store and drugstore in town, and build a carrier-boy service for home deliveries in Riverton and its suburbs. The work would consume the Sunday school hour but would not interfere with church attendance.

Getting up every morning at five o'clock to deliver the local paper had been hurting my school work. Father knew this, but $3.50 a week was important money in the ministerial household. By transferring my activities to Sunday only, I could earn at least five times as much money. But how to persuade father? That was the problem, and there seemed no solution.

Meanwhile Betty did not phone.

It was noon on Monday before I saw her. I went into the *Panther* room to study Latin, and she came in after her lunch.

"The flowers were wonderful," she said. Her eyes were soft and large and enchanting.

"Glad you liked them."

"I—I hoped to see you after the basketball game."

"I was busy. I didn't get there."

"I know. I saw you through the window."

"You mean you came past our *house?*"

She nodded.

"Didn't you go to Mary Edith's?"

"I didn't want to."

After that everything was all right. We were together again.

Now I made amends for neglect by being with her constantly. When I was not in school or at the *Panther* or working my paper route, I was at Betty's. The parsonage car was oftener parked before her door (she was an Episcopalian) than before that of any Methodist parishioner.

The first time father urgently needed Old Maud and it was at Betty's, he observed that I was rarely home any more except for meals. The second time he said if I had to moon around Betty all the time, I'd better leave the car at home. Then one afternoon a rural parishioner was reported dying, and father, in a desperate hurry, telephoned Betty's mother, who sent me racing home with such speed that father, already in a dudgeon, had to listen while a woman complained by telephone that I had almost run down her child while roaring past her door and that I was in the habit of driving that way, to the peril of all the children on Fifth Street. The next evening he made an announcement.

His son, he said, seemed to have an uncanny adaptability for asininity. He had thought that a lesson had been learned over the holidays, but it hadn't. He did not particularly mind if his son made a fool of himself. That was the son's privilege and, apparently, his natural inclination. But it was common talk that the pastor's boy was camping on a certain doorstep with a mooncalf expression on his face that nobody could interpret as other than idiocy. Betty was a fine girl, a lovely girl, of a splendid household, and perhaps there was some excuse for a man's making a sublime ass of himself over her. But I was too young to appreciate all the perquisites of making a fool of myself over a woman. When it came time for a man to be a fool, he should be old enough to get the full benefit.

Therefore it was now the rule in this house that no son of his younger than seventeen (I was sixteen) was to have more than one date in the same calendar month with the same girl, except to repay obligations or to carry out a social duty imposed by the hostess of a *bona fide* party. Was that clear?

It was.

There was only one thing to tell Betty, the truth, which I did. She was all understanding and sympathy. She returned my Clisthonian pin, which she had been wearing at school but not at home and promised me a date whenever we could arrange it.

I was both surprised and disappointed by her calm attitude. I had imagined our parting as a tender and sacred scene in which, after felicitations of devotion, we would allow ourselves to be torn apart by cruel fate. Somehow I had muffed my part.

For a half hour I drove around town. Father knew I was breaking off the romance and would not expect me home for a while. The more I reviewed the miserable scene just enacted, the more dissatisfied I became. I determined to go back and do it again, this time with the proper romantic filigree.

But I didn't. Ray Somerville, the best looking fellow in school, was parked in front of Betty's, and she was in the car with him.

I did not even honk as I drove by.

Betty was not so hard to get over as Eleanor had been, for the very day after we stopped going steady Miss McGregor, the public schools' music supervisor, announced tryouts for the operetta.

This was the big stage event of the year, involving more students than any other enterprise, and it was best patronized by the townsfolk. Any student who sold five tickets to outsiders was admitted free.

In chorus classes we had been rehearsing the group music to a musical for several months, and we suspected it would be the year's operetta. There were two good male roles and one flashy soprano score. Of the feminine lead there was no doubt. Any girl who even tried out for the big part would know that the best she would get was a secondary character, for Phyllis Danielson really had a voice.

Among the boys there was one very good tenor, Elmer Rolls, a popular football player, and we all assumed that he would get the complicated part of a set of twins, around whom the plot swung. But the comic part of Jason, the thwarted suitor, was also a beauty, and I coveted it as soon as I heard that it would probably go to Ray Somerville. In fact, he told Betty he had it in the bag.

So I tried out. There was no use singing one of Elmer's songs; I'd shoot for Jason. I memorized a sad, rollicking lyric about a fellow who always was left swinging on the gate while the beautiful girl passed by on another man's arm.

After school the hopefuls assembled in the high school auditorium to display their vocal wares. Miss McGregor sat critically in the middle of the house. In a corner, obscure and alone, sat Mr. Martin, the dramatics coach, who would be responsible for acting, scenery, and make-up. In the balcony fidgeted those hopefuls who, having already tried out their favorite songs, now bit their fingernails and prayed no one would outshine them.

For a long time I waited in the wings. It seemed that everybody in the boys' chorus had chosen the song I was to sing. Even Elmer, who everyone thought would shine out with *In My Garden There Are Roses,* the lead's best number, sang the plaint of unrequited love. Ray Somerville was the only one who attempted *In My Garden,* and he made it ring.

By the time I was called, I had lost confidence. I walked onto the stage trembling, and as I sang my right ankle got away from me and shivered up and down, angling off by itself as though urgently seeking the sanctuary of the curtain. My voice tightened and grew husky. Somerville, secure now in the balcony, laughed happily to his companions. When the song ended, I withdrew miserably with visions of lining up with the boys in white pants and a sailor straw hat for the choral numbers.

Only one thing was in my favor. Both Elmer Rolls and Ray Somerville took private vocal lessons from Miss McGregor, and if she gave them too prominent positions she might be criticized. One of them might get a starring part, but not both.

Next day I discovered that Miss McGregor had not overlooked this hazard, for the operetta's leading part was withheld from both her pupils and was given to me.

I was terrified at the announcement. I did not want to be the hero. I knew I couldn't sing well enough. I knew that whoever played the unrequited lover would steal the show out from under me if he had any voice at all. Who was singing Jason? Elmer Rolls! The only consolation was that Ray Somerville, in sailor straw and white trousers, would be submerged in the chorus.

The rehearsals were a battle against terror and inferiority, a clash with Phyllis every time we were together (we had never gotten on very well), self-consciousness when I looked at Elmer, who could have handled my role so much better. I did not even object when half a dozen boys showed me they could reach a high B-flat I couldn't touch, nor when Miss McGregor took one verse of the garden song from me and gave it to Phyllis.

Father suffered with me throughout the chore of learning my songs and my lines. He pounded out the arias on the piano with forthright, hymn-song cadence, which Miss McGregor converted into syncopations at the next rehearsal. He labored over my lines also to get the emphasis just right and was disgusted when he learned that Mr. Martin had drilled me differently.

By the time the operetta went before footlights, I didn't know how to sing a note or read a speech, and as a result Phyllis was entrenched in dislike for me.

Particularly she showed animosity during our tender moment in the second act. We had rehearsed the scene oftener than any other. The hero sings his best number, then proposes to the heroine. She says "Yes," and he is about to fold her in his arms when the Chinese houseboy, goaded by the forlorn, unrequited suitor, breaks up the clinch with a crash of breaking dishes. It was a good thing the script didn't call for a kiss at that point, as Phyllis was taking no mushy stuff from me.

The night of the performance I sang my melodic aria (cracking badly on the high B-flat) and bumbled over to my heroine with arms outstretched. My embrace began to enfold her. The houseboy did not appear. He had deliberately missed his cue. Ray Somerville had taken care of that.

I didn't know what to do, but it seemed logical that, having made a gesture to envelop the heroine in my arms, I'd better go ahead with it, so I kissed her. But the houseboy did not come in. We clinched again. Still no houseboy. Thoroughly stage-frightened now, I moved in for another embrace. But Phyllis was having no more.

"Hartzell Spence," she trilled, "don't you *dare* kiss me again!"

The audience cheered, and in came the grinning Chinese houseboy, who dutifully smashed his crockery to a great burst of applause.

The operetta was a great success, but not for me. After it was over, father and mother met me in the hall.

"What in the mischief happened in the second act?" father asked, and I explained that Howard Forrest, the houseboy, had been in league with Ray Somerville in a practical joke.

Father was amused. "It's not a good idea," he said, "to get in over your depth. You're a choir singer, son, not a chorus boy."

He was immensely pleased. Here, completely outside

the parsonage, I had learned a lesson he knew would have a lasting effect.

The following Sunday my Sunday school classmates razzed me about the operetta. Even my Sunday school teacher joined the sport, and that made me angry. When the class did not settle down and when the teacher appeared again to have prepared no lesson, I walked out with appropriate words.

"I thought," I said, "that we came here to study the Bible. I don't mind getting the bird, I earned it. But Sunday school isn't the place for it."

At noon father inquired. He had been told that I'd left Sunday school before it ended.

"I did," I said, "and I'm not going back."

"Why?"

"I haven't heard one thing in that class since September except small talk. Not one Bible lesson, not one good discussion. Instead I've heard a dozen dirty jokes and a lot of gossip. I've had enough."

Father investigated among other boys of the class, confirmed that we had been taught nothing. Coupled with his anger over this state of affairs was a crushing disappointment that, when the heat was on me, I had not stood up to it. He could not realize that my indignation had welled up as a product of my home training. The injustice was not that the boys had jumped on me, but that Sunday school time had been utilized for it.

Under the impetus of this Sunday school experience I accepted the *Register* job and then told father about it.

He was very angry. This was merely a dodge to avoid Sunday school, he said. I didn't have guts enough to go back and face the class after a fit of temper. I was concealing my real motive in the lure of a substantial income.

"But," I said, "the *Register* has canceled its contract with the old distributor and signed with me."

"Makes no difference," father said sternly. "You can't execute any contract without my approval, and I won't approve anything that takes you out of Sunday school. You're going back to that class and learn to take your medicine like a man."

He had so missed the whole point that tears came to my eyes.

"If I can't take it," I mumbled, "it's you who taught me."

He was hard hit. His hands trembled across his desk, looking for flecks of erasure rubber.

"I don't see that," he said.

So I explained again, clearly and gravely, concluding, "You taught me to be a sissy. Have you any idea what they call me around town? A 'Christer,' father. Do you know what that means?"

"I won't tolerate blasphemy in this house!"

He roared, but he understood me. He walked to the window, his refuge against temper. Perspiration stood out on his broad nose and on the hairy backs of his hands. He breathed in gusts, like sobs. Then heavily he resumed his chair and spoke, without looking at me:

"All right," he said, "do anything you like."

CHAPTER NINETEEN

$\mathcal{T}$HAT spring Fraser and I did as we pleased. Father paid little attention to us, for he was up to his bushy eyebrows in work.

We had been through similar experiences. In Fort Dodge during a church-building program even mother had to make an appointment to see father. In Sioux City during the 1918 influenza epidemic father was scarcely home for several months. In Denver when he was interested in the election of a bishop, father was out of town for six weeks prior to the General Conference.

This time father was in a jam that required every waking moment. He had done a job he called "boss busting," in order to break a one-layman domination of church activity. He had been forced to clean out the choir loft and had antagonized many persons. The job took three years, but he did it.

His enemies, however, would not stay beaten. Every day there was some new harassment. He could not relax for a moment or take a vacation lest the old crowd jump back into its former domination.

As soon as I started the *Des Moines Register* job, my absence from Sunday school was noticed and an issue made of it. Father scotched it, though, by asking the official board at a meeting how many members subscribed to or regularly purchased the *Register*. More than a majority did so.

"All right," father said. "And my son delivers the papers. If anyone is going to be taken out of Sunday school to do a necessary job, my son perhaps can be best spared for it. He is in church, goes to Epworth League, and has regular devotions with the family at home."

Then a letter from Eileen arrived that enraged him.

"What do you think?" she wrote. "I'm being shadowed. I haven't the faintest idea what for. Several times lately I've seen this man hanging around the soda fountain where we have cokes after class, but I didn't connect him with me until last Friday, when Eddie spotted him looking through a window at a Phi Gam dance and later saw him again outside Monett Hall when Eddie was saying good night. Eddie recognized him as a flatfoot they used to hire at the rubber plant where Eddie works summers. He doubled back on the man and discovered that he's watching me!"

Father had not been paying much attention to Eileen's letters lately, except when they asked for money. But he stormed over this one. He knew no detective would uncover any scandal in the life of his daughter. Eileen was above reproach.

"Attacking me through my daughter is cruel," he said, "but it won't work."

Several times Fraser and I took problems to father that he settled on snap judgment or parried with the comment, "Don't bother me now, please." But we were at an age that needed guidance. Fraser was the first to find it.

We were throwing baseballs around a vacant lot with

the neighborhood gang late one afternoon when Fraser, who had no fielder's glove, let a hot one roll through his fingers. The ball jumped across the street and rolled up Mr. Tracy's drive into his garden.

Fraser went after it cautiously, sharp-eyed for the gardener or the dog. Neither appeared. Instead Mr. Tracy ran out of his solarium and retrieved the ball. He had been watching the game. Fraser was about to run. None of us knew what Mr. Tracy might do. A man with a mean dog was likely to have trained the animal after his own disposition.

"Catch!" Mr. Tracy called and threw a fast one. Fraser stopped the ball, but he could not hang on.

"Haven't you a mitt?" Mr. Tracy asked, walking back across the street with Fraser.

"No, sir."

"Who are you?"

"The preacher's son."

"Well, you ought to have a mitt."

He took Fraser downtown and bought him a first-baseman's glove, which was what Fraser wanted. Before long Fraser was spending most of his time at the Tracys'. George Tracy was past sixty, fat paunched and merry eyed. His own children long ago had left his twenty-six-room house. He liked Fraser, and Fraser liked him. The friendship was instantaneous and enduring.

Fraser's manner began to change. He developed confidence, acquired additional vocabulary, became more articulate. And he stopped asking me questions. Evidently he was asking them and getting the right answers from Mr. Tracy, who even began coming home from his lumber mill about four o'clock in the afternoon to spend an hour with Fraser before dinner. From our house we could see the two of them in the solarium huddled over a plant, spraying roses, or tying up vines, laughing and talking and having a great time. And on Saturday mornings they were throwing balls over the garage or kicking a football. Mother welcomed the companionship, imposing only two rules: Fraser must not take money, and he must come home at six o'clock sharp.

But one day a jibe was shot at father in the barber shop, and he hurried home.

"Son!"

"Yes, sir," I responded quickly. But for once I was not the son he meant.

"Where's Fraser?"

"Across the street at Mr. Tracy's."

"Please get him. I want to talk to him."

When Fraser arrived, father was on the porch.

"Do you spend all your time at Mr. Tracy's?"

"Gee, he's swell," Fraser responded. "He just gave me a pair of spiked track shoes. Want to see 'em?"

"Not now. Don't you think you ought to ask your father when you need athletic equipment?"

Fraser hesitated. Apparently something was up that required caution. Even I couldn't figure this one out.

"I did ask twice, father," Fraser replied, "but you asked me not to bother you."

"Oh."

"I didn't exactly ask Mr. Tracy for the shoes. I was running up at school one afternoon and he saw me. He comes by once in a while and lets me drive him home. In the Dodge, though, not the Lincoln."

Father nodded.

"Did you know Mr. Tracy has a cabin cruiser, father? We're going fishing Saturday. It's all right, isn't it?"

"Of course, of course. I just heard somebody downtown say that the neighborhood had had to take on the obligations of a father for the preacher's son."

I trembled. In that case, he had questions to ask me. But evidently he hadn't heard about Mr. Hedge.

"Just a lot of nonsense, I guess," he concluded.

I was relieved, for I too had a friend. Our house was on a corner, with Mr. Tracy across the street on the northeast and Mr. Hedge on the southeast. Mr. Hedge was a bachelor.

One evening about eleven o'clock I was passing his house enroute from a late orchestra rehearsal just before our spring concert, when Mr. Hedge called a greeting from his porch. I stopped, and we had a chat. Bud, as everybody called him, was an aristocrat and very much in demand for bridge parties. He had been in the war, had worked for a newspaper, and had a sister in Paris of whom he spoke with respect akin to terror.

He was exactly my height, and his manner was free and boisterous, an excitement after the parsonage. My training of respect for my elders amused him. Before we had been talking five minutes he exclaimed, "For Heaven's sake, stop calling me 'sir.' Who do you think I am, God?"

We got along fine then. I was curious about a man who had so much money he didn't have to work for a living. I wanted to know how he spent his time. Bud answered all my questions, giving me quick character sketches of the three old ladies with whom he played cards once a week and of the "family grub" twice a month when his entire clan gathered for dinner at one house or another to discuss family matters. He seemed to be related to everybody in town who had money enough to live behind a stone wall, but he made light of his connections.

"I'm the bastard child," he said. "I'm the one who didn't get married. Why should I? I didn't need anybody to support me." He broke into an old song, a rowdy one as I discovered later, but he gave me only the first two lines:

> *Oh, I used to know a ballet girl,*
> *Her name was Kitty Wells—*

That led to a discussion of plays. Twice a year Bud went to New York for ten days to catch up on the theater season. He subscribed to the *New Yorker* and carefully pasted in a notebook reviews of such plays as he wanted to see on his next visit to the city.

"Look," Bud said, breaking into his description of New York and Yale 1900, "let's have some cookies."

We paraded to the kitchen down a paneled, gas-lit hallway. Through doors I could see a living room furnished in Georgian antiques, a Governor Winthrop dining room in which the last embers of a fireplace fire were burning. The long table was set for breakfast: one place, an egg cup on the service plate.

On the kitchen table, neatly placed, were a glass and a plate covered by a fine linen napkin.

"Well," Bud sighed, "let's see what Mary has left tonight."

He picked up a note from the table. "Milk in icebox. More cookies in rose-painted crock."

"My housekeeper," Bud said, pointing to the note. "She's eight years older than God and was in this house when I was born. Naturally she gets things confused. She still thinks I'm about six years old. Every night she leaves this stuff out for me, and if I don't eat it she hard boils my breakfast eggs."

I attacked the molasses cookies hungrily. After all, I'd been blowing the flute in an orchestra for three hours. Bud's eyes gleamed as he filled my glass with a second pouring of milk. He pointed to a faint ink mark on the bottle.

"She marks the line of the milk, like a bartender with a whiskey bottle, to be sure I've taken some out at night. Sometimes I have a hell of a time getting rid of this stuff. You're a lifesaver."

I suggested that I'd be only too happy to consume this snack any night he wanted to get rid of it. I often studied until eleven o'clock anyway and was always hungry.

"Fine," said Bud. "Tell you what. Every time I need this stuff eaten, I'll turn on the porch light. If it's on, come in."

Thus began a friendship with Bud. Night after night I saved him from Mary's cookies and milk, and he entertained me with lively stories of bachelor doings in the city, of life in Paris, where he had lived several years, and of Yale 1900. He had kept a big scrapbook of his college days, mainly photographs of young dudes dining in New York restaurants, and I wondered how he had studied any when he was so much away from New Haven.

Bud knew many things about which I was curious. He had schemes for breaking dates with girls and for getting dates with girls who weren't responsive.

If father knew about my close association with Bud, he did not mention it. I doubt if he was aware of it until the warm evening when, as he was puffing up the steep hill at dinnertime, I approached in a flashy cream and green Chrysler coupé, honked, and stopped.

"Want a ride?" I asked.

"Where did you get that thing?" he asked.

"It belongs to Mr. Hedge. I just drive it."

He climbed in, admiring the upholstery.

"So you're cultivating the neighbors, too."

I explained that Mr. Hedge, who had driven Model T Fords for nearly twenty years, was having difficulty mastering a gearshift drive on Riverton's steep hills and that I had been chauffeuring him around a bit in his new car. Besides, if I took him to a dinner party and didn't have to pick him up until eleven o'clock, I got the car meanwhile. Not bad, was it?

"Not bad," father admitted.

"That lets you have Old Maud more often."

"Very generous," said father. "This cream and green business was your idea?"

"I had a hand in it."

"It looks more your taste than that of Mr. Hedge."

"Oh, he's flashy," I said.

"Is that so?" Father immediately became suspicious.

"Sure. He plays the best game of bridge in town."

"Hm-m. Has he taught you?"

"Nope. Says he will, though, if you'll consent."

Father beamed.

"He asked you to get your father's consent then?"

"Yes, sir. And he says if you'll let me and I can get a substitute to handle the *Register,* he'll take me to New York in August. I could help drive. He wants to show off his car to his eastern relatives."

"We'll think about it," father sighed. "I had planned a little vacation for us at Okoboji Lake, but I may not be able to get away. And I won't try to compete against New York."

CHAPTER TWENTY

FATHER found that he could not compete with Eileen either.

She arrived home with one college year behind her and immediately asserted herself.

Asked if her heels were not just a little high, she breezed, "On the contrary, they're too low, father. The next ones will be higher. Like 'em?"

She held out a very trim leg and pulled up her skirt.

"I don't need all that foreground just to see the horizon," he said, blushing, and retired from the field. In one year Eileen had come a long way. I told her so as soon as father was out of sight.

"You don't know how wonderful it is," she exclaimed, "to be able to make up your own mind."

She made it up the next night too on a date with Bob. There were repercussions. While she was out, a church member telephoned father that she had been seen at the entrance to a traveling carnival that had set up a noisy, bawdy show on the circus grounds. He waited until morning to confront her with her crime.

"Sure I was there," she replied casually. "Why not?"

Father was stuck. He didn't want any more skirts swished in his face. But he didn't know what to do.

"I've never allowed you," he said uncertainly, "to attend carnivals."

"That's old fashioned," Eileen scoffed. "If the dean of women lets us go and the president doesn't object, what's the harm?"

Father was not sure he had heard her correctly.

"You mean the school doesn't object to such things?"

"Why should it?" Eileen's toes kept tapping a step I knew was the *Charleston,* but father certainly didn't.

Father swallowed and took off his glasses to wipe them.

"Well, I don't like it," he concluded, "but I suppose the college authorities know more about your generation than your father."

Eileen didn't tell him what she had already told me, that she was going to Dreamland that night. She had definitely developed a will of her own, and father did not understand. He worried over her all afternoon, and when she did not appear for dinner he inquired for her.

"She's having dinner with some young people at Crystal Lake," mother said.

This was a club across the river where, it was said, people gambled and played slot machines, and there was known to be liquor in some of the lockers.

"Mother, I don't like it," father fussed. "She ought to find out if we approve of these things."

"I think Eileen's all right," mother defended. "Children grow up rapidly when they get away from home. She's been making up her own mind for nearly a year now. You can't expect her to slip back into old habits."

"I want her to make up her mind," father went on, "but is she doing it?"

Mother asked what he meant.

"I think it's this Eddie person she has written about. Her letters have been full of him. Eddie says this, and Eddie says that. I'm afraid she's fallen under the influence of a strong personality."

"Not Eileen."

"Yes, she has. She didn't learn that trick of throwing her knee in a man's face from any professor."

"She was teasing you, Will."

"Maybe so, but suppose she elopes with Eddie before her schooling is over? She'd regret it all her life."

"She won't do anything like that."

"You bet your sweet life she won't," father said grimly.

He had cause to remember his words two days later, for he was dislodged from his study by a scream in the lower hallway. Eileen was on the telephone.

"Eddie, you darling! Where *are* you? Not here in town! How did you—you *hitchhiked!* Come up to the house right away. Bring your things!"

Each exclamation brought father down the stairway another step. When she hung up, he was standing beside her.

"Who was that?"

Eileen forgot her caution.

"Eddie. That wonderful boy. He's come all the way from Ohio to see me."

"Hitchhiking?"

"Yes, isn't it wonderful? You'll love him."

The whole family was in the hall as a brawny, handsome youth every inch Joe College A.D. 1925 leaped up the front steps and poked out his hand in the accepted fraternity manner. His arm was half around

Eileen as he was introduced to father, and father noticed it. Father observed also that Eddie's shoes were very much down at the heels.

He did his best that day to become acquainted with Eddie, but he did not succeed. Every few minutes the telephone summoned him to his work, and constantly in his mind was his church problem.

This young man from the industrial East, product of the rubber industry in Akron, reared in a crowded city, utterly confident of his own abilities, utterly Tory in his point of view, spokesman for the good life of industrial independence and dog eat dog, was not father's idea of a fit influence upon a nineteen-year-old girl.

Eddie paid part of his college expenses by stock-market speculation. He admitted his athletic scholarship was a joke—he had not even been inside the building of which he was janitor at $30 a month. Why should he? He worked playing football. He was promoting this and that scheme for great riches.

We of the family, listening to this talk at the dining-room table, were astounded but not at all doubtful of Eddie's ability to do whatever he desired. He oozed moneymaking ability from his whole being.

He and Eileen talked in college slang, danced to Victrola records, enchanted mother with their flirtation. But father was as worried as a biddy hen. He fussed every time they held hands, went into the kitchen to work off his steam when their collegiate conversation drove him from the living room.

And he knew this Eddie was not religious. He said so—in the kitchen. Eddie didn't even close his eyes when the meal was blessed. Father had made this discovery in the same manner as I—by peeking.

Father was bewildered and frightened. He did not understand his adversary. He did not realize that a college campus had descended upon his house.

On the third day he trapped Eileen in the kitchen. She was juicing oranges for Eddie's breakfast. The football hero was not yet downstairs. Making large black tracks across the floor I was at that moment scrubbing, father stormed.

"It's a pretty pass when a man can't even get into his own bathroom to shave in the morning. What's that fellow doing anyway?"

"He's probably dressing," Eileen answered.

"He's had time enough to hitchhike from here to Galesburg."

That remark seemed to give father an idea. Galesburg was forty-eight miles due east, a good spurt on the way back to Ohio.

"Eileen," father threatened, "I won't have that round-heeled bum camping on our doorstep another day. Get rid of him."

"What's the matter with him?" Eileen demanded.

"He's disgusting. He's not wholesome. I don't like what he's doing to you, and I won't tolerate his presence in the house any longer."

"Why, father," Eileen exclaimed, "he's the pick of the campus. There isn't a bishop's daughter in school who wouldn't grab him if she had the chance."

"Well," father replied grimly, "this preacher's daughter isn't going to."

"What's the matter with him? Tell me one thing wrong with him."

"He's seedy, down at the heel, needs a haircut."

"Nonsense. The boys are just wearing their hair long. It's distinguished."

"Well, that may be, but no man with any pride would go around with his ankles on the ground."

"But, father, if you hitchhiked all the way from Ohio, your beautiful heels would be rounded off too."

"That's another thing I don't like—begging on the highway like a common tramp."

"Where have you been?" Eileen scoffed. "Practically every boy I know beats his way to school to save train fare."

"Well, I don't like it. Get rid of him before dinner."

Eileen arose to the tips of her toes and defied her father.

"I won't!"

"Then I will," father said and, brushing her aside, stomped into the hall. Eddie was descending the stairs.

"Young man," he said, "pack your things. You and I are going for a ride."

"What's the trouble?" Eddie asked, looking at Eileen, who was tearful and stinging with fury.

"Get your things," father repeated and headed for Old Maud in front of the house.

Eddie gazed after father, looked at Eileen, and laughed.

"I get it," he chuckled. "The bum's rush."

Banteringly, treating the whole thing as a joke, Eddie

packed his bag while Eileen served him his breakfast. Father sat honking the horn from the curb.

"Come and see the fun," Eddie invited as he shut his suitcase, and drank the last of his coffee. Eileen and I climbed with him into the car.

We had scarcely closed the back-seat door when father was off with the roar of a seven-year-old engine racing to keep up with its driver's determination. Across the Mississippi River bridge we clattered, around two curves to a spot where the paved highway stretched straight across the bottom land as far as we could see. Here father stopped.

"I want you to give me an exhibition," he said, turning to confront Eileen's guest, "of the technique of hitchhiking. We'll wait right here until you have flagged a conveyance, *eastbound.*"

Again Eddie laughed.

"Your old man's really something to see," he told Eileen, kissing her lightly in final defiance.

He yanked his bag from the car and walked away with dignity. A moment later he stopped a truck. Throwing his suitcase aboard he turned, blew another kiss to Eileen, took off his hat as he bowed to father, and departed.

"Disgusting," father said, jerking the car around to return home.

"Exceedingly," Eileen spat at him. "I wouldn't brag about it around town if I were you."

We returned to the parsonage without another word. Eileen, tears long since frozen into cold anger, sat rigidly beside me.

But that was not the end of it.

In midafternoon the telephone rang. Eileen had gone to the movies with Fraser, and I answered. Western Union had a telegram for Miss Eileen.

"Telegram for Eileen," I told father.

"You can read it to me," father said, picking up the phone. "I'll relay it."

He heard a loud giggle at the other end of the line. Even I, three feet from the receiver, could hear it.

"Are you sure?" Western Union inquired.

"Yes, I'm sure," father snapped, his patience at an end.

"All right," said Western Union. "It is a telegram from Galesburg, Ill., signed Eddie."

"Read it."

"Very well, sir. It is: 'Your old man's nuts but I love you anyway.' Have you got it, Doctor?" Again the giggle from Western Union.

"I've *got* it," father replied and slammed the receiver.

Soon after Eddie's departure I secured a reporter's job on the *Courier*. The editor needed a vacation relief man. I had gained a little experience with high school reporting, and I was willing to work for less money than anyone else he could find, because I was able to retain my lucrative *Register* distribution on the side.

I went to work without consulting father, and at the dinner hour discovered that I would not have time to join the family. The *Courier* was a morning paper. My day began at two in the afternoon.

By six o'clock I had made the rounds of the mortuaries, firehouses, and hospitals and had all sorts of chit-chat, which in the morning would appear in a column like this:

—Hats cleaned at Renner's. 50¢ (& up).
—A son was born to Mr. and Mrs. George Gunnison of Wapello at Mercy hosp.
—Be kind to your furs. Don't let moths get them. Trust us—Superfine.
—Fire yesterday noon gutted the garage at 166 Stone St. Three cars burned.
—Doris Supel, 5, of 1281 Emerson Ave., was admitted to Riverton hosp. for an operation.

It was not very exciting stuff for a beginner, but it must be written. In half an hour I had to be at police headquarters to check the blotter, then again make the rounds of the mortuaries.

I telephoned my excuses to father.

"You mean you're to work nights?"

"Yes."

"What time will you be home?"

"About one o'clock."

"Son, your mother won't like this. You're supposed to be in *every* night at twelve."

"Well, that's changed now. G'by."

The new job did not involve Sunday work, as the *Courier* published a Sunday paper from Saturday's news and skipped a Monday edition. By midnight our work was cleaned up, but we had to stick around until the presses turned at one, in case a big story broke at the last moment. During that hour the staff wives wandered in, and a game of hearts was played for pennies. I took to it quite handily.

After two weeks I found another diversion. Across the street from the *Courier* plant was a mortuary, the owner of which had been in business for sixty years. Mr. Hanson remembered wild stories of Riverton's younger days, tales filled with blood and dead men and savory saloon murders and grim jokes played with vagrant corpses upon police and newspaper reporters. To me they disclosed another entirely new life and a large and picturesque vocabulary. Mr. Hanson sat before the door of his office each evening until midnight, hoping for business, and often when my work was completed I joined him until the game of hearts began.

One night I was listening to a story. Some forty years earlier, when the mortuary was located near the railroad tracks, a tramp was brought in by the police. He had been found dead along the track. About to go to dinner, Hanson put the body in the backroom. At home there were guests, and it was quite late before he remembered his charity case. Returning to his establishment, he was surprised to see the front door wide open. A survey of the premises revealed that the alley door likewise was open and that the corpse was gone.

Hanson sat down to think it over. He was still thinking when the night police officer poked his head around the corner and whispered.

"Burt, git out o' there quick."

"What's the trouble?"

"Git out o' there, I tell you. There's spooks."

Hanson sauntered to the corner.

"Where's my corpse?" he asked. A vanished body didn't disturb him too much. But the night officer was inarticulate. He kept pointing toward the front door.

"There's nothing in there," Hanson said. "I looked."

"Of *course* there's nothing there. Your dead man just walked down the street!"

Now Hanson was concerned, for the man had been unmistakably dead when he was brought in.

"Alone?" he inquired.

"Alone—and very light on his feet."

At that moment the *Courier's* managing editor shouted through an open window. The police had a report that a liquor still was operating on the West Side. I'd better go with them and, if they made an arrest, phone in the story.

I never heard the rest of Hanson's tale. Officer Joe Sheehan picked me up, and we went to an address a block from the iron works, a shabby, soot-black house behind a lumberyard. He loosened his revolver in its holster and stepped to the front porch. I was directly behind him.

"Open up," he shouted, rattling the locked screen.

"Who's there?" A bulky Negro appeared in the door.

The next I heard was a double shot, and as Officer Joe fell in front of me I dived off the porch into protecting shrubbery. There was a scuffle of feet through the house, the slam of a back door. The Negro was running away. Joe Sheehan lay heavily unconscious.

Across the street I found a telephone, which brought reinforcements. Joe was dead. His gun, from which a bullet had been fired, was in his hand. Blood trailed through the house and down the hill to the railroad track, where it disappeared. A freight train had passed that way a moment before.

An alarm went out to stop the freight up the line, and a large still in the house was confiscated.

Meanwhile I telephoned the story in "takes." Officer Joe's death was sensational. There was no game of hearts that night.

When there were no more details to be telephoned to the managing editor, I hurried back to the office. We caught the westbound trains with half a column, the northbound a half hour later with a full column and a spill over inside. The managing editor himself wrote the story from facts I supplied. By three o'clock there were four columns and pictures for local consumption, complete to details of a man Joe Sheehan had shot in the line of duty six months previously and the ominous prophecy of the victim's widow: "God will punish you, Officer Sheehan, for this."

Proof sheets of the final edition displayed a masterpiece. This was journalism in the raw and at its best. The managing editor barked a compliment and patted my shoulder as he sped to the composing room with the last proofs.

The presses rolled. The paper, damp with the ink of its gaudy headline, came up from the roaring, vibrating room below. Underneath the headline, but on top of the story, was my name.

There was the eye-witness account by the preacher's son, in a torrid vocabulary supplied by the managing editor, who was an old Hearst man. Words I had never heard of bristled through the account, phrases dripping with crime and gore and sensation. And they were my words; the line over them said so in capital letters.

Wearily I crawled home, ignoring the light that still burned on the porch at Bud Hedge's. I went to bed.

In the morning father awoke to the sensational headline and saw the family name attached to a recital of murder and lawbreaking. This could not have happened to *his* son!

But it had. I confirmed the details when I arose at eleven o'clock. Father sat by me as I ate breakfast.

"And you *like* this kind of life?" he sighed finally.

"Boy, do I *like* it!" I responded. "I *love* it."

"Well," he said, shaking his head, "you have completely disproved the theory of heredity and environment."

CHAPTER TWENTY-ONE

*F*ATHER was glad when I quit reporting to accompany Mr. Hedge to New York. But the trip did not cure me of an interest in newspapering.

Offered the task of patrolling the hospitals and mortuaries and proofreading on the *Courier* while attending school that winter, I accepted. My *Courier* salary was spending money, and income from the *Des Moines Register* route could be saved for college.

The journalistic lessons I learned at the *Courier* came in handy at school, where I was editor of the *Panther*. Problems of make-up and composition too advanced for the English instructor who labored with the school publication I took to my boss downtown.

The result was that at the annual high school journalism convention at Grinnell that year and at the University of Iowa's journalism banquet, six of the seven cups awarded went to Riverton. Even Mr. Haskins, who had doubted my editorial judgment, was impressed when the news came.

So too were the fraternities at the University of Iowa. On the lookout for material, two squads showed up on our porch during Easter week. They were my first reminder that high school was about over. I had spent little time in normal school activity except for some of the largest parties. Now suddenly they wanted to know where I was going to college in the fall.

All I knew was that by almost any strategy I wanted to duck junior college. This was a pet of Mr. Haskins' wherein the high school offered the first two years of college work to students who could not afford any other. The credits were accepted by most universities, and the instruction was excellent. But it was not college. Mr. Haskins treated the students like high schoolers, even compelling them to sit through high school assembly programs.

After the second delegation of fraternity men had visited me, their hands indifferently riding a hip pocket so that the casually opened coat would reveal their well-polished Greek badges, father came downstairs. He was naturally curious about strangers.

"Who was that?" he asked.

"A couple of guys from Iowa. They want to know if I'm going there to school next fall."

"Is that what you have in mind?"

I knew that any wavering at this point would commit me to junior college for sure, since already father was worried over the financial problem of supporting two children in college at the same time. I sparred carefully.

"I don't know."

"That's fine. Don't be coerced into anything. You don't know what your lifework will be yet. Until you decide, you can't intelligently select a school."

There it was, and the time to destroy the foundation on which surely he would build was that moment. I must decide, and I did.

"But I do know this much," I said. "I'm going to be a newspaperman."

That jolted him, but scarcely as I had intended.

"Come here, son," he said, retiring to his leather chair.

There was something he wanted to say, and he didn't know how. He could think, probably, only of all the opportunities that an ordinary father and son would have to talk about the future: hikes and fishing trips and ball games, sessions of conversation such as Mr. Tracy shared with Fraser and Mr. Hedge with me. These proxy fathers knew more about our ambitions and aspirations than he did, and now when he wanted to talk to his son as man to man he was a preacher and a father, but not a "dad." That discipline that he had imposed, which compelled Fraser and me to call him "sir," was hard now, when he wanted softness. Here was a son who had decided upon his lifework without even consulting him, him who was adviser to the whole town, but not to his own family.

"You are eighteen."

"Yes, sir."

"You may change your mind many times yet before you take on your lifework. At your age I was a farm boy, determined to be a teacher. At twenty-two I was a teacher, bent on medicine. I was ready for my internship before I discovered, at the age of twenty-nine, what my life would be. Keep your own mind open; look about you."

"Yes, sir." It was another sermon.

He squirmed.

"Have you—have you ever given any thought to the ministry?"

"No, sir."

"Any particular reason why?"

"It doesn't appeal to me, that's all."

"Have I set you too bad an example?"

Now it was my turn to squirm. "Of course not."

But this was not enough. He was waiting for more, watching me, waiting.

"Well—" I fumbled. "I like the ministry all right, but—" I couldn't speak frankly to father, not when he looked like that. Someday, out in the car, perhaps, with the river to look at, I could speak, but not now.

"But what?" he prodded.

"Well—you're a good preacher. I couldn't be that good."

Very faintly he smiled. "You don't know yet. You have shown in school that you're a leader, you speak well, you know your Bible."

"Yes, but—" There it was again, that awful hurdle a fellow couldn't jump.

"It's that 'but' that I'm waiting for, son."

He had to have it, then. There was no escaping it.

"Someday," I said, "I might be a father."

He cleared his throat. "Yes, son?"

"I'd want to get out and play football with my boys, and baseball. I'd want to be to them all the things you've never been to us, things you're too dignified to be. I don't want to live with my problems; I want to leave them in the office and be a dad when I get home. I'd want to understand my kids so"—I was about ready to cry now, and, I fancied, so was he—"so thoroughly that when they asked something of me it would be a discussion, not an issue. I don't want to be so busy worrying about everybody else's life that I have no time for my own. That's the price you pay for being a good minister."

"Don't think I haven't thought of these things," he answered. "Don't think they haven't tormented me. I'm trying to be more liberal with Fraser."

"Then play catch with him over the garage roof."

"I can't do that. The neighbors would talk."

"Then talk to him, don't preach at him."

"I'll try."

"And—and make him feel that his life is as important to you as Mrs. Littleton's lumbago."

He took out his fine linen handkerchief and blew his nose.

"Am I that bad?"

"You're a wonderful man, father, and I respect and love you. But I wouldn't have a job like yours for anything in the world."

He arose quickly and left the house. I had said too much.

Next day, however, he was lively again.

"Son," he said at breakfast, "I have an idea."

He had, too. Where he had fallen down, he analyzed, was not so much in his lack of intimate contact with me as in his failure to see that I played baseball more often with boys my age. His mistake was in denying me permission to go to Culver Military Academy that summer in Sioux City when I had coaxed so hard and to Mr. Seeley's woodcraft school in Denver and on that three-week bicycle tour with Bud Eaton and the Marsh boys.

Lacking normal outlets, I had gone to work when too young; now I had the habit of working when I should be playing. This newspaper business was a substitute for clean, wholesome play with other boys. He was a fool not to have realized it. Before I went anywhere to college, I needed mental and physical competition and camaraderie with boys. How would I like to go to the Y camp in Estes Park for the summer?

He had hit a bull's-eye.

"You could have three months out where there's nobody to keep an eye on you, and I know you love the Colorado mountains."

"I sure do."

"All right. I'll write to Ira Lute about it. I'm sure he can find you a summer job in the Y organization that will be more fun than work."

"Swell!"

But there was a catch to it.

"Son," he went on, "if I do this for you, will you do something for me?"

"What?"

"Give up the *Register* immediately and take things a little easier."

"But what about the money? It's my college money."

"We'll find it somewhere else," he said, and I should have been suspicious. He continued quickly, "Besides, I want you to teach a Sunday school class. There's a group of twelve-year-old girls who badly need an instructor. After you've taught a couple of months and had a summer under the influence of the Y.M.C.A., you may have other ideas about your lifework."

"What will Fraser do?" I asked. "You know he gets 50 cents a week out of the *Register* too."

"I'll take care of that. He won't lose."

"Okay," I agreed. "It's a deal."

The Y.M.C.A. camp was a covey of buildings on a plain in a valley of Estes Park, four miles from the exciting temptations of the village, surrounded by spectacular mountains. There during the season were entertained a sequence of conferences, each lasting from ten days to two weeks. The Y.M.C.A. secretaries held a retreat there, and also the Y.W.C.A. workers, the Girl Reserves, the Hi-Y, and other quasireligious groups. Delegations totaling 600 were housed on the grounds in cottages, ate at the cafeteria, sought pleasures in the main lounge, worshiped in the chapel.

To minister to these transients there was a permanent staff of housekeepers, maids, kitchen and dining-room help, bakers, bellhops, porters, postmen, and stewards. My idea that work would be subsidiary to pleasure was immediately dispelled when I reported to Mr. Lute.

My job was to run the commissary storehouse, in which capacity I checked in foodstuffs for the cafeteria and employees' dining room and guarded them until they were checked out to the cook and baker's chef. Hefting 150-pound sides of beef on a truck from the village to camp, toting hundreds of cartons of canned goods up and down stairs, keeping an accurate ledger inventory of stocks on hand and their disposal were all part of the assignment. I would live in the men's dormitory where lights were turned out at ten o'clock; I must not leave the grounds without permission; and one week end each month I would be free to do as I liked, within the rules. The routine was a long haul from father's prospectus of the summer. About the only use I'd find for my new hiking boots was when driving a truck.

The manager of the cafeteria impressed my duties upon me as she gave me the storehouse and auto truck keys. Last year, she said forbiddingly, some supplies had disappeared, and the truck had been utilized to take employees into town after hours to iniquitous public dances. Did I understand?

I did and set to work.

The male employees' dormitory was north of the administration building, a similar layout near by housing the girls. The staff was composed of college youngsters, the manager having made an exception in my case.

The third evening one lad, who had been a garbage collector the previous year and now waited on tables, appeared at the storehouse about eight o'clock, as I was closing.

"Hey," he whispered, "bring out a hunk of cheese and some crackers, and we'll have a bull session." He disappeared.

When I reached the dormitory, five boys were in my room awaiting the feast, among them my roommate. Seeing me empty handed, they set up a howl.

"What's a matter, you scared?"

"No," I said, "I'm not scared, but I can't lift things out of the commissary."

"Why not, you're the bookkeeper, aren't you?"

"It wouldn't be right."

"Nuts. Who's going to know?"

"That's not the point. I just can't do it, that's all."

A few days later, a lad from Simpson College, who was studying for the ministry, sauntered into my office.

"Look," he said, "I had this job last year. You've got to be a good sport. Nobody's going to miss a little cheese or maybe some chocolate bars and cocoanut."

I refused, however, to become involved, nor would I turn my back while he and an Oklahoma half-Cherokee Indian appropriated from my shelves. My orders were to prevent pilfering. The fact that I had a job at all proved such guardianship necessary. My loyalty was not to my coworkers but to my boss; every syllable of my parsonage training said so.

Another week went by, during which I worked as hard as in the basket factory, and again the delegation appeared. They wanted the keys to the truck for a spree after hours in the village. If I wanted to come along, that was okay; they had a date all lined up.

"Look," I said, "I'd like to go as much as the next guy, but I was told particularly not to let the truck out after hours."

"Nuts," exclaimed the theological student, "they say that every year. There's no lights on the truck, and they're scared somebody'll get killed, that's all. But it's easy. You just wait till a car comes along and follow *his* lights."

This sounded like real sport, and I was about to consent, when I thought about father. Mr. Lute had given me this job because father petitioned him, and if I was caught in an overt act it would reflect on father.

"We've got to stick together, pal," pleaded Oklahoma Joe. "We won't have any fun all summer if we don't."

Gloomily I admitted this. The summer certainly held no promise, within the rules. But there was that matter of loyalty. Which came first? Loyalty to what father expected of me or to the boys? If I had ever been with young people in a summer camp, the decision would have been easy. But I didn't know the ropes; and I *did* know father.

"Sorry," I said.

They did not take the turndown charitably, and there was some talk of taking the keys from me forcibly. For such an offense, however, they could be expelled from camp. Finally they departed, and I remained a long time among my stores before I had courage enough to return to the dormitory.

At ten o'clock the lights went out. The boys would be in bed now. Furtively I hurried across the dark grounds. If they had intercepted me at that moment, I'd have given them the keys. But no one was around, and I couldn't offer the truck even to my roommate; he wasn't in his bed.

Either they had abandoned the enterprise or had hiked the four miles into town. If I had been sure they had gone to the village, I would have driven down and saved them the walk home. But I wasn't sure.

So I went to bed. An instant later the door banged open, and dark figures surrounded me.

"Get up, sister!" commanded the theological student. "We're going for a little walk."

A blindfold was clamped over my eyes, and I was yanked into the yard in my pajamas, without shoes or socks. The chilly mountain air whipped up my legs. Cactus bristles snipped at my feet. Crushed stone ham-

[269]

mered my toes. Resistance was useless, and I began to
think more clearly of the obligations of a boy to a
group.

At the reservoir from which the camp got its water
supply we stopped. The bandage was taken from my
head. Holding me securely were the Indian and the
theological student. Solidly behind them were the other
thirty male employees of the camp. My pajamas were
torn off, to snickers and certain anatomical comments.
A rope was put around my waist. I was pushed onto the
dam. Struggle was useless; the older lads held me in a
tight grip.

With a mighty splash I landed in the icy lake, came
up shocked and chattering. Seeing I could swim, the
boys vanished, taking my pajamas with them.

It took me half an hour to get back to the dormitory.
The conference meeting at the camp was of Y.M.C.A.
secretaries, who had no curfew hour. In serious groups
of twos and threes they roamed the grounds. From
tree to tree, from cover to cover, I ducked in frigid
nudity, stumbling over brambles and rocks. I decided
what I would do on my return. My coworkers would
be in the yard if ever I succeeded in getting back.
They'd laugh, and I'd laugh with them and suggest a
good midnight snack for all hands. It was obvious they
wanted to be friendly, else they would not have bothered to teach me a lesson. We'd have lunch, and everything would be all right.

But the camp was without sign of life. No one
loitered in the yard. Not a head showed in any window. The dormitory seemed to be empty.

By flashlight I pulled brambles and thorns from my

feet, nursed them with iodine, put two extra blankets on the bed and jumped in, every muscle aching. Just as I began to relax, a restless coil wrapped itself around my ankle.

A snake!

With a roar I leaped from the bed and groped for my flashlight. But before I could find it, a bright torch illuminated the partition that separated my room from another. Laughter arose from all sides.

This was the moment to be a good fellow and produce cheese and crackers, but I did not see it.

Oklahoma Joe took a harmless, six-foot bullsnake from my bed, grinned at the basket-factory vitriol I poured forth, and refused to see any reason for getting sore over a bullsnake. It should have been a rattler for a guy like me, he said.

Next morning I was greeted at breakfast as though nothing had happened. But somebody told somebody else, and by midmorning Ira Lute had heard the news. He intercepted me as I was inquiring for mail. Behind the cage, within earshot, was the mailman, who had tied the rope around my waist.

"I hear the boys did a little hazing last night," Mr. Lute began.

"Nothing special," I said casually.

"I hear you were dumped in the reservoir."

"What for?" I evaded him.

"That's what I want to know. It's a wonder you didn't get pneumonia. And that snake might have frightened you into St. Vitus' dance. Who did it?"

"I have no idea."

"Why was it done?"

"Search me."

"Either you'll tell me, or I'll have to send you home."

"I really don't know," I said. "I was blindfolded."

"All right," he concluded, "but if it happens again, remember that you could have avoided a second dose."

The news of this conversation was well received. The boys waited hopefully for me to invite them to a party. If they had approached me, I'd have given them the whole storeroom. Instead they waited, and after a week they were still waiting. Gradually they lost hope that I had learned my lesson and began to ignore me. Despairing of getting close to them, I retired to my storeroom and remained there the rest of the summer. My companion on a three-day mountain hike each month was a Chinese student at Denver University, who acted as baker's helper.

On the train going home I figured out what I should have done. I should have gone to the theological student and Indian Joe the next morning. For the remainder of the summer I'd have been included in their sport. But it was too late now. All I could do was profit *in absentia*. In three weeks I'd be off to the University of Iowa, and when I pledged a fraternity I'd be careful not to let anything like this happen. That was it! If there were things I wouldn't do, that was no reason they might not be okay for somebody else. Maybe they'd be okay for me too if I tried them. I thought of the thrill it would have been to drive the truck to the village on a black night, chasing the lights of another car down a winding road across four narrow bridges. There would be thrills like that at college. All I need do was look sharp, and not let the parsonage keep too tight a hold on my coattails.

Just three weeks, and I'd be set. By the time the train pulled into Riverton I was tense with excitement.

Father met me at the station.

"You look very fit," he said. "Did you have a good summer?"

"Sure," I said. "I played flute solos for three conferences and broke two fingers falling off the side of Mount Chapin. I climbed Long's Peak and the whole Mummy Range."

"Who did you hike with?"

"A Chinese missionary's son."

"Did you make a lot of friends?"

"No."

"Why?"

"I just didn't, that's all."

After a few days he cornered me on the front porch.

"You didn't change your mind, did you?"

"About what?"

"About being a newspaperman?"

"Oh, no. I've got the curriculum from the University of Iowa School of Journalism right here."

He sat down and cocked his heels on the porch railing.

"Son, you didn't have much of a summer after all, did you?"

"It was heavy labor, father. I could have earned more money right here in town and not worked so hard for it."

"But the other fellows—didn't you get to *know* any of them?"

"Sure."

"Not well enough to correspond with them now?"

"No."

He thought a moment. "Son, I wonder if you're ready for college."

"How's that?"

"You aren't very adaptable, I'm afraid. You're very precocious in some respects, exceedingly naïve in others."

"That's not my fault."

"I know. The shoe fits me, and I'm wearing it. That's why I don't think you'd better go to the university this fall. I don't think you'd fit."

"Why not?"

"You just wouldn't, that's all. You stay right here in junior college this year, and I'll show you I can be a dad as well as a father. By next fall you'll be more mature, and college will come naturally to you."

Junior college! It was like a sentence to Devil's Island. The same high school building, the same old teachers, the same parsonage influence. That wasn't what I needed.

I defied his judgment. A moral lecture followed. With all his might he was doing what he, not I, thought best for me.

Besides, he summed up, if I remained in town another year, Eileen would be within a year of her graduation, and he could manage financially our joint education. As it was now, he couldn't swing it. The $1,000 I had in the bank would be equally valuable next year.

"You will stay here," he said finally. "You can have

your Sunday school class back. The girls say you're the best teacher they ever had."

So that was it. Father's reasoning was obvious. He would have another year in which to talk me into the ministry. Nothing could have more securely cemented me into journalism.

"I'll stay if I must," I answered, and it was my turn to be final, "but I'll be darned if I'll teach in Sunday school. I won't even *go* to Sunday school. I'll get my old job back on the *Courier.*"

CHAPTER TWENTY-TWO

*D*URING the summer I had maintained ardent correspondence with three Riverton young ladies, not dreaming that I would be home to face them in the fall.

Junior college began, therefore, with trouble which pursued me all winter. And because the postgraduate high school studies required little mental application and the college extracurricular activities did not interest me, my major emphasis turned to social affairs.

All three girls were high school seniors, but there the similarity ended.

My favorite of the three was Louise, a tall, extremely comely blonde. As early as my junior year in high school I had suggested she wear my Clisthonian pin, but she was uninterested. She preferred to scatter her affections so that no matter what crowd gave a party she was there. Louise could do this, because she was very much in demand. Her father was a tailor and insisted that she make her own clothes. A steady beau, particularly one as flighty as I, might not ask her to a dance until too late for her nimble fingers to construct a sensation for the occasion. And Louise went nowhere unless she was a sensation.

Next came Mary, an exceedingly quick-minded minx who flirted joyously but cold-bloodedly with any boy who could advance her social position. She was also a specialist at entertainment. No matter who gave the party, Mary contrived to be the consulting expert, for this assured her an invitation. Mary was compelled to this opportune conduct by circumstance. She was not of a "best" family. Her father was dead; her mother supported three children by dressmaking. Mary could not compete dollar for dollar, but she could outclass any of her friends in wits. When she was not working at her job of being clever and gay, she was another person, tender, romantic, poetic, responsive to little compliments; and she could cook a dinner for a fellow that was unbeatable. This latter Mary had emerged from our summer's correspondence.

Finally, there was Marjorie. She was the prettiest of the lot and the simplest. Not a resident of North Hill, she was very happy to be included in social affairs but not resentful when she wound up at the movies instead of in somebody's game room. Black-haired, sparkle-eyed, quiet, the daughter of a salesman who retired from the parlor whenever a boy called, Marjorie was relaxation from the strenuousness of North Hill girls. She was also the most dangerous of the three, strictly a one-man woman and jealous.

I was with the girls each day at school, and no matter which one I went out with, I was almost certain to bump into the other two.

The winter promised to be lively, if nothing else.

When social affairs closed in ominously, I could plead my work on the *Courier* as an excuse to cancel a date to a party where all three girls would appear.

Technically I worked from three in the afternoon until midnight, but except for special occasions, the *Courier* managing editor let me arrange my own schedule. I could always get away if I wanted to. During the summer a new sweetshop had opened conveniently a block from the *Courier* office. It was equipped with a small dance floor and an Orthophonic Victrola in a back room. And it was almost deserted between four and five-thirty in the afternoon.

So I began to invite my girls there for an afterschool malted milk and a few dances: Louise one afternoon, Mary another, Marjorie a third. I would duck from the *Courier* for an hour for a bit of romance and then return to work.

The system functioned elegantly at first. John Scorio, proprietor of the Honeymoon, was a good fellow who advanced credit, bought my favorite records, and co-operated. He did not mention when I appeared with Mary that Louise had been my companion on the previous day.

Then one afternoon, bound for a tryst with Marjorie, I met him at the corner.

"You can't go in today," he gesticulated with his chocolate-stained apron, waving me back. "They all show up. The black-headed one, she's waiting in the dancing room; the other two are inna the booth up by the door."

This was an *impasse,* indeed. Louise and Mary evidently had compared notes. No accident sent them together to the Honeymoon. Their preference, when together, was a little place where a tall glass full of ice

cream, dry malted milk, marshmallow, and crushed pecans sold for a dime.

"Look, John," I said, pulling him into the sanctuary of a cigar store, "this is tough. Stall Marjorie. I'll phone her from the office. The others couldn't overhear, could they?"

"Trusta me, trusta me," he replied.

[280]

Marjorie accepted graciously the excuse that I had to work. But at dinnertime I got this report from the owner of the Honeymoon:

"She comes outa the dancing room, and she see the other two. She sita down. The other two finish their soda and freeze up, like this—" John hunched his big Greek shoulders into his coat. "They finish their soda, and go out."

For a week I left the Honeymoon strictly alone, although twice I drove past each girl's house and tooted the car horn to let them know I was faithful. Some high school activities in which I, a college man, couldn't be interested, occupied the trio meanwhile.

Then I took Louise to a concert of the visiting Minneapolis Symphony Orchestra. I hardly expected either of the other two to appear, but for safety bought balcony seats, where we would not be observed. Our arrival was timed to the first tap of Dr. Verbruggin's baton, and we were among the first to leave.

"Let's go down to the Honeymoon and wipe that sticky Tschaikowsky off our hands with some Paul Whiteman," Louise said.

"Nah," I countered quickly, shoving her into the dilapidated, eight-year-old Ford. "I know a better place."

We went to a suburban nook with high-backed booths that I had found when Eleanor was visiting Mrs. Dawson. Not a soul there knew either of us.

I was exceedingly proud of this maneuver until Mary asked next day, "Did you and Louise have a good time last night? We sort of hoped you'd show up at the Honeymoon—after the concert."

To make amends I invited Mary to the first DeMolay dance of the season, always a big event. But now—what about Louise? She'd surely go to the DeMolay with somebody. I needed an alibi. And one occurred to me. I'd wait until I was sure Louise had accepted another date, then ask her. She'd think Mary was second choice, and everything would be all right.

To keep Marjorie quiet I invited her to the Saturday football game at Ottumwa and sat back to await developments. But it was not until the DeMolay dance was only three days away that I learned Louise was booked. When I asked her for DeMolay, she was very much surprised.

"Why, I thought—" she said. "Oh, I'd *love* to go. And I'm giving a dinner Saturday night. Won't you carve the roast?"

I was flabbergasted.

"But I—"

"Yes?" she inquired innocently.

"Oh, sure, that's swell," I said, thankful for the bell that called her to Latin and me to French.

But it wasn't swell. It was awful. I had two dates for DeMolay and could not possibly get Marjorie home from Ottumwa in time for Louise's dinner. The only brightness in the whole glum prospect was that Louise would not be at Ottumwa and Mary would be helping Louise with the dinner. So they wouldn't see me with Marjorie.

All day I fretted, finding no solution. I even consulted Fraser, but he was no help. He had just passed his twelfth Boy Scout merit badge and was about to become senior patrol leader. Girl troubles weren't yet in his line.

That night Bud Hedge's porch light went on at eleven, and I confronted him with the dilemma. Even he was stumped.

"You'd better break your leg," he said, "unless you want me to take Louise to DeMolay for you. You can chauffeur us."

I rejected the offer, but had an idea. Louise's brother had told me that Louise was attending DeMolay with George Kitzel. If that was right, she had two dates too. There was still time for plenty to happen.

So I called her brother. "Look, chum," I began without introduction, "you gave me a bum steer."

"How?"

"You said Louise was going to DeMolay with George Kitzel."

"Well, isn't she?"

"No."

"Just a minute," he interrupted. "I'll find—"

"Hey," I shouted in alarm, "for Pete's sake don't *ask* her."

"Why not, she's right here."

"Not so loud, please. You're sure, though?"

"Sure I'm sure."

"Okay, and don't mention I telephoned."

The next call was to George Kitzel.

"Look, pal," I said, "just who's got a date with Louise for DeMolay?"

"I have," he answered promptly. He had been trying to break into her company since midsummer, calling week after week only to discover that she was dated up far in advance. He had gone straight home from the DeMolay meeting at which the dance date was set and telephoned her. Caught, she could not refuse.

If I could just impress upon George that his date was in peril—

"Listen," I said, "Louise is going to DeMolay with me."

"When'd you ask her?"

" 'Way last summer, in a letter from Estes Park. She promised me the first DeMolay of the season, no matter when it was."

This last was not an untruth, I had just forgotten it until that moment.

"She can't do that."

"Then you'd better call her and insist on your rights."

"I will, and thanks for the tip."

In a few moments he phoned back.

"Hey," he said, "there's dirty work going on."

"What's the trouble?"

"I told Louise about my talk with you, and she says she remembers very clearly the promise she made in her letter, and she can't break her word. She forgot about it when she accepted me. Now, what'll I do?"

If I could get George and Mary together, that would fix everything.

"Look, George, how about Mary?"

"I'm tired of asking her," he answered. "She's always busy."

"If I fix it, will you take her?"

"Boy, that would be wonderful!"

"Okay. You sit by the phone until I call back."

Telephoning Mary, I asked casually if she was going to George Kitzel's party. That was the only thing I could think of in a hurry.

"George Kitzel's?" she queried quickly, in a voice that expressed sorrow for all the times she had refused him.

"He's going to give a whopper in his grandmother's barn—a hard-time party."

"In costume?"

"Sure. Everybody comes dressed like a tramp. He wants to invite you and doesn't dare."

"Why, I'd *love* to go with him. Be a real friend and let him know, will you?"

"I sure will."

Pause.

"Who's he taking to DeMolay?" she said.

"He hasn't got a date yet," I answered blissfully.

"How about trading a dance with him?" she went on.

"I don't know whether we'll have time."

"What do you mean, time?"

"Well—for one thing, we'll be late. I may have to work at the *Courier* until ten o'clock."

"Oh, that's terrible."

"You angry?"

"No, not angry, but after all—first DeMolay and everything."

"Well, I know how you feel," I said after a thoughtful interlude. "It's too bad you aren't going with George Kitzel."

"Yes, isn't it," she sighed.

"Well," I said, "I hate to do it, but since my time is all messed up, I'll make a deal with you."

"How?"

"I'll persuade George to call you for this DeMolay, if you'll promise me right now that you'll go with me to the *next* one."

"If you really don't mind too much," she rushed in, "I'd love to go to the next one with you instead."

Now all I had to do was talk George into giving a party. From the promptness with which he answered the telephone, I judged he had taken literally my request to sit by the instrument.

"It's all fixed," I announced. "All you got to do is phone and ask Mary. But don't mention talking to me."

"Oh, no, I wouldn't."

"Okay then. But listen, George—to be popular, you've got to give parties. Why don't you have a swell hard-time Hallowe'en party in your grandma's barn? It would set you up for the rest of the winter."

"Oh, I don't know—"

"Sure," I coaxed. "You could ask Mary to help you—"

"Well—"

"Then it's all fixed," I concluded hurriedly. "You get Mary to help you, then she'll *have* to be your date for the evening."

My only problem now was to get to Louise's in time for dinner Saturday night. I thought that would be so simple that I did not even have a strategy in mind when I met her in the hall next day.

"You weren't serious about Friday night, were you?" she sparkled lightly.

"Of course, I was," I replied forthrightly. "Why shouldn't I be?"

"Because," she laughed, "you have a date with Mary."

"Oh, no," I corrected her. "What gave you that idea?"

"I heard it."

"But you couldn't have, Louise. She has a date with George Kitzel."

"George Kitzel!"

She stared at me incredulously for a moment, then her smile returned.

"And I," she said glibly, "have a date with Ray Somerville," and with that she slipped into her botany classroom.

I didn't like to admit it, but it appeared that I was being used. Mary had George, Louise had Ray, and I was outside looking in. About all I needed to hear now was that George Kitzel wasn't inviting me to my own Hallowe'en party in his grandma's barn.

Anger, cold and earnest, settled down on me. These high school kids couldn't do that to me. I'd get to Louise's party Saturday night even if I had to show up an hour late.

I would miss the DeMolay dance, but I was going to cut that roast, or else!

Saturday Old Maud was in one of her purring moods. She clipped off the forty-eight miles to Ottumwa in two hours flat, a record for her age and condition.

"Nice going," I applauded her silently as Marjorie

and I pulled up at the football field, "but you've got to do better, old girl, going home."

She did her best. We made twenty-six miles the first hour and came into Morning Sun before dark. There, according to father's instructions, I was to check the oil. But time was short. I grabbed five gallons of gasoline and sped homeward.

Just outside of Middletown Old Maud let out a throaty yell, and we rolled to a stop off the pavement. Five minutes of strenuous cranking did nothing to revive her.

Marjorie suggested that we get a shove into Middletown. We could telephone her mother from there. She didn't at all mind being out. There would be a full moon at ten o'clock. I began flagging cars that passed. One stopped, that of a farmer member of father's church.

He pushed us into Middletown, where the garage man was emphatic in his diagnosis. Bearings burnt out; no oil. That's what you got for letting a kid drive a car. No kid of his would—

Marjorie telephoned her mother, and I made a call of my own.

"Listen, Louise," I said. "I'm stuck out near Middletown. The car burned out a bearing. I can't possibly get to your dinner."

She was not at all upset.

"That's all right," she retorted. "I didn't really expect you, so I invited Ray. Have fun with Marjorie!"

The return to Riverton was long and torturing. The full moon arose unnoticed. Marjorie snuggled close, sheltering herself from the night wind, but it was only shelter as far as I was concerned. Behind me the good samaritan was shoving poor Old Maud, silent engined, back to town.

At ten-thirty we reached the garage father used for repairs. At a quarter of eleven Marjorie was safely home. At half past eleven a taxi deposited me at the *Courier,* where I tried to explain to a furious managing editor who was waiting for my story of the football game. Shortly after midnight I reached home.

Fortunately, father was not up. On Saturday night he always retired early. The following day, after a particularly successful sermon, he took Maud's demise nobly.

"It would have happened to me," he said simply. "Poor Old Maud was about gone. We'll patch her up and see if she'll last until spring. No use getting a new car in an Iowa winter."

That was the last time I ever used the Ford. I didn't much mind; I had Bud's new Chrysler almost every night.

But Louise wasn't riding in it. Nor Mary, who was busy planning George Kitzel's party. As a result, I settled down to Marjorie, escorting her to George's barn dance, and to the movies. I didn't have to worry about being seen now.

Mary and I still had a date, though, for the second DeMolay. And as soon as the Kitzel party was past, she dropped George and I had a new chance. As usual, however, I overworked the amends. I hung around Mary's locker so much, took her out in Bud's car so often, that eventually Marjorie saw us. Moreover, one evening when I was supposed to be working, Marjorie walked into the Honeymoon and caught me dancing with Mary.

This did not bother me until the night of DeMolay, where I should have been secure. Until then Marjorie had gone nowhere without me. That night she showed up with George Kitzel. And there I was with Mary.

Even then I didn't much mind. I had Mary. But the following Sunday, when I dropped around, Mary was busy. Not with a date at all, but with homework. It was a definite, unequivocal brush off.

Cruising up the street, I coasted slowly past Marjorie's without finding her home and rolled down the hill toward town. Then I saw her, walking with her little sister and brother, a Sunday afternoon stroll. They were a long way from home.

"Can I give you a lift?" I called.

They accepted.

"How's Mary?" Marjorie asked, while her sister giggled. That completely discouraged talk. I deposited them at their door, and they went directly into the house.

My pride was hurt. First Louise, then Mary, now Marjorie.

At the Honeymoon Marjorie's current recorded favorite was a lachrymosal rendition by Nick Lucas of a ballad entitled *It All Depends on You*. Often we had sung it over marshmallow sundaes: "I can be happy, I can be sad; I can be good or I can be bad. It all depends on you."

Maybe if I sent her the record, she'd thaw.

Immediately after school on Monday I did so, telephoning the order and requesting that it be sent by special messenger. Enroute home for dinner I stopped at Marjorie's to ascertain the effect of this tender memorial sentiment. She met me at the door, her eyes gleaming. Behind her stood her father, her mother, her little sister and brother, all smiling a friendly greeting.

What a reception! Even better than I expected.

"You got it then?" I asked.

Marjorie had the record in her hand.

"Yes. Which side did you intend for me?"

"What do you mean, which side?"

"There are two sides to a record."

"You know which one I meant. I didn't even look to see what was on the other side."

"You didn't!" The whole family was enjoying some kind of a joke at my expense.

"Was it this?" Marjorie held up the disk. There, exactly as I intended, was *It All Depends on You*.

"Of course."

Again the family laughed.

"It couldn't have been this?"

She turned over the record.

Aghast, I read the title: *I'm Looking for a Girl Named Mary*.

I took the record in my hands, broke the disk across my knee, and fled.

The family's merriment followed me to the car and down the street.

CHAPTER TWENTY-THREE

*W*HEN Eileen came home for Christmas, a simple action demonstrated to the family that this was the last yuletide we would ever share.

She had her picture taken and 100 passport-size copies made to attach to applications for teaching jobs. This year would be her last under the family roof. Next year she might be too far away to return home, or if she did it would be as a girl who was on her own in the world.

There was no doubt that Eileen would become a teacher. Father's unceremonious treatment of Eddie had discouraged her. What was the use of getting crazy about somebody if father was going to boot him out of the house?

Father had hoped, in sending her to a religious school, that she would fall in love with an embryo churchman, but she didn't. To his delight she had a collegiate crush in her junior year on the son of a missionary to India, a boy of such brilliance that a bishopric in time was a foregone conclusion, but the attachment was not enduring.

Father tried hard that Christmas to recapture the spirit of Fort Dodge, Sioux City, and Denver, but 1925 was a prosperity year. No one bothered to knit a scarf or a pair of socks, or to put up jelly. Except for an enormous box of candy from the daughters of the Buick distributor, everything that came to the parsonage was store bought.

No candy bags were packed in the parsonage for distribution to the poor. There didn't seem to be any poor; everybody was making money. Even the church janitor was in the stock market. No jovial Sunday school superintendent disguised himself as Santa Claus in our living room for a children's party on Christmas Eve. No affectionate choir came to the parsonage door before starting on a round of caroling. All that was behind us.

No longer need Eileen wonder whether the Canadian aunts would give her a red camisole or outing-flannel pajamas. She was almost through college, and the gift would be silk stockings. Fraser, the last of us to be wide eyed over mother's annual rendition of *'Twas the Night before Christmas* and father's melodious reading of Van Dyck's *The Other Wise Man,* was a Boy Scout senior patrol leader, a trombone player.

We were not a family growing up, but a family breaking up. To father we children were not two future ministers and a minister's wife, but a teacher, a newspaperman, and a Boy Scout.

But as soon as Christmas Day was past, father's spirits revived, and he attacked with gusto the task of finding Eileen a job. Hour after hour he sat at his desk typing application blanks, which flew from his machine to her hands for neat pasting of the passport photo. He certainly didn't want her teaching career to begin in the Mahaska County Consolidated School, where she might fall in love with a farmer, or in Cook County, Ill., where a guileful Al Capone man might steal her. Yet he did not let her forget that, so far as he was concerned, this teaching business was only an interlude until she met the right man.

"Let's not send this thing to Quapaw, Okla.," he said, looking up the town in an atlas given free with a three-year subscription to *The Literary Digest*. "You'll never meet a good man down there."

Or, "I'm taking out this application to Steelton, Pa. You'd be wasting your time among those miners."

Without saying anything, he also threw in the wastebasket all applications to schools in Ohio near enough for Eddie to commute week ends, and Eileen just as stealthily returned them to the mail. But he did not discard the towns where there were theological seminaries or where, from his vast knowledge of the Methodist church, he knew there would be an eligible young circuit preacher.

After Eileen returned to college, father's typewriter continued to hum, and each night I went to the post office with a score of envelopes. Each was addressed to a preacher in some town where Eileen had applied for a job. By the time mother left for Eileen's graduation, father's file burst with answers to his inquiries. The only difficulty was, he admitted, that unfortunately it wasn't the preachers who picked new school ma'ams.

Father and I were to attend Eileen's commencement, too, a week later than mother, while Fraser went to scout camp. On the train father found his opportunity to concentrate on me. He still believed, he said as we crossed Illinois and again after we left Chicago, that I would eventually decide to be a preacher. A lad with my environment and heir to a great theological library would jump to the top of the profession in a few years. And, frankly, it would be a great day for him when he sat in General Conference and helped elect his son a bishop.

I did not respond. There was nothing to say.

"Perhaps another year at home will help you decide," he said finally, deeply disappointed by my lack of enthusiasm.

I was frightened then and immediately resolved to escape another year at junior college if I had to run away from home to accomplish it.

As we approached Delaware, Ohio, father put on his most elegant morning coat and Ascot tie, complete to starched white facing on the vest and a star-sapphire stickpin. To his usual splendid attire he had that day added a silk hat, bought at Chicago enroute, and a gold-headed stick that had been in the attic since we left Fort Dodge. He was shined up as for a congressman's funeral. In the whole of Ohio that day there was no man to match him in elegance.

Even Eileen was overawed as we descended from the train. She had brought mother and five sorority sisters to meet us.

"Delighted," father beamed, tucking his arms around a couple of girls as though he was the rich uncle who had financed their education.

At breakfast in Eileen's dormitory, Monett Hall, he was a sensation. Wit poured forth so uproariously, so entrancingly, that two of the girls volunteered to go down to Gray's Chapel an hour before the exercises to save the family three good seats.

And when, in the chapel, the academic procession started, father almost stole the show. Certain professors with whom he had been a political accomplice and crony at church General Conferences paused to shake hands with him, and the bishop who was to make the principal address nodded to father from the stage. To all father beamed, until the girl sitting next to Eileen hurriedly whispered, "Who's that big handsome guy in the aisle seat? Part of the endowment?"

"He's my father," Eileen whispered proudly.

After the ceremony Eileen approached him with a matter that she had withheld until the last minute.

"Father," she said, "the rule is that a diploma isn't issued unless the seniors pay up all charge accounts at stores. I've a couple of little ones that my budget couldn't quite meet."

"Fine, fine," father expanded, jubilant that his daughter had just graduated from what he considered Methodism's best school, "let's take care of them."

What happened then was an eye opener to me. Father was led into a drugstore where, without quibble, he paid for two months of chocolate malted milks. At the jeweler's he nobly settled for costume jewelry and bric-a-brac, which at any other time he would have condemned as extravagant nonsense. Finally, at a department store, he was presented with a bill for hat, a bag, and a pair of shoes.

"Graduation costume," Eileen whispered. He whipped out his pen, wrote a check for ten dollars more than the amount, and gave the change to mother.

On the street outside, Eddie was waiting. I had wondered whether he'd show up and, if so, what father might do.

But after paying all these bills, father evidently could survive anything.

"Hello, Eddie," he said, pulling the gray glove from his right hand.

"Howdy, Doc," Eddie replied, his eyes bulging a little at father's elegance.

Before this reconciliation had opportunity to be ruined by further conversation, mother began to talk rapidly. Eddie had taken her over Ohio in his car pointing out landmarks, she told father, and to Marion for a look at the new Warren Harding Shrine and to Columbus for the dress she was wearing.

"That's fine," father said, and as we walked back to Monett Hall Eddie and father had a friendly visit. Eddie seemed to me a little too casual to win father's friendship, and sure enough, when we reached the door father indicated that Eddie had come far enough. Again he held out his hand.

"I apologize for my conduct when you visited us in Riverton," he said. "It was not a Christian thing to do."

Mother, Eileen, and Eddie all fell silent on that one. Eddie recovered first.

"Good luck to you," he said, and withdrew.

"He's a fine boy, Eileen," father said then, "but he's not the type for you." Father had forgiven, but he was not prepared to forget.

"No," Eileen admitted, "he's not. But he's an all-right guy, just the same."

We were scarcely home from Ohio when the telephone rang. A member of father's Denver church had come in from Chicago and was stopping over until evening for a visit with his former pastor.

He was principal of one of the Denver high schools. As soon as he discovered that Eileen sought a teaching job, he inquired about her education credits. Oddly enough, he also was a graduate of Ohio Wesleyan. Immediately he became interested in the possibility of Eileen's entering the Denver school system, and offered to sponsor her. This was, of course, a dream coming true for Eileen, who preferred Denver to any city in the world.

Father had another name for it.

"It's the hand of Providence," he said after the guest had departed. "He comes in here unannounced, on the merest whim, after we haven't seen each other for five years. He's an educator, an Ohio Wesleyan graduate, and here's Eileen, dreaming of Denver. Nothing could be a better manifestation of the hand of God. We won't send out another application."

During the next fortnight a few tentative offers trickled in, but they were uninteresting. One was from a rural school at $744 a year, another a small town at $1,050, provided Eileen would guarantee to oversee a school club, help with the Girl Reserves, and sing in the Episcopal choir. Several others stated flatly that she would be required to teach in the school-board chairman's Sunday school. One secondary school had an opening for someone who could teach home economics, interpretative dancing, and bookkeeping. Another needed a freshman and sophomore English teacher of sufficient versatility to conduct courses in musical appreciation and manual training, put on two plays and an operetta, and sponsor a zoology club. This teacher must also guarantee to be active in community life and spend only two week ends out of town during each semester and, it was hinted, the principal's wife ran a boarding house where the teachers "always lived."

"I know just what kind of food and beds she's got, too," father commented.

Then came a genuine offer, from Ollie, Wyo. The salary was excellent, $1,600. Back father went to his correspondence with the preachers.

"We have to pay a lot of money out here," he read aloud to Eileen, "because men outnumber the women eight to one in these parts, and it's hard to persuade a teacher to stay more than a year. When school's out some rich rancher helps the schoolma'am lock the door, after which they go into town to get married."

Eileen was for accepting immediately, but father cautioned against haste.

"You are forgetting Denver," he said. "That's your best opportunity. Give it a little time."

She and father stalled for nearly a month, while Ollie became more and more insistent by letter and finally sent a telegram demanding immediate answer. Fortunately, it arrived on a Saturday morning.

"We mustn't encourage anyone to make a decision on the Sabbath," father said. "We won't answer until Monday. By then we should hear from Denver."

But no word came from Denver in the Monday-morning mail. Father paced the floor, the telegram from Ollie in his hand. About noon he telephoned his friend in Denver. A few minutes later he summoned Eileen.

"What's holding it up is your credits," he said. "You've the right credentials to teach in the grades but not in high school. Would you be willing to teach fourth graders?"

"Sure," said Eileen.

"Then hop on the train this afternoon and get out there. They want you for a personal interview."

Such a bustle and renovating of dresses as went on then. The gay clothes Eileen had worn to college needed toning down for the Denver school board. Mother was too busy to get lunch. By three o'clock Eileen was ready, and at 3:17 she was on the train.

As soon as she had gone, father sent a telegram to Ollie: "Miss Spence absent few days will reply later. Please wait."

But Eileen returned without the job. She had been interviewed by a half dozen persons separately and by a group. The matter was under consideration.

"It will go through," father repeated every day that no further report came. His friend was to telephone the news, good or bad.

Again father and Eileen stalled Ollie, this time on a technicality. There had been so many collateral considerations involved in other jobs, they wrote Ollie, that they could not believe that Ollie's bid to instruct in English and history without even organizing a May fête was true. It would take three days for this letter to reach Ollie, and three days for a reply to be received. But Ollie jumped the gun.

"No strings," the school board replied by telegraph. "We hire teachers to teach. Reply immediately."

"That's a fine kettle of fish," father fussed. "What can we do now?"

He was still thinking about it twenty-four hours later, when the call came from Denver. Eileen had been accepted.

Father took us all to dinner that night at the Hotel Riverton. Not until we had returned home did he remember the unanswered telegram from Ollie, Wyo. He recalled also that the daughter of one of his members needed a teaching position. By telephone he verified that she was at liberty and willing. Then he wired a night letter:

DAUGHTER ACCEPTED DENVER POSITION BUT HAVE FINE CHRISTIAN GIRL HERE BEAUTIFUL CAPABLE EDUCATED UNIVERSITY IOWA MAJOR ENGLISH MINORS SOCIOLOGY HISTORY WHO WELL QUALIFIED AND AVAILABLE APPLICATION ENROUTE.

"Ollie's just the place for Sally," he laughed heartily. "She's never had a beau in her life."

Sally went, and married a rancher at the end of the year.

"You see," father remarked to mother when he heard of the wedding, "it was the hand of Providence, all right. You certainly wouldn't want your daughter married to a cowman out in the wilds of Wyoming."

Eileen went to Denver. Once more the entire family escorted her to the train, on the afternoon of Labor Day. It was the first year in sixteen that father had declined an invitation to make a Labor Day address.

The train pulled out. Father shoved mother, Fraser,

and me unceremoniously into the car and raced to a grade crossing a quarter mile away. As Eileen passed, we waved.

But when the last coach had disappeared and father stepped on the throttle to take us home, his mind jumped to the next problem on his list.

"Son," he said, turning toward me, "I've neglected you lately. Now that Eileen is gone, we'll think about your future."

I recognized this as the opening speech in an argument persuading me to remain a second year at junior college. I was ready.

"Never mind," I answered, "I'm all set."

He was still being jovial.

"Are you? Tell me about it."

"I've enrolled at Iowa, my high school credits have been accepted, and I'm entering the School of Journalism as a sophomore. I'll have to take freshman and sophomore English at the same time, but they're allowing that. I leave a week from Monday."

"I can't send you away this year," he said. "I'm sorry, but it's financially impossible. And I think another year here is just what you need."

"It isn't," I replied, "and I don't need help. I have money enough for two years, and then we'll see. Maybe I won't need help at all."

"You have it all figured out, haven't you?" he remarked, wincing.

"Yes, sir," I said, and he made no reply.

CHAPTER TWENTY-FOUR

WITH high expectations I set out for the University of Iowa, where college life could do so much to prepare me for the life of a newspaperman. After eighteen years of tempering in the ecclesiastical fire, I wanted to try my steel in a profession where men were permitted to see life as it is rather than as it should be.

Charlie Romwell, son of the local Coca-Cola distributor, went with me. His family had moved to Riverton that summer, and I did not know him well. But every other boy entering Iowa expected to move directly into a fraternity, so Charlie and I teamed.

Charlie was an open-faced devil who had only to look at a girl to know whether he could safely make her acquaintance. Some higher instinct told him when feminine protests were simulated or genuine. During the two-hour ride from Riverton to Iowa City he flushed the train for potential conquests, and by the time we reached our destination he had three telephone numbers and a date for that evening.

"Why didn't you fix me up too?" I inquired as the last of his lovelies departed in a taxicab. Charlie busied himself with his luggage.

"I don't think you'd like 'em," he answered.

Thus, before I was even on the campus, the preacher's-son barrier was up.

Charlie had rented a room for us on a trip to Iowa City the previous week. We gave the address to a taxi driver and our trunks to a drayman and set out along a broad maple-lined street that marked the eastern boundary of the campus.

To the right was the shabby residential section of any town of 15,000 population, to the left the county courthouse. But after two blocks there was a sudden change. On the west, in a great park, shining out from a frame of oaks, emerged a stately building of ancient gray stone, fingered with ivy and capped by a gentle golden dome. This was the university administrative office, onetime capitol of Iowa.

Situated on a hilltop, Old Capitol lifted its golden head above two nestling buildings as though protecting them and looked out across the slope of a green-swarded hill to a river and beyond to gothic spires a mile to the west. All this was campus.

A few figures strolled the walks that ran from the four corners of the park to Old Capitol, and they were in keeping with the scholarly tone: a black-bearded professor with a walking stick, two girls in bright sweaters and sports shoes, a flat-heeled woman carrying many books, three college men in well-cut checkered coats and snap-brim hats.

"That's something, isn't it!" I exclaimed as we drove by.

But Charlie was noticing something else.

"Sorority row begins here," he said, pointing to an imposing Georgian mansion. "The sorority houses run up this street for six blocks. Then the prexy's home overlooks the river, and then the fraternities start."

The houses were huge and magnificent, their porches swarming with girls.

"They're rushing, all right," Charlie said.

That brought up a problem of our own. Both Charlie and I had cards in our pockets introducing us to fraternities. The system at Iowa was for scouts to make dates with prospects during the summer and pass the hopefuls through the house in a lunch, dinner, and evening parade during registration week at school. Sometime during six days of fraternity and sorority parties, students took time out to interview professors and to make out their study schedules. By the time classes began both fraternity and sorority membership drives had ended. It was important, therefore, to get a good start.

I had given more thought to fraternities than had Charlie, and from the long range of Riverton I had decided to be Phi Psi or nothing.

The reason for this decision was simple. I had only one real ambition, to be the editor of the *Daily Iowan*. If I could land that $75-a-month job during my senior year, I would not need money from father, and I would prove to every newspaper in the state that I was a reporter worth hiring. The editor of the *Iowan* always found employment after his graduation. To become editor more than talent was required. One had also to be a deft politician. I reasoned that a campus record, plus strong political connections, would ensure the fulfillment of my ambition. Phi Psi appeared to be the most potent political voice. But, though I had engagements with twelve of the thirty-six fraternities, I had none with the club of my choice.

And the rooming house Charlie had selected was not one that would attract the aristocrat of fraternities to my doorstep. It was a three-story one-time-white frame structure, as dilapidated as a Methodist parsonage, on North Dubuque Street fronting Fraternity Row. To the north, on a bluff above the river, reared the fraternity palaces.

Our room was the worst in the house. A postgraduate zoology student and his fat wife occupied the ground floor and ran the establishment. The second story housed a quartet of double-occupancy student rooms, and the third floor, reached by a narrow, unlighted stairway, contained a renovated attic with two dormer windows. This was to be our home. Charlie had not been able to find better for the $15 a month we had decided to pay.

"How do you like it?" he asked, settling his valise on one of the two iron cots and depositing his coat on one of two identical square desks.

"We are being robbed," I said.

"Rooms on the floor below are $30 a month. Think they're worth the difference?"

"No."

"Good. They're taken anyway."

Charlie consulted his notebook to discover which fraternity was about to call for him.

"I'll meet 'em on the porch, I think," he said and went downstairs.

Through the dormer window I could see two battered Fords in the yard. Beyond the trees a block away were the white pillars of the president's home. And to the north that imposing succession of luxurious fra-

ternity houses. What, I thought, did college men need
with such splendor?

Our obese landlady, Mrs. Weems, dragged her 250
pounds to our penthouse and bowed a cot with her
weight.

"Everything all right?"

"Yes, I guess," I said.

"You didn't bring no sweets with you, did you? Cake
or anything?"

"No, I didn't," I answered, still looking out the window.

"Well," she said, "you could have saved me a trip
up here, if I'd known. Maybe you'll get some in the mail
tomorrow."

She creaked her way downstairs, and I followed. My
first fraternity date was not until dinnertime. By then
I could complete my enrollment in a couple of courses.

But I did not get to the English building. Eight
blocks down the street, within sight of Old Capitol and
the liberal arts offices, I saw a ramshackle red-brick
structure with a spiral frontal tower. Outside was a
bulletin board, on which was printed: *Daily Iowan.*

I went inside. Evidently this structure at one time
had been a church, for the main room was long and
high ceilinged. Newspaper racks hemmed an aisle, behind which was, as at the *Courier,* the city room. From
an adjacent cubbyhole came the unmistakable thump of
a teletype.

Slipping my fingers under the gate, I released the
catch that every newspaper plant has to keep out in-
truders. I was reading the AP report when a figure
joined me.

"Anything going on?"

It was the old shoptalk greeting, and I responded to it.

"Everything quiet," I said. "What's new with you?"

The one who had joined me was the editor, Harry Boyd. He had been publishing the paper singlehanded during vacation and must continue to do so until classes began. Then he would have plenty of help. Meanwhile he was having a difficult time.

"What do you want done?" I asked, sliding onto the rim of the copy desk.

"You can write heads?" he asked, hopefully.

"Try me," I responded.

Two hours later, when I left for my first fraternity date, the market page and small stuff for half the inside of the paper were in the composing room. And I had a friend. Harry knew that I was enrolling in journalism and that my newspaper experience was considerable. A week later he appointed me city editor, a post usually given to a third-year student.

As I began to visit fraternities, I noticed that the glee of pledging a man under Phi Psi's nose was hilarious, the sorrow of losing one to Sig Alph assuaged by the comment, "Well, anyway Phi Psi didn't get him." Phi Psi became more than ever my goal.

But on the third day, when two groups were beginning to put on embarrassing pressure, I was as far away from Phi Psi as ever. Then, as I emerged from the Beta Theta Pi house, I bumped into Louise's brother.

"Hello," he said, "you being rushed Beta?"

"I suppose," I answered indifferently.

"Is that so. Well, good luck."

Ernie moved on and then, for politeness, called back over his shoulder, "How about dropping around to the house (Phi Psi) for dinner?"

His manner was strictly that of a landlord inviting a tenant in to see the new Doberman pinschers.

"I'd like to," I said, "but I have a date at Sig Alph."

"Oh." There was a bit more interest. "They rushing you, too? Well—come around after dinner."

"Can't. I have a date with Phi Delt."

"Is that so?" He came back up the street. "What dates have you got free? Let me see your card."

I produced the appointment book dotted with the names of Phi Psi's leading rivals.

"Not bad," he admitted. "How come you haven't any Phi Psi dates?"

"I got enough," I said.

"You sure have, but you haven't got Phi Psi."

He filled in Thursday lunch, Friday lunch, and Friday evening. That was too late in the week to do much good. Everybody who could possibly pay his bills in cash was buttoned before Friday. But Phi Psi prided itself in taking its own time. The cream of the crop, they boasted, would wait for them. And they had no financial worries anyway.

Phi Psi was the oldest fraternity on the Iowa campus. The second generation was coming along in such numbers that the problem was to find housing. Phi Psi spent the first half of rush week eliminating legacies, then got down to the serious work of maintaining an illustrious house. By that time only the most talented freshmen, spiked during the summer, could be pledged, for the house was full.

At Thursday's lunch Ernie was so condescending that I knew I didn't have a chance. The active chapter, mustering every letterman in his sweater and every campus politician in his honorary keys, crowded around the all-state quarterback from Oelwein, the state champion half miler from Laurens, the boy orator from Waterloo.

Ernie and I went down to lunch unaccompanied. During the meal a button was hung on the quarterback, and a song honored the occasion. Across the table the rushing captain decided to let the boy orator go. He had a flashy car, but Phi Psi didn't need it.

The athletes went upstairs arm in arm with the half miler and invited him to inspect the dormitories. This was a signal to the active chapter that if anyone had any objections he was to speak them now, as they were going to work on the prospect in the quiet of an upstairs chamber.

From the main hall I watched the trackman climb the stairs, then heard the telephone ring. The president answered, emerged from the phone booth and bemoaned to Ernie, "What do you think? Roy Peters from Riceville just pledged A.T.O."

"But we had him sewed," Ernie replied. "He has our button in his pocket."

"Yeah, they're sending it back."

The chapter was upset. Peters was the best piano player among the new crop and the son of a high state official. I had met him four times in my own travels from house to house, and every fraternity had made him feel important.

Ernie had no further interest in me. "Well, it's nice to have seen you," he said, and I knew what that meant. There was no use my keeping two dates with Phi Psi on Friday. They had to concentrate now on getting even with Buzz Kennedy, A.T.O.'s rushing chairman.

My appointment for that evening was at A.T.O., Phi Psi's next-door neighbor. Curious about the fraternity that had taken away a Phi Psi cinch, I dropped in at mealtime with pleasant anticipation. There was no doubt that I could pledge A.T.O. It didn't have anybody in journalism. The debaters, the orators, the actors, and the football center crowded me into a leather lounge, sat with me during dinner, invited me to see the house. I didn't want to go upstairs. I'd been through one of those ordeals at Beta.

But I went. From room to room we wandered, led by the ultrasmooth Buzz Kennedy. Then by lifting his brow Buzz scattered the small fry, and I was ushered into a dormitory room that housed two men, though scarcely big enough for one.

I sat down on a bed, flanked port and starboard by debaters and faced by Buzz, the football center with his gleaming old-gold "I" sweater, and the business manager of the yearbook, who sat on the opposite bed.

Buzz went to work, abetted by the others. He extolled the glories of Alpha Tau Omega. Albums displaying A.T.O.'s campus achievements were thumbed across my knees. Then came facts and figures of the house financial budget and the money obligations of members. The two debaters, having drawn closely to

explain the scrapbook, did not withdraw. They were
sitting so tightly against me that I could not even reach
into my hip pocket for a handkerchief to wipe my per-
spiring brow. The room was growing hotter and hotter.
The window remained closed, despite the fact that the
day had been one of Iowa's hottest and most humid.

Buzz Kennedy leaned forward.

"Now you know all about us, how about it?"

He took a pledge button from his pocket and displayed it temptingly. His eyes casually measured the distance to my left lapel, underneath which he knew I was a soaking, steaming mass of flesh. The air was suffocatingly close now. The stale fumes of almost endless cigarettes cloyed my nasal passages with burning irritations. The idea clearly was that the sooner I put on the button, the sooner we'd be outside in the fresh air.

"I'd like to think it over," I said.

The tension relaxed in exasperated sighs.

"Why think it over? Either you want to or you don't. Tomorrow won't make any difference."

"But it might."

"How could it? Look. The right fraternity for you is the one in which you'll be most congenial. We have just the kind of men you can like, as man to man. Isn't that true?"

"Y-yes."

"Then what more do you want?"

"I have some other dates I'd like to keep."

"We'll cancel them for you. That's the accepted thing, you know."

I thought of Buzz Kennedy's call to Phi Psi about Roy Peters.

"I know that," I replied, "but—"

"See here, Hartz," the football center came in, "I know this is a hard decision to make. Probably the hardest and most important of your entire college career—maybe of your life. You're a smart boy; you don't want to muff it."

"Sure," Buzz took up the play, "of course he's smart. That's why we want him. And"—turning back to me—

[313]

"that's why you'd be happy in A.T.O. We don't pledge a man, Spence, just because we think he'd make the track team. He's got to have something else. Get what I mean? You know—he's got to be a good fellow too because, after all, we're living together here. It's a family. You don't invite just *anyone* into your family."

"I appreciate that," I said, sweating more than ever.

"Then what's holding you up?"

"Well—I don't know. I think I'd better keep those other dates."

Again the exasperated sigh.

"You can go all over the campus," Buzz went on, wiping his blond, short-cropped hair, "and when you're all done, what have you seen? Nobody like A.T.O. Does it occur to you that when you've been the rounds, we might not be interested in you any longer?"

"I know, but—"

"But what, man!" Kennedy was getting sore.

"I know what it is," said the footballer. "You've got something on your mind, haven't you, Spence?"

"To be honest, yes."

"What is it? Maybe we can help you solve it."

"No," I answered sadly, "you couldn't do anything about this."

"Why not?" Kennedy asked enthusiastically. "After all, we want you to get a good start in college. That's even more important than getting a pledge, isn't it, fellows? What can we do for you?"

"Nothing."

"Is it some other house?" the footballer asked. He was a big fellow, full of sympathy, his eyes friendly and encouraging.

"Yes," I admitted huskily.

"Which one?"

They hung on the question, parachutists picking a landing spot.

Now what was I to do? Admit I wanted Phi Psi or nothing, when Phi Psi didn't want me? I decided to be honest.

"Phi Psi," I said.

They all nodded.

"A swell house, and don't think it isn't," the footballer answered. He had his hand tightly on Kennedy's knee, signaling the rushing chairman not to interrupt. "I don't mind saying that it's a tough decision to make. Of course, we think A.T.O. is better. That's what a boy from Riceville thought, too. He came in here this noon with a Phi Psi button in his pocket, but he pledged us instead. I think he made a wise choice."

Kennedy stared at me, perspiration running down his face too. He was ready to quit.

"I want Phi Psi or nothing," I said.

The debaters inched away. The footballer crushed his cigarette under his heel.

"Okay," said Buzz Kennedy quietly, and he reached around to a desk and picked up a telephone.

I thought the interview was ended and arose. But Kennedy's words stopped me with a horrible chill.

"Phi Psi house?" he was asking. "Buzz Kennedy at A.T.O. There's a boy here who says it's Phi Psi or nothing. Want him? Name of Spence—from Riverton."

A long silence. I wanted to run; it would soon be over now.

"Okay," Kennedy said. "I'll meet you at the door."

Like jailors in charge of a prisoner they marched me downstairs. Fresh blasts of air almost dizzied me. What would Phi Psi say to me now?

There in the door stood Phi Psi's rushing chairman, Olympic high-hurdles champion Bab Cuhel, a gleeful smile on his face. But he addressed Buzz Kennedy, not me.

"I hate to do this, Buzz," he said.

"I'm sure you do."

"Thanks for helping us out."

Cuhel turned to me and ostentatiously inserted the pledge button of Phi Psi in my coat lapel on A.T.O.'s front porch.

"Congratulations," he said.

Phi Psi was even with A.T.O.

CHAPTER TWENTY-FIVE

I RETURNED to my room with a blissful glow.

"Well, Charlie," I exclaimed enthusiastically to my roommate, "I made it!"

"Made what?" He was gnawing his fountain pen over a letter to his mother.

"Phi Psi."

"That's swell," he said, turning so that I could see the Delta Upsilon button on his own coat.

"Congratulations to you, too," I said.

"They didn't like it much that I can't live in the house this semester."

"They didn't like it at Phi Psi either," I admitted.

"You're taking meals there though?"

"Of course."

"So'm I, at D.U. We'll move out of here in January."

With that we settled down to our letters. We both had a lot to write. My typewriter thundered on the flimsy desk. Once or twice Charlie looked over at me as though to protest against the clatter, but I didn't take the hint. Then from below came a bellow.

"Cut out that damn noise."

And up the stairs, a beer bottle in his hand, swayed a tailor-clad young man with black hair and black eyes.

"What the hell kind of a coffee grinder you got up here?"

He stared belligerently at Charlie, then at me.

"Jeez, more freshmen. When will people get wise to themselves?"

He sat on my bed, swigged his bottle, and passed it over to me. I looked at it, handed it to Charlie.

"You don't drink?" Aghast, as though I was a snake, the newcomer edged toward the door.

"No, thanks," I said. "But enjoy yourself."

"Enjoy yourself!" the drunk repeated. "What kind of talk is that? And from a freshman too. What else we come to college for 'cept to enjoy ourselves? You didn't come to study, did you?"

He seized the bottle from Charlie and menaced me with it.

"Did you?"

"I don't know," I answered.

"You don't know." He pulled again at his comfort. "College freshman. Doesn't know why he came. Typical of a degenerate civilization."

"I'm a sophomore," I said.

Our guest sat down again.

"Can't be," he stated emphatically. "Nobody but freshmen don't drink."

Again he offered the bottle, and turned to Charlie when again I refused.

"I suppose you're a junior," he said sarcastically.

"Sure," Charlie humored him. The drunk was a big fellow.

"Le's see, le's see you drink. I'll tell you whether you're a junior, same as me."

Charlie, who had never touched a drop in his life, reached for the bottle, drew a deep breath, and emptied half its contents down his throat.

"Yep, junior all right. My name's Peeler. What's yours?"

"Romwell," said Charlie.

"Good. Romwell. Peeler. Juniors. Let's get out of this disgusting company."

They went below. But I didn't care. I was a Phi Psi.

Classes began, and I was loaded with English courses, making up the lack of freshman English as well as keeping up with other sophomores. And I had elected three hours of description and narration. For a companion in the latter course I had Clem Ogilvie, a Phi Psi first-string football player. He was a senior and had flunked this elective the previous year. His father had insisted on his retaking the course for discipline.

But my major interest was the *Daily Iowan.* I had to work hard to keep up with other sophomores, who had become acclimated to the university while I had wasted a year in junior college. I was city editor because of my experience on the *Courier,* and the task required that I familiarize myself with the town and university in a short time. In liberal arts I was a year behind my age group, too, and was required to attend freshman-orientation lectures, study public speaking, and participate in other time-wasting neophite activities, while carrying a full sophomore course. The routine left no time for relaxation.

I was also a member of the university band. I signed for band because it paid $50 a year and because it opened a free door to all athletic events. I was second flute in the concert hall and piccolo player on parade except at football games, where there was no place in formation for a piccolo player. Then I ran half the length of the field to support the bass drum. Band practice was three afternoons a week from four-thirty to five-thirty. The *Iowan* swallowed my day from my last class until nearly seven, and many nights until much later. Saturday until midnight I was at the *Iowan*. On Sunday I slept and studied.

Such a schedule did not appeal to Phi Psi. As a pledge, I had certain disciplinary obligations. Phi Psi was not so interested in my campus activities as in making me a true Phi Psi. Each night at dinner I was supposed to stand on my chair to recite certain facts, such as the names of all Phi Psi chapters, or to sing any of a score of fraternity songs. Two hours a day I was expected to answer telephone and doorbell, entertain company, shovel ashes, and mow lawns. And I was required to spend all my idle moments in the house, where I could watch real Phi Psi men in action and profit by the observations.

But I was never around, except that I made a point of attending pledge meeting on Monday night, when we lined up before the active chapter for a detailed accounting of our transgressions during the previous week. I became increasingly unpopular with both the active chapter and the pledges because of my consistent absence.

Halfway through the football season Phi Psi caught up with me. Clem Ogilvie, the football player in my description and narration class, was placed on the dean's list in that subject. He had been unable to write an 800-word description in which the only verbs were those of action. Unless this deficiency and a 1,200-word character sketch were turned in before Friday, he could not play in Saturday's football game against Indiana.

About ten o'clock one night Clem turned to the three law students who were helping him with his composition and growled, "That pledge Spence gets an A on everything he turns in. Where the hell is he?"

A delegation called on me at the *Iowan* and ordered me to the house as soon as I finished my work. I arrived at midnight, and immediately Clem and I sat down to an 800-word action-verb essay. We decided to describe a football game. By half past three we had exhausted Roget's *Thesaurus,* and the paper was written. Clem went to bed, leaving me to type his masterpiece.

The next evening I had dinner at the house, and Clem caught me on the way out.

"You've got another job, son," he said.

"I can't do it tonight, Clem," I answered. "I have two pieces to write myself."

"That's just too bad," he replied.

We set to work, this time on a character sketch of football coach Bert Ingwersen. After a few lines Clem grew restless.

"I'll be back in a minute," he said. For a long time I heard him playing bridge downstairs, and at eleven o'clock he went to bed. I worked on.

Had the theme been mine, I could have completed it in half the time. But I had to make the writing sound

like that of a football player who had flunked the course
once and was likely to do so again. I must accomplish
something midway between acceptability and failure.

Both essays were accepted, and on Saturday Clem
played football. During the next four weeks I wrote all
of Clem's work, but as soon as the football season ended
I refused to assist him any longer.

"If you were trying," I said, "I'd be glad to help.
But when you play bridge and then go to bed without

looking at what's been written, my responsibility and the football season end simultaneously."

Clem beat me with a barrel stave for my impudence, but he could not insist on my ghosting him through the entire course. He talked, though, and my unpopularity grew.

At the *Iowan* I learned that my fraternity was not mighty on the campus. It had no political consciousness. What I had mistaken for power was prestige, an entirely different thing. Phi Psi belonged to the Panhellenic clique, composed of the nine oldest fraternities on the campus. Panhellenic men dated only in the seven so-called "best" sororities, played bridge only with Panhellenic comrades, and were socially rather than politically active. Political control rested in a shrewd organization of Delta Upsilon, Phi Gamma Delta, and the university dormitories across the river from Fraternity Row, commonly called "The West Side."

Important journalism jobs were controlled by the Student Board of Publications, composed of three professors and four students. Campus members were elected for three-year terms. One holdover that year was a Panhellenic, and I knew that when I applied for the editorship, two years hence, I could count on him. Another holdover was the Delta Upsilon's political strategist, a law student named James Carroll. The other two student chairs on the board were up for election. If I was to satisfy my ambitions, it was important that Panhellenic elect one. That would leave the balance of power to the professors, of whom I was not afraid. They did not dabble in political shenanigans.

In all Panhel I could not persuade one man to run

for office. Even Phi Psi would not put up a candidate or permit me to post my own name.

"Pledges stay out of the limelight," they told me, "and if you were elected, it would be bad taste to vote for yourself for editor when the time comes."

I became a candidate anyway, campaigned among the freshmen and sophomores in my huge English classes, whittled at the school of journalism, at members of the band and their friends, at all the girls who dated Phi Psi men. I sent notes to all Panhel chapters, exhorting them to vote.

By election day I had quite a following and plastered the campus with handbills. The West Side had taken for granted that Panhel would give them no opposition and had not organized. At the last minute, in fear of defeat, they rushed their men to the polls.

I lost by eight votes. In my own house, of thirty-six men, only four had voted. I had been beaten by my own fraternity.

At pledge meeting the following Monday night I stepped from the line to tell the active chapter what I thought of their lack of loyalty. They were not impressed.

"Before you expect any support from us," the president said, "you'd better learn to cooperate, yourself. You're never around the house. You shirk all your duties. You are just using this house as a boarding club three nights a week, and that's all. Besides, we told you not to run in the first place. Pledges don't step out of line to tell their betters how to behave."

I was paddled after the meeting. This was part of a game called "ringing the bell," in which six freshmen bent to the waist and lined up head to tail. A bell was placed around the neck of the boy foremost in line. A stout oak paddle was swung by an upper classman on the end man. The object was to strike so hard that the vibrations would carry through the entire line and ring the bell.

Naturally, I was end man. Several of the active chapter tried their skill before Clem Ogilvie succeeded.

I arose from the game with a red face.

"How did you like it?" Ogilvie asked.

"All right," I answered.

"It may be all right with you, but it isn't with me," Ogilvie went on. "I don't like your attitude."

I said nothing.

"Sullen, are you? Point."

I assumed the angle, and he swung again.

"How's that?"

"Very good."

Ogilvie pointed me again, struck hard.

"When you speak to me, call me 'sir,'" he said.

"Yes, sir."

"You're a cocky guy," he went on, "but you've got nothing to be cocky about. Don't forget how you got into Phi Psi. It wasn't because anybody wanted you."

He flung down the paddle and left the room.

After that I avoided pledge meetings. I buried myself in work. Studies, the *Iowan*, the band, anything to escape Phi Psi. The orchestra needed an extra flute for a concert. I volunteered. The Memorial Union needed captains to help raise funds among the students to pay off the mortgage. I enrolled. The fencing team sought sparring partners. I was one of them. I even began to play tennis.

And all over the campus I made friends, except in my own house.

Despite my many activities I could not avoid probation week. As soon as first-semester grades were posted, I said good-by to Charlie Romwell and moved from the rooming house to Phi Psi's second floor, where I shared a room with Bab Cuhel, the hurdler, and slept in the upper half of a double-deck bunk on a sleeping porch.

Probation at Phi Psi was vigorous. Late one night pistol shots, raucous cowbells, and war whoops woke the freshmen. The sleeping porch seethed with maniacal activity.

"Hump yourself! On your feet! Get going!"

We moved, fourteen of us in bare feet and pajamas, down the darkened hall to the stairs, spurred on by actives who swiped at us with paddles and barrel staves. Downstairs we ran a steeplechase across chairs, under a rug, into the basement and back upstairs again, to pause breathless in the front hall. The ordeal of probation had started.

For a week we were kept on the go. Sleep was prohibited, conversation outlawed. Every moment we were not in class we were in the house whitewashing walls, scrubbing floors, polishing furniture, redecorating the housemother's suite, and submitting to the pranks of the active chapter. One day we were stuffed with saltless oatmeal at all three meals, the next deprived of all nourishment except water. Violent beatings were the punishment for insubordination. But it was fun.

The suffering we pledges experienced drew us together. I began to understand the basketball player from Odeboldt, of whom I had been contemptuous—he was a mighty good man with a whitewash brush and through many nights kept the whole gang from breaking by his own display of dogged strength.

We helped each other with special chores. Monty Hakes, top scholar among the pledges and a long-distance runner, exerted no pressure when ordered to sandpaper the soles of my feet, and I reciprocated by feeding him sandwiches at the *Iowan* on a fast day. Joe Crookham, engineer and half-miler, tipped me off on the number of railroad ties between Iowa City and Coralville so that I sneaked three hours' sleep instead of counting them one night. In return, while Joe slept I wrote a poem for him on the shortcomings of our pledge class.

I began to see that such chastisement as I was getting I had deserved. No one in Phi Psi said so. They let me discover it for myself. Those long nights when I pushed a floor-waxing machine or carried out some other assignment were thoughtful hours. Now that I was living among the Phi Psis, I was beginning to appreciate them.

On the sixth night, when we were hard at work building a new ping-pong table, Clem Ogilvie entered the house with another football player, a Kappa Sig. They were plastered.

Ogilvie called me from the line and challenged his companion to a game of breaking barrel staves. The one who broke the least out of five staves across my posterior would pay the bootlegger.

"Point!" Clem ordered.

[327]

I did not move.

"Point!" He seized my neck, forcing me to bend. But as soon as he withdrew I straightened.

"I said 'Point!'" Clem shouted. "Are you deaf?"

"No," I whipped back, "but I'm not pointing."

"Why?"

"No drunk is hitting me, and nobody outside the house either."

Clem headed for me with a roar, but he did not reach me. Up behind me surged the other pledges. Lifting Clem and his friend bodily, they heaved them out the front door and returned to work.

Clem made no attempt then to reenter, but the pledge master, whose job was to maintain discipline, lined us up at attention.

"What's the big idea?" he asked.

No one spoke.

"Answer me." He looked at Joe Crookham.

"No drunk beats me," Crookham answered.

"Nobody was beating you."

"It could have been me."

"That's my business, not yours," the ringmaster retorted. "Twenty staves for every one of you. Point!"

A growl of dissension moved down the pledge line, and I heard it.

"Run," I shouted and dived at the pledge master. He went down, and the pledges rushed for the door, I following them. But Clem Ogilvie blocked the way. We ran toward the back door, but actives now were rushing down the stairs in answer to the pledge master's yell for help.

Trapped, we piled through windows onto the lawn

and up a fire escape into Ogilvie's room. Monty Hakes had acquired the pledge master's paddle. All of us had seized barrel staves.

We shoved Ogilvie's bureau across the door, piled his bed on top of it. The first head that appeared on the fire escape was a target for Ogilvie's heaviest textbook, thrown by Crookham.

Actives were now battering the door from its hinges, smashing the window glass. The state governor's son, aroused from legal studies, got in the way of an ink bottle hurled through the window, and that was our undoing. For Ned Turner was tough. He was up the fire escape in three strides, taking away the window sash as he smashed into the room. His fists kept us so busy that we did not see the door cave in, and in ten seconds more the fight was over. We pledges were down, our chins buried in the debris that cluttered the floor.

Our pajamas in tatters we were lined up downstairs. Crookham's lip was bleeding. Monty Hakes had an elegant shiner, and a trickle of blood rolled down my scalp, but we were grinning. The entire active chapter inspected us admiringly.

"Wow!" someone exclaimed. "What a class! Who started this?"

The pledge master pointed to me.

Silence greeted this. Then Ogilvie staggered in, complaining about his room. But the pledge master was ready for him.

"You won't need it, Clem," he said quietly, "you're moving out tomorrow. You'd better find a rooming house."

The pledges straightened immediately, and the pledge master noticed it.

"I think we'll end probation right now," he added, "while there's something left of the house. Any requests?"

We had been told that when probation ended, each pledge would have the opportunity to avenge himself on any active who in his opinion had abused him during the week. This meant he could swing a barrel stave on any man he chose. If he broke the stave, the active could not strike back. If the stave failed to splinter, the active could swing on the pledge until the stave broke.

Not one of us exercised his privilege. We had already expressed ourselves.

"Good," said the pledge master, pleased that none of us was nursing a grudge. "Class dismissed."

But he had a surprise coming to him. While the actives stood by cheering, we stripped the pledge master, carried him into a shower bath, and made him sing the chorus of the school song, *On Iowa,* before we let him go.

He emerged from the shower chattering but laughing.

"Whose idea was that?" he asked good-naturedly.

Joe Crookham pointed to me.

The pledge master looked me in the eye, man to man. "Nice going," he said. "You'll get on."

CHAPTER TWENTY-SIX

*T*HE PLEDGES celebrated their initiation with a party. We had Edam cheese and crackers and prohibition beer. But when one of the group suggested we adjourn to a roadhouse for sterner liquid, I excused myself.

"I've got to get back to the *Iowan*," I said. "See you later."

I wasn't the only one who didn't drink, but I was the only one who made an issue of it.

"Okay, Deacon," Joe Crookham said. "Have a good time."

I was inundated with work. All the duties I had acquired to avoid Phi Psi now commandeered the time I wanted to spend at the house. I was particularly busy at the *Iowan*, where I must establish a record no one could match when the editor was elected the following year. The annual spring band concert was approaching also, and there were flute passages that required extra practice.

And there was the Union drive. I had not known, when I consented to captain the journalism school team, that soliciting funds would require my attendance at half-a-dozen banquets. Four dreary evenings I sat in the sumptuous Memorial Union, listening to speakers beg for money. The Union was a campus-activity building where students received their mail, lounged between classes, sipped lemonade on a balcony overlooking the Iowa River, and on prom nights danced to a New York orchestra. Begun as a memorial to Iowa's soldiers of 1917-18, it had added wing after wing on promissory notes. Now the mortgages were coming due.

In past years students had been blackjacked into subscribing by appeals to their school spirit. But this plea had worn too thin. This year there was a new bait. We were exhorted to raise enough money to build a theater wing for the production of plays written by Iowa authors.

I liked that and set to work. My team was composed of journalism majors who had spent a summer vacation selling magazine subscriptions. With such experience it was easy to get student signatures on pledge cards.

My strategy was to arouse competition within my squad rather than against other teams. I put up a gold watch, which had been awarded to me as first prize in a high school essay contest, for high man in our contingent. But I became so enthusiastic over my own sales talk that I worked night and day for two weeks setting my team an example.

The result was that we raised more money than any team in the eight-year history of Union drives, and I was high individual scorer with $3,800.

My success was quite a story for the *Iowan,* particularly since I was unable to attend the victory banquet. I was down in bed from exhaustion. That, as the *Iowan* pointed out, was school spirit beyond the call of duty.

The university president wrote me a commendatory letter, and the Union board gave me a gold cup.

Phi Psi was impressed. It had not added a cup to its mantel that year, and the publicity was worth clipping for its scrapbook. The fraternity wished to pay me a tribute. The procedure, when Clem Ogilvie had scored a touchdown and Jack Hasson had pulled a basketball game from defeat with a well-timed shot, was for the brothers to retire by night to an acreage known as the North Forty with a case of near beer and a quart of alcohol.

That wouldn't work on me.

I was invited, and wanted very much to accept, but the parsonage dictated my refusal.

"Aw, come on," they said. "You don't really know a fellow until you get tight with him."

My observation told me this was true. The inseparable friendships in our house were drinking companionships. The great men were the drinkers. A man was not quite a comrade, no matter what his attainments, until he had been on a binge. Once he had come in well oiled late at night and the fraternity had greeted his bleary eyes the next noon at lunch with the raucous song of brotherhood, he was one of them. The difference was subtle, but it was there.

Only recently one of the bashful boys, who had been treated casually in the fraternity, had come in drunk. The next noon every face at the dining table beamed, and every throat burst out with song:

Here's to Herbie, tried and true,
He's a Phi Psi through and through.

[333]

So fill 'em up again, boys, celebrate the day
When we go to Heaven, he'll go the other way!
Drink! Drink! Drink!

There was another blood brother in the house.

My blood, however, had been strained through the white ribbon of the W.C.T.U. Drinking was a sin.

As school ended for the year, Phi Psi added another clipping to its large scrapbook. My picture had been in the paper again, this time playing flute obbligato for a coloratura soprano who sang at commencement.

There was some talk of putting me on the rushing committee, but it was overruled. I had been asked to edit the *Iowan* during rush week, while the editor took a vacation after working alone all summer. Unlike the students, the *Iowan* took no vacation since half its circulation was among townspeople.

I went home for the summer to a new town. The family had moved during April.

Father had remained in Riverton for six years. He had defeated the church boss, but the incessant wiles of Preston Thurston to recoup lost power had hurt father. His heart had begun to flutter, and his strength was dissipated.

Feeling himself a little old, father wanted to return once more to the North Iowa scene in which he had begun his ministry. As a young man, barnstorming the circuit churches of Wesley, Laketon, and Clarion, the *big* congregation had been Mason City.

Now he was pastor at Mason City. It was the completion of a cycle, the reward of a lifetime. Happily he could round out his career with six or eight soul-comforting years before retirement.

Mason City was dull for me after the excitement of the campus, and father's continued appeals for me to enter the ministry reemphasized my need to edit the *Iowan* during my senior year.

At the first excuse—the illness of the managing editor—I returned to Iowa City and in six weeks clinched the job of assistant managing editor for the autumn term. Since the editor and managing editor must be seniors, my appointment was to the top junior position available. It brought in $35 a month.

But money was not a problem now. I had found a gold mine. Experimenting in Mason City, I had picked up one of father's dinner-table stories, rewritten it luridly under a feminine pseudonym, and sent it to a confession magazine. Back bounced a check for $75 and a letter of encouragement from the editor. Twice a month thereafter I shipped off a story of unrequited love soothed by a strong Methodist moral, twice a month banked a check for $75.

In the band I was elevated to first chair, and I continued to play in the orchestra. I was appointed to several all-university party committees and became a contributing editor to the humor magazine, *Frivol*.

But I did not forget my first ambition: the *Daily Iowan,* nor would my fraternity let me forget, for the editor of the *Iowan* was always elected to A.F.I., the honor society of the twelve senior men who during their campus careers had "done most for the university." It was the top campus honor. Since A.F.I.'s organization in 1912, there had always been a Phi Psi member, an unbroken record no other fraternity could claim. An A.F.I. was no political prize. Membership was self-perpetuating, and diligence was exercised to prevent chicanery in the selections.

As winter melted into spring, I thought my record had assured me the editorship of the *Iowan*. The appointment would be announced late in the spring, and on the same day A.F.I. would name its selections. Phi Psi had no other eligible. I was their one chance.

As the day of the announcement approached, the house became excited.

"What's new?" they asked, clustering around when I returned from the office late at night. Burton Jerrell, himself formerly editor of *Frivol*, was particularly interested. He made sure that the Panhel representative on the Student Board of Publications not only would vote for me, but fight for me.

In the band too there was excitement. I had played with these eighty-five men in snow, sleet, rain, and heat and had rehearsed Tschaikowsky and Sousa with them three days a week for two years. I was excused from band practice to appear before the Publications Board.

The political line-up was clear. Two faculty members favored my appointment, as did the Panhel representative. Three students definitely were opposed, organized by James Carroll, political leader of the West Side; they favored the selection of Virgil Lewis, a member of Carroll's fraternity and the *Iowan's* capable campus editor.

The balance of power lay in a faculty member who could not be influenced. He was a crusty surgeon in the college of medicine, who sat on the board from duty, much to his annoyance.

Whoever sold himself to Dr. Rowlles would become the editor. This I believed I could do on my record.

There were other candidates, but my real competitor was Virgil Lewis. He too had been working two years for this big chance.

Burt Jerrell stood beside me as we waited.

"You got it in the bag, pal," he whispered. "Panhel and non-Panhel are evenly divided this time. No chance for tricks. You'll win on your record."

The meeting began at four o'clock, would end at six. The closing hour was mandatory, no matter how important the business, for Dr. Rowlles became impatient for his dinner at five-fifty-five and abruptly adjourned the proceedings. Everyone knew this; it was a journalism school joke.

The candidates lined up in alphabetical order. Lewis was the third man in. With him he took a carefully organized scrapbook illustrating his work on the *Iowan*. I had no exhibits, preferring to rely on the improvements that I had already suggested and those on which I was experimenting. I doubted the board wanted to read a lot of clippings.

But apparently it did. Lewis remained before the board for nearly an hour.

"That robber!" Burt Jerrell muttered. "He's stalling, so that you won't have much time."

When Lewis emerged, another non-Panhel entry went in, then another. Both had held insignificant jobs on the paper. At fifteen minutes to six, when there were still three applicants ahead of me, Burt and I caught on.

Every one of the hopeless candidates had a name with an initial in the alphabet later than *L* (for Lewis), but ahead of *S* (for Spence). Jim Carroll, Lewis's "manager" had rounded up every possible editorial aspirant, so that by the time I appeared to present my case, Dr. Rowlles would be ready to go home. I knew that I hadn't a chance.

Dr. Rowlles had his watch in hand as I entered, and when I began my speech, detailing what I had done, he interrupted.

"We've heard that from half a dozen others," he said. "What do you propose to do?"

Again I began to elaborate, again was cut off.

"We've heard all that, too," he interrupted me. "I think we're wasting time now. We've decided who the editor will be." He picked up his hat, and I walked out.

"It's no use, Burt," I said. "They're dealing from a cold deck in there."

"Nonsense," he consoled me, "they don't need to know what you've done, pal. It's written all over the *Iowan*."

He offered to drive me home in his car, but numbed by failure I didn't feel like meeting the boys. I wasn't even sure at that moment that I could think. We saw Dr. Rowlles leave the board room and rush away. The Panhel member emerged to confirm what we already knew. An A.F.I. representative sprinted down the journalism building steps to attend his own election.

Burt went to dinner. I walked through a spring rain

to a shack near the university power plant, where I ate a hamburger and tried to reorganize. Everything I had planned for two years was frustrated. My future in the newspaper business was threatened. Father would accept this failure as proof of my journalistic incompetence, renew his persuasion that I become a preacher.

I went back to the *Iowan*. At the editor's desk sat Virgil Lewis. He had his coat off.

"Congratulations," I said.

"Congratulations yourself," he replied.

"For what?"

"For A.F.I."

In a jump I was over the rail, scanning proof sheets, locating my name and the explanation that followed: "For unselfish work in raising funds for the Union, for two years of faithfulness to band and orchestra, minor athletic teams, and for important posts on two student publications, the *Daily Iowan* and *Frivol*."

The bass-horn player from the university band strode in at that moment and slapped me on the back.

"It's the millennium!" he chuckled. "A bandsman in A.F.I." He was merrily tight. "I been culling hell for you. Where you been? Come here."

We went into the men's room, where he produced a bottle of alcohol and three cold bottles of prohibition beer.

"A little drink, chum," he said. "Firs' time in hist'ry a bandsman made A.F.I. And to think it was the piccolo player."

He bit the cap off a beer bottle, filled the neck with alcohol, and beckoned. "C'mere."

When I did not respond, he asked, "Din' you ever drink this stuff?"

Miserably I admitted my inexperience. The parsonage and liquor didn't go together, I said.

"Then it's time you got out of the parsonage," he answered and took my hand. He placed my thumb over the bottle opening, turned hand and bottle upside down so that the alcohol blended with the beer.

"Now," he said, and I drank.

It was bitter, biting, hot.

"I hear you got counted out by the Student Board," he said. "Tha's tough. I hoped maybe you'd get it. I was going to hit you for the city editorship."

Again I drank, a longer pull this time.

After the second bottle, when we foraged the town for additional refreshment, I felt better. Cares were far away. The tuba player was a great fellow. We picked up another bandsman in front of a near-beer parlor and added him to our party. The drizzle changed to rain, driving us back to the *Iowan*. I produced a key to the *Frivol* office, which was in the same building, in a small room lined with storage shelves. There was not a chair in the room or a desk.

We sat on the floor until that became uncomfortable, then climbed on top of the files. The tuba player had discovered a guitar somewhere. We sang plaintive songs. Several times the door opened, and we were warned to keep quiet.

Finally I found myself in the hall of the Phi Psi house, giggling and talking to myself. The bright light hurt my eyes.

"Look," somebody shouted, "the Deacon has broken out!"

A half-dozen boys helped me upstairs. I began singing southern airs, believing myself still on the filing cabinet with the guitar.

"Boy! he's really stinking." This from Burt Jerrell. "You can't blame him, though."

He put me through an icy shower, guided me to bed.

Next day I did not waken until noon and appeared for lunch a minute late. As I walked in, Burt struck up a song:

> *Here's to Hartzie, tried and true,*
> *He's a Phi Psi through and through—*

Two weeks later, at the final meeting of the year, Phi Psi elected me its president.

CHAPTER TWENTY-SEVEN

*W*HEN my senior year began, I was not invited to work on the *Iowan*.

The new editor posted the list of his staff on the bulletin board, and when I saw that my name was not included I was disappointed. But after a few days I was thankful. I found that I had time for two difficult but very interesting lecture courses and for an experimental subject which that year was inaugurated. Instead of completing my requirements for a degree in journalism, I turned to electives that would give me a major in English and graduate me a Bachelor of Arts rather than a Bachelor of Science.

Three professors interested me. One was Nellie Aurner, who had turned my sophomore English from a routine into an adventure; another was Leigh Sowers, whose modern drama I had taken as a junior; and the third was Benjamin Franklin Shambaugh.

Mrs. Aurner's senior study was early English romance: Scottish, Irish, and Welsh folklore and literature. Mr. Sowers' great course was playwriting, in which he accepted only twelve students. Bennie Shambaugh was seeking students to serve as "guinea pigs" for what he called a campus course which, if it succeeded, would be offered to underclassmen the following year. Enrollment in all three was by personal application, and no one looking for a "pipe" went near them.

My grade average, however, was high—a straight A in my junior year, and the professors accepted me. Mr. Sowers even offered me the opportunity to be his "reader" in modern drama, which meant correcting examination papers for a stipend of $100. I accepted.

Senior lectures, I discovered, were at advantageous hours. No more racing across the river to an eight o'clock. No more bolting of lunch in time to walk eleven blocks to one-o'clock French. And since I was no longer with the *Iowan,* I could study in the evening, sleep eight hours, and walk downtown for a leisurely nine-o'clock appointment with Mrs. Aurner or Bennie Shambaugh.

There was still band practice from four-thirty to five-thirty, but even this could be absorbed at leisure. I studied in the library in the afternoon or strolled by the river or bought a girl a lemonade in Memorial Union or played bridge in the house, where now I was president. I had time to think and to play.

And I soon discovered that there was a lighter, but no less important, college course taught by the students themselves. It could have been listed in the catalogue under the title: "Getting along with people. Undergraduate instructors. Required laboratory work: formal dances, fraternity proms, sorority dance exchanges. Car parked on road behind Kappa Sigma house optional but recommended."

The fraternity presidency was absorbing too and gave me an idea. Somehow father must be impressed that I was not destined for the ministry. And since I was no longer majoring in journalism, I decided to prove by harmonious fraternity life that what was natural to me was the worldly outlook of these college men, not the strict ways of the parsonage.

Mr. Sowers assigned the composition of a one-act play and the reading of nine others during the first week. Mrs. Aurner prescribed stiff researches from the *Chanson du Roland* and the *Cuchulain*. And Professor Shambaugh began to show me how to think.

Shambaugh was a celebrity and an actor. He strutted the campus in a tweedy suit and racy hat, flashing a cane and flourishing his eyeglasses at the end of a black cord. As master of ceremonies at university lectures he was often wittier than the principal speaker. He electrified me when Cornelia Otis Skinner visited Iowa. Leaving her in the wings, he strode to the proscenium, extracted a handkerchief, which was Miss Skinner's principal prop, and proceeded to satirize her delivery in what might well have been Cornelia lampooning Cornelia. He thought of a new approach for each introduction all winter.

His classroom was a lounge with easy chairs before a fireplace. As we entered the first day, a phonograph was playing classical music. Shambaugh's assistant invited us to smoke if we wished or walk about the room or enjoy the comfortable chairs. We were to register disgust or approval at any time.

Promptly at nine o'clock the assistant stopped a recording of the Brahms' *Fourth Symphony* and started the *Ride of the Valkyries*. To the militant Yo ho, to ho, Shambaugh strode into the room, bowed to his class, ascended a rostrum, and seated himself ceremoniously behind a mahogany desk, where he resembled a Supreme Court judge about to read a constitutional decision.

The record ran out to its end. Automatically the phonograph stopped. Shambaugh did not speak. Minutes ticked by in silence. He seemed to be waiting for something.

Suddenly he whirled on a girl who was using this interval to sharpen a pencil and shouted: "What are you thinking?"

"I beg pardon?" she gasped.

"What are you *thinking?"*

"Why, I—"

"Exactly, exactly. You were not thinking. Thought is of the essence of this course. It is the chemical unknown we will analyze in our laboratory, the human mind. We will find out what others have thought, what great minds have produced. And we hope, after dipping into the vast caldrons of thought that have boiled since man began to think, that we will teach you too to think. I'm afraid it is asking too much—but we'll find out."

With that introduction, he proceeded to outline the course. He would suggest certain reading: from philosophers, poets, and teachers; from scientists, warriors, and lovers; from engineers, agronomists, paleontologists, musicians, plumbers, and bricklayers; from lawyers, doctors, and dentists. He would introduce us to every science and art.

We were not required to follow the bibliography he would suggest. We could read Zane Grey's *Riders of the Purple Sage,* or Lawrence's *Lady Chatterley's Lover,* if we desired, so long as what we read inspired us to think for ourselves.

We would come to class prepared to discuss our ideas. And we would keep a diary of our thoughts hour by hour. At the end of the year he would read the diaries, and our grade would be determined by the original thinking shown by our recorded secret thoughts. There would be no examinations.

"My assistant will now pass out mimeographed lists of suggested reading," he concluded, "for those who want to prime the pump of their thought wells."

He descended to our level and started walking toward the door.

"And by the way," he called as an exit line, "when I enter and leave this room I expect all of you to rise."

We rose.

Succeeding classes were as interesting and as unconventional as the first. Usually a student brought the initial ceremony to an end with a question which members of the class were encouraged to answer. When an argument started, Shambaugh goaded us to self-expression, rousing our anger if necessary. Always he was contemptuous of confusion, snapping, "Sweep out the attic of your mind!"

If a classroom discussion or debate proceeded smoothly, he would await the moment when he could pounce back into control with the words, "No, NO! You have not thought that through." Then he would lecture for the remainder of the hour, glibly citing Jacob Wassermann, Pythagoras, Will Rogers, Lafcadio Hearn, or Fred Waring. Sometimes he credited the source; sometimes he didn't. He wasn't scrupulous except with regard to the goal: to compel us to think.

In the midst of all this, the stock market crashed, and the entire student body became gloomy. Within a month most of the Packard and Chrysler roadsters were gone, their owners with them. Phi Psi was hit too. Seven men left the house in one week. Boys who relied entirely on checks from home became frightened. Hopes of years' standing dissolved. Medical seniors discovered that hospitals were decreasing the number of interns. Seniors in the law school found legal firms closed to them. There was no position for me either. Not even the Riverton *Courier* could use a journalism graduate. In journalism, banking, insurance there were no openings.

Bennie Shambaugh snapped the philosophical trend of his campus course and converted it into a laboratory. His students became applicants for jobs, he a personnel manager. We researched the requirements of oil companies, chain stores, and the few big businesses that were expanding despite the depression. We learned how to write application letters.

"Get the man who hires men to *think*," became Shambaugh's new motto, "and see that he thinks about you."

But our letters of application came back or were unanswered. Nobody wanted the Class of 1930.

The week before graduation I wrote father that I had been bid to Phi Beta Kappa. I expected a special-delivery letter in reply. Father would make a great deal of scholastic honors.

Instead he jumped in the car and drove to Iowa City.

[347]

I was sitting out a very dull dinner in Memorial Union, at which a national officer of Phi Beta Kappa endeavored to impress us with his knowledge. He had talked halfway through his third glass of water when I saw a familiar figure on the lawn outside.

Father stopped pacing and waved. Another glass of water disappeared. Father began to gesture. Broad pantomime of shoveling. Of using a pair of shears on long hair. Of drinking water. He also gestured for me to unbutton my coat so that he could see the key swinging from my watch chain.

When the banquet ended, he was waiting at the door. He was a great deal older than he had been at Christmas. His hair, coal black for so many years, was mottled in white and gray veins, like fine Italian marble. Creases that had grooved his face only when he smiled were now permanent. The laughter had been superseded by shadows. The fire had burned out of his eyes.

But he was still father. And there was more on his mind than applause for a son who had studied his lessons.

He suggested that we take the river lane that led from the Union to the Phi Psi house past the back yards of the university president and the fraternities. Bright moonlight reflected by the river lighted our way.

"I had dinner at the house," father began. "They're a fine group of boys, and they seem to think a lot of you."

I could have told him that they had put on an act developed to impress parents, but I remained silent. I wanted him to see them as the honest, broad-minded group they were, a little racy, tolerant of a glass of beer, liberal in their religious beliefs, men who would make excellent laymen, but not preachers. And I wanted him to see that I was like them.

But he didn't. He returned to his old theme.

"I could see your hand at the controls in that house," he said. "You have a way with men, son."

"I haven't influenced them," I replied quickly. "It's they who have changed me."

But he refused to accept this and began the monologue that obviously had brought him on the 120-mile drive to Iowa City. The depression, he said, was a good thing. Sometimes he thought it was Heaven-sent to break people from worldliness, force them to reconstruct their values. He could see manifestations in his own church of people whose souls were better for the trials that had been forced upon them.

"Have a job yet, son?"

"No, not yet."

"Well," he went on, "that may be a good thing. It may be part of the greater plan. Perhaps you were not meant to be a newspaperman."

The road was still open to the ministry, he went on. After what he had seen at the Phi Psi house, he was more than ever convinced of my calling. And with a Phi Beta Kappa key, admission to the Methodist clergy would be easy.

"I'm caught up again now financially," he continued. "Stop looking for a job and let me finance you in theological seminary next fall."

"I can't do that, father," I said.

"You're sure?"

"Positive, father."

His pace quickened.

"All right, son," he said. "I've got to be getting home."

At the Phi Psi house he jumped into the car and departed unceremoniously.

On graduation day he and mother returned to see me parade in cap and gown. As guests assembled for commencement, the band played a concert on the grass before the ivy-draped pillars of Old Capitol. Father and mother were among the earliest arrivals and secured seats in a front row.

Father's whitening hair shone among the mass of heads, and twice the old grin sweetened his countenance as my piccolo flashed like a streak of lightning through the landscape of the Tschaikowsky *Fourth Symphony*.

Then the senior members of the band joined the academic procession, and when next I saw father and mother they were tipping their heads one around each side of a flowery hat that had lodged in front of them.

I was among the first group called, the *cum laudes*. The band saw to it that I received a round of applause by breaking out a chord in A flat. Father blew his nose appreciatively.

After the ceremony I still had another band concert to play, at Memorial Union where the president received the parents of graduating seniors. Father and mother, veterans of a thousand church receptions, did not attend. They sat on the porch, where they could hear the music.

At last I was ready to leave. I had only to turn in my band uniform and return my cap and gown to the store from which I had rented them.

We walked up the hill from the Union to the steps of Old Capitol. Its west face was genially sunlit.

I paused on the rim of the hill for a last absorption of the river-valley view, which had been my first sight of the university. There outspread were the hill on which the band had drilled in formation, the concrete bridge I had crossed six times a week for three years, the ugly building in which chemistry had made my life miserable, the gothic-spired hospital that had cured a streptococcic throat, the field house where I had swum and fenced and played baseball and tennis, the football stadium where the band had brazened out many an athletic defeat.

A last look finally at the *Daily Iowan*. Lights burned there even at midday, but I did not enter. My farewells had already been spoken.

We loaded the back seat of the car with my trunk and suitcases and headed north.

"Well, son," mother said, "it was a beautiful graduation. But those poor children. Where on earth will they all find jobs to do?"

"About one in ten has a job," I replied, quoting a survey in the *Iowan*. "The rest are going home."

"Have you any prospects for a job yourself?"

I explained that I had leads out all over the state. One might strike at any time. All I could do was wait. "But I won't be a burden to you," I added quickly.

"You always have a home, son," father said quietly.

"Sure, and I'll be paying for my board this summer.

I'm playing in the Clear Lake Band." This was an admission that I did not expect to find permanent employment until autumn.

"Well, you'll be home anyway," father went on, appreciating the implication. "You can work at the lake and sleep at home. That's more than we bargained for, isn't it, mother, another summer with Hartzell?"

CHAPTER TWENTY-EIGHT

$\mathcal{F}$RASER met us on the front step.

"Well, well," he shouted, "and how is the alumnus?"

Fraser had grown so that I scarcely knew him. He had stretched to father's height and was as handsome as father, but mother's eyes were there yet, although their snap was his own.

As we unloaded my luggage and carried it up to a bedroom I discovered that he was as witty as father and as shrewd as mother in getting his way with father. When I had left Riverton for college, Fraser was a Boy Scout senior patrol leader, with twenty-one merit badges, and his idea of a good time was to put Ex-lax in cocoa. Now he was smooth and smart, a little of the bond salesman and the backslapping insurance man. Evidently a good deal had happened to him, for his manner was not that of the parsonage at all. He had just graduated from high school and already resembled a college campus politician.

The modernization of Fraser, I learned later, began with an experience in Mason City.

The scout troop sponsored by the church was composed mainly of tenderfeet. Fraser wanted to enroll in another troop with advanced standards, but this was not allowed. The scoutmaster, a church member, might

[353]

have been insulted, thus giving father a bad start in his Mason City ministry.

For more than a month Fraser struggled with the little boys and then went to scout camp at Clear Lake, which was twelve miles west of town. He had looked forward to his fifth camp year to complete requirements for scouting's highest honor, the Eagle badge.

The camp ruled, however, that no awards or merit badges would be honored except those given by itself. None of Fraser's Riverton credentials was acceptable. He could not believe the decision. The executives to whom he protested admitted their action was arbitrary and probably contrary to national scout rules, but they had to impose it to save the morale of a camp crowded with beginners.

Fraser packed his bedroll, walked three and a half miles to the interurban line, and returned home. His scouting days were ended. He hunted up a job repairing tires in a garage.

When school began, he was invited to parties, and for two months father complained of mysterious ten-cent toll calls to the neighboring village of Nora Springs before he discovered that Fraser was interested in a girl there, named Catherine Jean. Shortly before Christmas she gave him a date during a huff with her "steady." In preparation for the gala event he bought a new suit and went proudly out with the car. In an hour he was home again.

Mother, who still sat up when Fraser, the youngest of her children, was out, watched him return and perch in a window of the atrocious parsonage, which faced the main business square of the city. For a long time he twiddled the radio dial without saying a word.

"What's the matter, son?" she asked at last.

"Oh, mother," he said in disgust, "you wouldn't understand."

But she did understand, and in a short time had the story. Catherine Jean's regular beau arrived in a contrite mood, and Fraser had been forgotten. Mother suggested that he try another girl, and in ten minutes he was on his way again, happy and buoyant.

By the end of the school year he was dating all over town, and one night he went to Clear Lake with a girl mother was inclined to believe was "fast." He did not return until three in the morning. By that hour both father and mother were waiting up, according to Fraser's version.

"Where have you been?" father began.

"Out," said Fraser.

"Out where?"

"I was at a party at a cottage on Clear Lake, a perfectly decent party."

"No one doubts that, son," father soothed him, "but we like to know where you are when you stay out all night."

"I can get along," Fraser said. "You don't have to wait up for me like a delegation. I'm not a baby."

"Of course not, dear," mother answered. "But it worries us when you stay out so late."

"Look," Fraser protested. "You don't have to watch me. I haven't gone to the dogs yet. But if you keep this up, I can't promise."

No one waited up for him after that.

During the next year he greatly enjoyed his trips as trombonist with the national-champion Mason City High School band to contests at Flint, Mich., and Tulsa, Okla. He forayed up and down the aisle of the sleeping cars, leaving only left shoes in one car, rights in another. When this escapade resulted in the permanent loss of the high school principal's left shoe, he was not disciplined. The principal returned home laughing at the joke.

Fraser's chief recreation was the Secret Seven. The other six members owned dilapidated Ford cars, called "jalopies," in which they cruised the streets looking for mischief after Epworth League on Sunday night. When this sport became dull, they retired to a two-car garage for ping-pong and other games.

One evening they conceived a new entertainment. From the club treasury a $5 prize was posted for the boy who, while driving his own car, could throw rocks accurately enough to knock out the most street lights. Fraser had the new parsonage Model A Ford, which was handicapped with a rigid top, but he entered into the sport. He was ahead with five bull's-eyes, when one of the other lads careened around a corner and, to avoid crashing into the pastor's automobile, wrapped his jalopy around a lamppost. The resulting short circuit knocked out sixty lights at once. He won the prize.

Inspired by such fun, the club members began to look farther afield. A natural-gas pipe line was being constructed from Oklahoma to service the towns of northern Iowa and southern Minnesota. Out riding one Sunday night, the boys saw the construction and coveted the bright-red lanterns that warned of danger.

They decided to string 100 lights on a jalopy, light them all in a dragon burst of red, and drive past the fire station shouting "Fire!"

For three weeks they worked to assemble enough lights. All were hidden in the garage of a respectable businessman whose son was a member of the club. They had about reached their quota when a private detective found the cache. He attended church one Sunday evening and gave the businessman exactly one hour to replace all the lights that had been stolen, or the seven boys would be arrested.

The culprits were nowhere to be found. They were hiding behind the sugar-beet factory. So seven of the town's leading citizens, led by a Methodist parson, bogged through muddy excavations at the side of a six-mile stretch of country road, replacing and lighting all those lanterns.

This prank almost broke up the Secret Seven. The next day there were six jalopies for sale in front of the high school.

Shortly after my college graduation Fraser secured a summer-vacation job as helper at a gasoline chain's superstation two blocks from the parsonage.

His aptitude for salesmanship immediately became evident. In addition to laboring eight hours a day six days a week in the station pumping gasoline into cars, changing oil, greasing, and wiping windshields, he was expected to sell a weekly quota of the company's own brand of automobile tires.

Theoretically this could be done while he was filling gas tanks, but he learned that a man or woman usually is in a hurry at the gas pump and resents being kept waiting with a sales argument. So to hold his job, Fraser spent three or four hours a day outside the station ringing doorbells, which jumped his working hours to eleven or twelve a day. As he met his quota, the company increased it, hence he never completed his job. He could not protest; there were too many unemployed men to take his place.

Early in August there was a series of filling-station robberies. Father and mother were worried for Fraser. The holdups were identical in technique: an automobile drew to the main pump just before closing, when the attendant was about to lock up his receipts. The driver dallied in the washroom until he heard the safe open, then stepped out, flashed a gun, slugged the attendant, and made off with the day's cash.

After the third such robbery Fraser saw that a shadowy figure had begun to pace back and forth among the elm trees across the street from his station. He watched, believing the man might be a spotter for the holdup gang. But when Fraser locked up for the night, nothing happened.

The next night the mysterious person arrived again, promptly at nine-thirty. Obviously the fellow wasn't going anywhere, as he would pause and peer toward the oil station from behind tree trunks. His job evidently was to ascertain exactly what time Fraser opened the safe.

But Fraser could not summon the police. His company disliked nervous employees, and the man might have been an innocent citizen walking a dog.

The following evening when the stroller appeared, Fraser lifted down the big fire extinguisher from its mounting and carried it inside his shack. If any gangsters went into his washroom, he planned to open the safe, seize the extinguisher, and shoot burning fluid into their eyes. While they were blind, he would knock them out and call the police.

Then, in a flash of automobile headlights, he identified the prowler across the street. It was father.

Fraser said nothing, but he felt more comfortable, knowing father was backstopping him. A week went by, during which father continued his vigil, remaining on guard until Fraser locked up. Father did not know that Fraser had observed him.

One night about ten minutes before closing a car drew up to the station. Its two occupants went to the washroom, and Fraser knew he was in for it. He strolled to the safe, took a tight grip on the extinguisher.

At that moment father appeared. In his hand was a heavy grease wrench with which he pounded on the rest-room door.

"I'll give you ten seconds to come out of there, or I'll come in after you," he roared.

Two young men came out hastily, jumped in their car, and fled, while father calmly telephoned their license number to the police. Later that evening they were caught in another holdup.

"Thanks," Fraser said as he locked his safe.

"It's nothing," father said. "I just happened to be across the street."

Meanwhile I played in the Clear Lake municipal band and hammered at my newspaper applications.

Occasionally father would dash over to Clear Lake

in midafternoon with the mail if the envelope bore the masthead of a newspaper. This was really an excuse to listen to the band. Every afternoon and evening we played in a bandshell on the water front to attract visitors to the lake. There were no rehearsals. From an enormous musical library Director Dan Gioscio, a former Metropolitan Opera harpist, would extract any number he or a band member fancied, and we played it at sight.

With only thirteen instruments, we sometimes sounded a little thin. But we played all the notes indicated in the score and doubled, when our own parts indicated a rest, for some instrument that should have been heard but was not in our ensemble.

Father sat in a front row on the same bench with the town simpleton, who never missed a concert, and chuckled to himself whenever I executed with reasonable accuracy some unusually difficult passage on the flute or piccolo. During intermissions he joked with the bandsmen and occasionally requested a number that Gioscio was glad to play. His selections ran to British compositions: Elgar's *Pomp and Circumstance,* Sullivan's *Iolanthe,* and a medley of Irish ditties extremely difficult for piccolo.

One afternoon he thought he'd show off a bit and request a number not in our library. He asked for Karl Goldmark's *Suite from Atlantis.* But the director found it, and we went to work. During the second movement the simpleton leaned over to father knowingly and said, "I love you, I love you, I love you."

Startled, father cocked an eyebrow.

"That's the name of it," the simpleton explained.

[360]

After the concert father discovered from bandsmen that a popular song had been borrowed from the Goldmark work. He went downtown to hear the record but did not buy it.

"I prefer the original," he said on his return.

Frequently father and I dined at the lake, after which he remained for the evening concert. We argued, we talked, we confided in each other. But there continued to be an ecclesiastical and personal barrier between us. If I lit a cigarette after a concert, he did not approach until I had extinguished it.

One afternoon, however, I lit a pipe, and he was in no mood to wait a half hour to talk to me.

"What pleasure do you get from that thing?" he asked, pointing to the pipe.

"I don't know," I said. "It's soothing. Makes me think more clearly."

"If I thought that," he remarked drily, "I'd take it up myself. But I can't see that your generation, for all its puffing, has developed a race of superior thinkers."

In mid-August father appeared at the bandshell waving an envelope. It was a letter from a university of Iowa journalism instructor saying that he had recommended me for an opening at the United Press in Des Moines.

Father and I went to Western Union, composed telegrams to every editor in Iowa for whom I had done college work, asking them to send the United Press manager a recommendation for me. This was father's idea. He thought a shower of unsolicited applause might get me the job before I appeared on the scene. In those days of fifty applicants for each position, you

couldn't overlook anything. Later that night I wrote a letter of formal application to the United Press.

A prompt telegram invited me to Des Moines for an interview. Band Director Gioscio let me go. The season was about over anyway, he said, and I was to forget the band if I had a chance for permanent employment. He could get along for three weeks with twelve bandsmen. He had never liked the idea of thirteen in the stand anyway.

I drove to Des Moines in the Model A, arriving at half past eight in the morning. I thought I'd sneak a look at the United Press office before the manager arrived. With extreme difficulty I found the place. It was a rabbit warren behind a storeroom in the *Register* building. From the door emerged the deafening clatter of teletype and Morse machines. A fat grouch slouched with a green shade over his eyes, copying the Morse wire report. Operating a teletype was a sleepy young man, behind whom, at the main desk, sat a tall, gangly, big-handed kid with a long impassive face.

The kid looked up. In his hand was an editor's stylus, behind his ear a pencil, at his side a typewriter holding a half-written story.

"Are you Mr. Gillette?" I shouted above the noise.

He scrutinized me quickly and acutely, with eyes like blue steel.

"You must be Spence." Apparently he had learned to speak below that machine clatter, for he did not raise his voice.

"Yes, sir."

His hand continued to edit copy, which he fed to his teletype operator. He glanced at a pile of telegrams beside him.

"You seem to have friends, but they're all Associated Press editors. Do you think that's going to sell a U. P. man?"

"I did some work for U. P. once at school," I said.

"Take off your coat then," he remarked drily, "and do some more. The salary is $30 a week, and we don't keep hours in this shop. We work until we're through."

Two weeks passed. Fraser brought down my clothes and drove the car home. I had no opportunity to return to Mason City. I was busier than I had ever been before and was enthusiastic about the work.

"This is the life for me," I said to Fraser, and he quoted me to father.

In the next mail I received a letter and a package.

"I'm told," father's note said briefly, "that editors are addicted to these things."

The package was a box of cigars.

CHAPTER TWENTY-NINE

*B*y the time Eileen decided to be married, I had been working for a year and Fraser was a college sophomore.

Eileen motivated her matrimonial choice carefully by letter, remembering father's consistent opposition to her adolescent heartthrobs. But this time he was enthusiastic, for by now he considered Eileen old enough to make up her own mind. And Paul was the son of one of his best Denver friends, handsome, stabilized in a Telephone Company career, and respectable. Paul wasn't much of a churchgoer, but father believed Eileen would change that.

Then Eileen communicated to father her desire for a quiet wedding. Because she anticipated opposition to this request, I went home by prearrangement for a week end to support her arguments when her letter arrived.

Except for three brief vacations, Eileen had never known Mason City and did not feel that a big church wedding would be appropriate. She wished to be married in church because of the organ and altar, but that was all. Two of her sorority sisters and the bridegroom's sister would stand up with her. Paul would bring his best man; Fraser and I would be in the bridal party.

But no fussing. No elaborate, expensive costuming for the girls, no long guest list.

Father read the restrictions imposed in her special-delivery letter and let out a roar that halted passers-by outside. She had chosen a husband, but a wedding was something she knew nothing about.

He had performed 2,200 weddings. How did *she* know what was proper?

Actually, what he meant was that for twenty-five years he had been awaiting the moment when, in his handsomest pulpit regalia, he could perform the ceremony that married his daughter. No obscure giving the bride away for *him!* No parading down the aisle while everybody admired the bride, answering with two syllables the unimportant question: "Who giveth this woman to be married to this man?" and then receding to a seat beside the bride's mother.

No, siree. He was going to stand up front, facing the audience during the whole business. This was his show. He had even figured a way around the problem of escorting his daughter down the aisle. Dr. MacDonald, who had been foster grandfather to us all and had inducted father into the ministry in 1904, would come from a near-by town to hand the bride down.

And you couldn't perform a job like that without spectators! Father had never preached to less than a comfortably full house in his entire ministry, and he wasn't putting on a show for his daughter with any empty pews. This was an occasion that called for a spread. It had to be worthy of the bride—and himself.

At least that's what he said, and so I reported to Eileen.

During hundreds of elaborate church weddings he had been gaining experience, experimenting with dramatic effects at the expense of the daughters of bankers, lawyers, and businessmen in three states. Now there would be a wedding such as nobody had ever seen—of the essence of his experience. It could not be any other way.

In the fall Fraser, having completed a year of junior college, would begin a three-year business-administration course at the University of Iowa, leaving father and mother alone. This wedding was more than the marriage of a daughter. It was a symbol of a family grown, educated, planted in the soil, embarked upon its own life.

It was a chance to show off a daughter and two sons reared in Christian environment, an opportunity to point and say: "This is what can be accomplished when the home is as it should be. Here is my daughter, gracious, beautiful, a successful schoolteacher, bride of an upstanding young man. Here is my older son, who is steadily employed at a job with a future. Here is my younger son, and you have only to look at him to know he'll get on in the world. They are clean-cut children, conscientious, molded by a firm but not too narrow hand into the kind of stuff that survives economic and spiritual upheavals."

He couldn't very well point with pride unless the whole town was there to see. And this time he concealed his ulterior motive so craftly that neither Eileen nor I realized it. We were busy with details.

"You don't need," Eileen wrote, "to have any invitations engraved. I can write personal letters to the few

[367]

who will attend. But I should appreciate it if you will have some nice announcements printed up—about 200 should be enough. I'll need only half of them, and so you can send the rest to the relatives and your friends."

"What does she mean, no engraved invitations?" father objected. "In northern Iowa alone there are 200 people who would like to see Will Spence's daughter married. They remember her in long curls. There are family friends in Fort Dodge and Sioux City and Denver, yes, even in Riverton, who *must* be included; they'd be mighty hurt otherwise. And in Mason City—"

He seized pencil and paper and began to make a list, starting with his official board and ending with the mayor, who was a Roman Catholic and a very good friend.

He enumerated half the Masonic brotherhood, tens of Kiwanians, dozens of preachers, and the Jewish furniture dealer, with whom in his moments of greatest sadness over the depression he could swap stories until he was laughing again.

When more than 400 names were on the list, he began to remember Eileen's friends, a list twice as long as the one she sent home. Everyone she intended to remember with an announcement he wanted on hand in the flesh.

When Eileen reached home and discovered on a table 600 engraved invitations awaiting addressing in her own hand and not a single announcement, she decided it was better not to interfere.

"Evidently," she wrote me, for I had returned to Des Moines, "it's to be his wedding, instead of mine. I haven't the heart to frustrate him; his excitement is so childlike."

She might have held out if he had not been so ecstatically proud of her. Her letters to me indicated that he followed her about the house, admiring her clothes, even mischievously suggesting that Paul was coming into the possession of a mighty trim pair of ankles, although his pastoral dignity prevented him from carrying this physical allusion farther.

Several times he asked her advice. What could he suggest to Mrs. Rhodes about her wild daughter? What could he tell Anna Ruthyea Sinclair that would turn her flighty head away from that ass, Hastings Cowley?

He even invoked Eileen's professional assistance in the matter of regrouping Sunday school classes. Would mixed classes be effective? Was all-boy and all-girl instruction more scientific?

Attention such as this from father was the supreme tribute, and Eileen recognized it. It was his way of telling her that he trusted her judgment at last. It was as though he was putting his stamp upon her: "Inspected, approved, and passed by the U. S. Department of Fatherhood. August 26, 1932."

So she wrote her college classmates that it would be a big wedding after all and advised Paul to invest his best man with the proper gloves and spats.

In only one particular did Eileen resist. Father wanted Elgar's *Pomp and Circumstance* instead of Mendelssohn for the wedding march, and that she would not accept.

"I'm not Queen Victoria," she objected.

He saw the point and yielded, not however without

adding plaintively, "But it would have been a nice touch."

Once the invitations were in the mail and he began to get replies from old friends assuring him that they wouldn't miss the wedding if they had to walk 200 miles, father became as busy as though he was dedicating a new church.

He rehearsed the organist, sitting on the bench with her and taking the keyboard himself now and then to inject subtleties known only to himself. He spent hours with the florist, preparing a list of altar decorations. He even considered having the postwedding reception in the church basement, fearing the parsonage would be too small. It was mother who put her foot down on that.

"Even though you haven't once acknowledged it," she told him, "this wedding is a family, not a church, affair."

"Of course it's a family affair," he retorted, not at all abashed. "The church is the universal family of us all."

And mother did not argue. She had lived with father long enough to know that a frontal attack upon his desires was never effective. She concentrated upon such details as Eileen's gown and the wedding supper and planned strategies for extracting from father's pocket sufficient funds to entertain the bridal party at a Clear Lake resort.

About two weeks before the wedding something began to occur that father had not anticipated. His previous experience had been ritualistic, not parental, and he had overlooked a matter of protocol. Presents began pouring in from the 600 guests.

"Holy smoke!" he exclaimed after the arrival of seventeen gifts in one mail. "I forgot completely that wedding invitations mean presents. People will think we're making a commercial enterprise of this thing."

"Well, we might have charged admission," Eileen remarked. "It's certainly going to be a good show."

He was seriously embarrassed when a Wedgwood platter came from the mayor.

"How did he know your pattern?" he asked Eileen.

"The town jeweler ordered a complete set of this Wedgwood in anticipation of the emergency," Eileen replied.

When the bridesmaids arrived, there was no place to house them. Even the beds were piled high with wedding presents, and scores of thank-you notes remained to be written. Furtively Eileen enlisted the aid of her friends to write from a form to those who would not recognize her handwriting. She herself had almost collapsed from writer's cramp.

In the matter of rehearsal, father knew exactly how everything was to be done. Even the bridegroom was silenced when he suggested the ushers wear gardenias.

"What's the matter with carnations?" father asked.

"They're funereal," Paul said, having arrived from Denver the day before.

"Well," father dismissed him, "you needn't worry. You'll be wearing lilies of the valley."

By the time I came home everything was in the groove. Eileen and Paul had surrendered.

As father repeated his instructions for the last time, Eileen turned to me and whispered, "Thank goodness, this show is only going to have a one-night stand."

Bossy as father was in details of the ceremony, he was a magnificent host to the wedding party, which indicated that mother had done her work well. He squired Eileen's friends as though each was the bride, without a word of protest carried out Eileen's suggestions for the entertainment of her guests. He was meticulous in little courtesies, gay at the dinner he gave for "the cast." He shelled out money. Everything had to be just right.

And it was. At the wedding he did not eclipse the bride. The marriage ceremony was a sacrament from the first musical chord. He was the preacher then, not the father, and he did not steal the show. Occasionally, like a good theatrical producer, he cast an eye over the house for flaws in the production, but no one noticed that.

At the reception father stood beside Eileen, supplementing her memory of the guests. She had a personal interest in perhaps one out of ten of those who shook her hand and wished her well. The rest were faces.

"Mrs. Hobson, silver cream pitcher," father would whisper, and Eileen would set her face in a smile.

"Harry and Eleanor Kipplinger, pewter candlesticks," and then in a louder voice, "How *are* you, Harry? It was mighty good seeing you in the pew again. You remember Eileen, of course? And this is Paul—"

Dutifully Eileen played her part, a little frightened as the parsonage became more and more crowded. Everyone she had ever known was in attendance. There was no doubt about it. She could only follow father's course, as mother was doing farther down the receiving line, and be friendly to everyone.

[372]

After a half hour I dropped from the receiving line and sat in father's old leather chair, from which I could see Eileen and bolster her with the glance we had exchanged in childhood when we wanted a second portion of roast beef at dinner.

"Yes," father beamed, "this is Eileen, Joe. Remember how she refused to eat her carrots at your house? You'd never know her now, would you?"

Or, "Yes, Sister Leighton, you never thought she'd

[373]

grow up to be such a fine girl, did you? Here she is."

Friends were there from all the towns father had served, recalling the memories of twenty-five years of parsonage living.

And as they passed in review, a change came over Eileen. Her eyes were tearful, and she clung affectionately to father's arm. Her "thank you" became personal, her voice soft, her manner genuinely friendly.

And a change came over me too. I began to think of those twenty-five parsonage years, what they had meant to us, and what they had done to us. All our past difficulties were smoothed out now into a long road whose end Eileen had reached, and perhaps I too.

It had been a road with steep hills, hills the climbing of which had given us an enduring strength, a strength upon which we had drawn many times since leaving home.

And what was that strength? An intangible something from the parsonage, composed of a little perspective, a little tolerance, an unwavering conviction that man and God are good, that the abiding constancy of faith is a shelter against the impacts of all manner of skeptics and cynics.

These people had not come to see Eileen so much as to greet father once again. It was he who had restored their faith, comforted them in sickness and in health, for them forsaken all other so long as he could live and work, even at the expense of his own family.

Perhaps, I thought, he had arranged this wedding in his own way to make Eileen see clearly, at the threshold of her married life, what the faith had meant to him and what it could mean to her if she too believed in it.

This was our heritage, the only legacy a child of the parsonage ever would receive.